A HISTORICAL RESEARCH GUIDE TO THE MICROCOMPUTER, 2nd EDITION

TULI BLOCK PUBLISHING HOUSE
Colborne, Ontario

A HISTORICAL

RESEARCH

GUIDE TO THE

MICROCOMPUTER,

2nd Edition

C. Murray McCullough

Manufactured in Canada

Tuli Block Publishing House
13866 County Road 21
Colborne, Ontario K0K 1S0

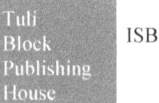

ISBN

This book is dedicated to

my brother ***Ronnie***

May God Bless

and

Kang, Son-mee

Korean language teacher and lover of English

who both have a special place in my heart

I wish to gratefully acknowledge the technical assistance of

Bob Cogle, Select Electronics, Colborne, Ontario,

and

Park, Tu-Young, The Computer Store, Pusan, Republic of Korea,

 in the production of this book.

ABOUT THE AUTHOR

C. Murray McCullough Murray is a computer teacher,
programmer (COBOL, etc.) and has taught
E.S.L.(English as a Second Language) in Botswana and
the Rep. of Korea. Murray was educated at York Univ.,
Univ. of Toronto, Cal. State Univ.(Dominguez Hills) and
Greenwich Univ.(Hawaii). He currently lives on the
family farm with his mother, a cat named Tiger, and
raises Belgian horses along with his sister.

You can contact Murray at:

Email: dunlee50@hotmail.com

Or at the Tuli Block Publishing House address
lettered on the Copyright page

Contents

PROLOGUE

The machine does not isolate man from the
great problems of nature but plunges
him more deeply into them.
_Antoine de Saint-Exupéry

Is this era of human history special? Why are we pursuing
personal-computing technology at a break-neck pace? Is
man in danger of being placed second on the totem pole of
intelligence? Is the microcomputer "the great transforming
invention of our time?[1]

These and many other questions I'll attempt to answer in this
book. But to conclude the introduction let's glance specifically at
its structure: In chapter one is an overview of the thesis defining
the structure of the argument while chapter two covers the
background of the art, science and technology of computers. This
is to provide a perspective and context for microcomputer
developments in the 1970s. Chapter three examines the inner
workings of microcomputers, i.e. its various parts.

In chapter four I'll examine the software side of micro-computing by looking at languages and applications in the early years. It's in chapter five where I'll look at important applications.

The early role of microcomputers played in the home with user groups, newsletters, BBSs and conventions contributing to the growth of home computing is examined in chapter six. Meanwhile chapter seven looks at the role microcomputers play in society, ie. in business, education and mass media.

In the conclusion, where I attempt to demystify microcomputing, providing a synthesis and analysis of published material, examining microcomputer's technological and sociological implications.

Chapter One

STRUCTURE OF THE BOOK

The intent of my paper is to debunk some myths surrounding microcomputers - to help disseminate non-jargonized, non-technical information of the early years. To help accomplish this task the paper follows a microcomputer history as outlined by D. F. Scott: the *Conception Stage(Altair 8800)*; the *Consumption Stage(Apple II)* and the *Consolidation Stage(IBM PC)*.[1] I view this approach as one of the best explanations for the early growth of micro-computing.

We must give consideration to the fundamentals or primitives of computers in understanding their power. What's meant here is a computer's superstructure: Its hardware and software interacting to process information, ie. data, and displaying a useful result. Over time we see a transformation from purely hand-held, mechanical calculating devices to electro-mechanical devices to pure electronic devices of today.[2] On the software side is an evolutionary process moving from binary machine-coding or assembly language coding to low-level processor and operating system coding. Both hardware and software combine producing a device that revolutionized society much faster than any previous invention. Maybe as Kundera says: *"Speed is the form of ecstasy the technical revolution has bestowed on man...when (he) delegates the faculty of speed to a machine...a speed that is non-corporeal, nonmaterial, pure speed, speed itself, ecstasy speed."* [3]

The following invention-revolution timeline demonstrates this dramatically:

INVENTION-REVOLUTION TIME LINE

Invention	Mass Produced	Time of Revolutionary Impact
AUTOMOBILE	1890s	1950s

Interstate highway system
Mass movement of people [The Mobile Society]

ELECTRONIC COMPUTERS	1940s	1970/80s

Internet [Communications revolution –
        movement of information rather
        than people]
Personal Computers
Remote-controlled electronic goods
Electronic banking
E-mail [The Information Society]

Most are familiar with the automobile's history; not so the electronic computer's. Out of the defense establishment of the 1940s; the Space Race of the late 50s early 60s we see miniaturization of electronic components ultimately culminating in the large-scale integrated circuit of the 1970s.[4] Further, because of military, academic and commercial competition during the 1960s and early 70s, computer technology surpassed that of every other country. It's not until the 1980s do we see Japan and Europe compete on the hardware-side. software-wise America still leads.[5] Only now is microcomputing technology spreading round the world.

This rapid revolutionary impact has left the layman puzzled. He knows little of its history, therefore not what continues driving it. This may be one reason why he fears the technological elite, the digerati, just as the literati were feared with the arrival of the printing press in 15th century Europe.

The substance of this paper expressed as knowledge of microcomputing is more and more in danger of being monopolized by computer-literate people, all who have power to manipulate information, menacing our freedoms.[6] It's as if we're revisiting the past: the literati having exclusive access to books until the arrival of public libraries and mass education; today the digerati, affluent, educated and computer-literate controlling technology and information if reasonable-cost access to computing technology isn't forth-coming.[7]

Concluding the introduction, my paper concerns itself with all stated issues and attempts, in some small way, to synthesize, analyze and explain historical forces propelling the microcomputer revolution.

Chapter Two

Art, Science and Technology
of Microcomputers

Computers have played a key role in the
acquistion of new knowledge and in its
dissemination and storage for later recall.
_Shirley Thomas

Computer science is no more about computers
than astronomy is about telescopes.
_E. W. Dijkstra

As stated earlier the microcomputer industry is full of jargon. I've included Appendix 1 to explain some of these terms which will help in understanding the terminology employed in this essay.

Russ Walter's writes "Let's look back. For many centuries people have dreamed of inventing a computerized machine that acts like a person. Let's look at those dreams...[1]

The story begins with men hired by astronomers to compute star positions, their duties including thinking about words, ideas and organizing information.[2] Hence the French word for computer - *ordinateur*. The historical literature relates the story of Pygmalion's scuplture brought to life; Ramon Lull inventing a machine in 1272 A.D. that knew all knowledge; and Pope Sylvester II creating a talking head.[3] Later, Paracelsus built *Homunculus*, a little man who could answer questions while a sixteenth-century Hebrew legend says Judah Loew ben Bezalel, Chief Rabbi of Prague, built a clay robot, *Joseph Gloem*.[4]

Beginning the era of mechanical calculators we see Blaise Pascal's *Pascaline* created "to give some numerical relief to the toils of his tax-collector father."[5] Building on Pascal's theory Gottfried Wilhelm Leibniz built the *Stepped Recknor*, with its nine wheel multiplier wheel concept still employed in 1960s electro-mechanical calculators. Leibniz like other computer developers said computing "is unworthy of excellent men to lose hours like slaves in the labor of calculation."[6] Such tasks belong to calculators.[7]

In 1804 Joseph Marie Jacquard perfected his namesake's *Loom* at the beginning of the scientific age. Yet his loom lacked a fundamental quality of modern computing:" It had no practical way of storing the answers obtained for subsequent operations."[8] For a true computing device we have to wait until the 1830s. In this decade Charles Babbage designed his *Difference* and *Analytical Engines*[9] establishing criteria all microcomputers employ today:

> A computing machine (was that it) must be
> composed of an input device (he used a
> card reader), a memory(which he called
> 'T*he Store*'), a central processing unit (which
> he called '*The Mill*'), and an output
> device(he used a printer). [10]

We know of these endeavors through his assistant Lady Lovelace, Lord Byron's daughter, the translator of his work.[11]

Probably of equal importance during this period is the work of George Boole, a British mathematician publisher of <u>Mathematical Analysis of Logic</u>. This work demonstrates how logic elements work on either a true or false relationship, now called Boolean Algebra.

Putting this new knowledge to work occurred in the 1890 United States Census with Hollerith punch cards allowing for tabulation of information giving rise to electrical tabulating equipment to analyze statistical data."[12] Yet it's not until the 1930s do we see the next computing step taken. Vannevar Bush's differential analyzer. (Incidentally, Bush is considered the founding father of American computing.[13]) Other developments take place in the early part of this century but they're best discussed separately.(See Appendix 2) With the U.S. military, academic and corporate sectors supporting computer research Bush installed a machine at the *Moore School of Electrical Engineering,* University of Pennsylvania.[14] Further research at M.I.T., Bell Telephone Laboratories and many other institutions moved computing technology from the mechanical to electronic stage.

Electronic computers fall into five generations. The first generation employed vacuum tube technology, creating special-purpose machines. Late vacuum tube and early transistor technology follows in the second generation with general-purpose computing becoming commercially available. Today's technology was established in the third generation - late transistor, early integrated-circuit era. The expansion of general-purpose machines, minicomputers and embedded-use microprocessors highlight this era. The fourth generation machines use large-scale integrated circuits. Finally the current era, are ultra, large-scale integrated circuits powering microcomputers in which smallness and processing are carried to extremes,[15] forming the core argument of my paper.(See Appendix 3 for details of generations one, two and three.)

Chapter Three

HARDWARE

In this chapter I present the hardware development of microcomputers. In essence what makes a small computer possible is the microprocessor.

A: THE MICROPROCESSOR

The 1970s was the decade of the chip, a super-session of transistors by micro-circuitry - tiny circuits of semi-conducting material sandwiched in a silicon matrix. Contained in a single chip the size of a baby's fingernail is all the components in the most complex computer ever built before the age of transistors.[1]

Yet the microprocessor's story is one of 'intrigue' and money. It begins with the 4004, invented by Ted Hoff, Stan Mazor and Frederico Faggin of INTEL, with the first working unit manufactured in January 1971.[2](Appendix 4) It was publicly announced in Electronic News, Nov. 1971. In rapid succession came the 8-bit INTEL microprocessors: 8080 (April 1972), 8080 (August 1973), 8080A/8080B(1974/1975)[3] while in 1978 INTEL invented the 8086 microprocessor building the foundation for the PC(IBM) industry.

However, INTEL isn't the only manufacturer of these micro-electronic chips, particularly the 8-bit kind.[4] As Steve Wozniak says:

> Then Chuck Peddle(MOS Technology) came
> out with the 6502 microprocessor and
> announced they were going to sell it over the
> counter at WESCON(a big annual computer
> show on the West coast). So a few friends of
> mine went down to WESCON and $20 went
> over the table and microprocessors came
> back...So for twenty bucks you could get a
> microprocessor. That put me in business.[5]

The low cost 6502 made the microcomputer industry possible.[6]

Around the same time Advanced Micro Devices(AMD) produced a faster 9080-A while Motorola, in April 1974, introduced the 6800 series. Zilog, maker of the 2.5 Mhz Z-80, was in competition with Texas Instrument's TMS-100, a 4-bit processor that by 1980 saw some 44,000,000 sold. They were used in such things as "toys, games, doorbells, washing machines and many similar appliances.[7] Yet, as in any business large amounts of capital are needed for mass production. According to ???(lost reference) "Zilog got money from Exxon while MOS Technology got money from Commodore."[8]

B: MICROCOMPUTERS

Microprocessors in and of themselves do nothing. Putting them to work as the heart of microcomputers begins with genius of Ed Roberts of MITS.[9] In 1974 MITS shipped the first viable microcomputer - the ALTAIR 8800.[10] (Appendix 5) It employed Bill Gate's and Paul Allen's Microsoft BASIC language interpreter and Gary Kildall's operating system CP/M(Control Program & Monitor).[11] The processor board or main board or mother board[12], all of equal value, is connected to peripherals by a 100 wire cable, hence the birth of S-100 computers.[13] Its success was due to hardware and software compatibility envisioned and implemented by Ed Roberts.

Yet as always there's debate of who came first. Stan Veit argues that SWTPC(South-west Technical Products Corporation) built the first real personal computer: "SWPTC sold a video terminal, a printer, a cassette interface, and even an early video graphics board"[14] enabling users to have what is regarded as a modern-day microcomputer.[15] Others say the Kenbek 1 was the first.

Another early machine, created by William Millard, valued by Stan Veit as a pioneering system, was the IMSAI 8080.[16] IMSAI, originally IMS Associates Inc., laying the foundation for the microcomputer industry is credited with spreading the personal computer revolution. However, all these earliest kit computers were very difficult to build and program.[17] Making them work was an exercise in patience and applying multi-programming skills[18] while the editors of <u>Personal Computing,</u> writing in the vernacular, say of this era: "In the early days of personal computing, assembling your own PC was often a rite of entry for would-be chopheads.[19]

The POLY-88, like many that followed, was sold as a microcomputer kit starting in Dec. 1975.[20] It was assembled by electronic enthusiasts, tinkerers, scientists, students, academics, and even by some who called themselves hackers.[21]

Since the earliest machines were sold as kits a fairly extensive knowledge of electronics was needed. Jonathan Titus in a 1974 article called *Computer!* In <u>Radio-Electronics Magazine</u> published the first construction microcomputer kit employing INTEL's 8080 microprocessor. He didn't call it a microcomputer but referred to it as a minicomputer, naming it the MARK 8.[22] Meanwhile in the July 1975 issue of <u>Popular Electronics</u> the SOL-10 microcomputer was introduced. This is regarded by experts to be the first assembled small computer, not in the traditional kit form, to be offered to the public. This machine is the beginning of the microcomputer revolution.[23] (Appendix 6 shows how it works.) Nonetheless many don't consider it a modern-day microcomputer. That begins in 1977 with four companies: 1) APPLE, 2)COMMODORE, 3)PROCESSOR TECHNOLOGY, and 4)

RADIO SHACK(TANDY).[24] The following is a brief synopsis of each companies first 'appliance' microcomputer made in 1977:

1)   APPLE founders Steve Jobs[25] and Steve Wozniak created the *APPLE I* [the first single-board microcomputer], later the *APPLE II*, showing the latter at the West Coast Computer Faire in San Francisco, April 16, 1977.[26]

2)   COMMODORE creator Chuck Peddle demonstrated the *COMMODORE PET* at the Jan. 1977 Consumer Electronics Show, publicly announcing the computer at the West Coast Computer Faire, Aug. 1977.

3)   PROCESSOR TECHNOLOGY was founded by Lee Felsenstein. He publicly announced the *SOL-20* in Jan. 1977.[28]

4)   RADIO SHACK's *TRS-80 MODEL 1*, internally designed by Tandy engineers, sold their computers with a built-in keyboard, cassette-tape memory and television/monitor control card.[29]

What made these computers possible was wave soldering technology. No longer did kit builders have to solder hundreds of connections. For the consumer had only to buy a video monitor or television and a cassette interface to have a complete microcomputer, ie. the APPLE story.[30]

Over the next two years technological advancement led to the *ATARI 400 & 800*, and Texas Instruments' *TI 99/4*. These micro manufacturers were the first to introduce the public to high pressure sales and marketing techniques borrowed with enthusiasm from IBM. [31]

Other inventors of note were Clive Sinclair of *ZX-80* fame. In 1981 his machine sold for $49.95 making it the cheapest manufactured microcomputer ever built and incidentally began the "Home Computer Price Wars" of that year.[32] At the same time Adam Osborne sold the *OSBORNE I* , a 24 lb. Portable business computer for $1800.[33] Sadly, this was to be the last year for innovation in the 8-bit micro-computing world. For IBM, on the 12th of August, 1981, entered the microcomputer business ushering in the age of 16-bit computing.[34]

However the 8-bit machine wasn't quite dead. With IBM's machine came Z-80 hardware and CP/M software emulators and by 1982 INTEL had pushed 8-bit chip technology to its upper limits with the 8051 having 60,000 transistors.[35]

C: MEMORY

Another dimension to microcomputer hardware is memory.[36] Internal memory, now and forever, called RAM - Random Access Memory - started off very small, chip-capacity wise.[37] Miniscule might better describe it - 256 bytes to be exact. The ALTAIR used 8 chips giving it a 2 Kilobyte capacity.[38] These chips were called static because as long as power was applied they retained their memory status.[Today most microcomputers use dynamic memory chips. The active locations must be continually refreshed to preserve their memory status.] With the arrival of the APPLE II in 1977 came 16KB memory systems. Even the ADAM in 1983 had only 64KB.[39] [Today the common memory capacity of PCs is 16 million bytes.[40] A multiplication factor gone wild.]

The most important factors in micro-computing are how to get information in and displaying processed information that require nothing more than typing and viewing a video screen. The input/output story is discussed next.

D: DATA FLOW or INPUT/OUTPUT

There are five stages in the historical development of data input/output: 1)programmer/user; 2) tape/tele-type/printer; 3) cassette drive; 4) floppy disk drive and 5) keyboard.

What came first were toggle switches that directly programmed the microprocessor.[41] Flashing LEDs(Light Emitting Diodes) displayed processed output allowing no storage capabilities. Their exact, albeit highly abbreviated, operation is as follows: they're called fetch-execute machines; they fetch(get) instructions and data, execute it accordingly, then return processed data to display LEDs. No wonder this system wasn't conducive to expansion.

Something easier was needed. The answer came in the form of a paper tape device called a teletype. It was an ASR-33 Teletype and Universal Asynchronous Receiver/ Transmitter(UART), a serial/parallel com-munications device with system programs and applications(written in machine language) stored as ones and zeros.[42]

These standard input/output devices were quite primitive. It begins with the Teletype Model 15 using 5-bit Baudot code, manufactured in 1925 selling through computer/ electronic stores. It was replaced by the Model 33 Teletype in the early 60s. Both served as input and output devices.[43] Most computer makers sold them for about $1500 until Integrated Data Systems came out with a 7X9 dot matrix machine selling for $949.[44] Centronics dot matrix and daisy wheel printers, both much faster, sold for between $2000and $3000.[45] In 1977 for the truly discriminating user there was the LA36 DEC Writer II selling for $2000 - a technology no longer primitive.[46]

The standard printer became the Epson line. First, in 1978 came the Model 797, a 7-pin, $1200 friction-feed device. In 1981 came the Model 70. It was unreliable, did 60 characters-per-second, and at $600 was too expensive. A year later came the Model MX-80. It was reliable, tractor-fed, doing 80 characters-per-second. According to Stan Veit it is the most popular microcomputer printer ever built.[47]

There was a key event in Kansas City, Nov. 7-8, 1975 that was perhaps the first major attempt to establish a degree of compatibility among different computer and peripheral makers, specifically of the cassette drive.[48] Its aim was to lower costs and expand the microcomputer market.[49] For a while the process was successful but around the same time Shugart eclipsed cassette technology with 5 ¼ inch floppy drive technology.[50] [Universally referred to as minifloppy-drive technology.] Its speed, reliability and random access capability relegated cassette storage to data-backup status.[51]

Finally we come to the universal input device - the keyboard.[52] According to Bruce Buckley "the keyboard (is) bad, the mouse is better but not (a) perfect" input device.[53] Yet keyboards, in a different fashion, have been around since the mid 1800s. It wasn't until 1875 and Byron A. Brooks that the shift key materialized. However in 1943, Dr. August Dvorak, proposed a clearly superior keyboard but QWERTY was too well entrenched becoming the standard for microcomputer keyboards.[54]

Is there something making all this fancy hardware possible? As we've seen its the transistor. Invented in the late 40s it's small, producing little heat, consumes little energy, faster than vacuum tubes, and most important, it's reliable.[55] The transistor makes possible integrated circuits, not only for microprocessors but very fast memories. The result is computer speed and memory capacity doubling, doubling again, etc., etc.[Moore's Law] However, what's more important to recognize is that cost per unit of processing has plummeted since the mid 70s. Christopher Evans puts it succinctly: This may sound like technology run riot - and that is exactly what it (is). Never in history has an aspect of technology made such spectacular advances.[56]

Hardware items operating under the control of a microprocessor advanced rapidly during the 1970s. We will see if software fares as well.

Chapter Four

SOFTWARE

T his chapter concerns itself with what makes computers work. Programs in many languages tell microprocessors exactly what to do. Serving this function are assemblers, interpreters, compilers and machine-language coders.[1]Just what is a program? Simply put it's control statements(code) and data: "*Code* (being) that part of a program that performs actions; while *data* is the information affected by those actions."[2] Meanwhile Jonathan Titus and Richard Hofstadter argue the logic programs employ are not complicated "thus it will allow the great unwashed public to actually(gasp!) program computers".[3] And as Greg Paschal Zachary writes: "A programmer tries to build something usable by all.[4] The chief impediment is general lack of knowledge among non-programmers who are afraid or of the computer itself.[5] Ron Mitchell puts it more succinctly:

When it comes to computer programming, you often hear a number of things being said:

- Programming is an activity best left to the experts.
- I don't know where to start. There's so much to remember.

- It's way too complicated for me. I just don't have the patience.
- Well. I really only use my computer for word processing.
- The computer makes me feel stupid.[6]

Paul Somerson's "programming conjures up unpleasant images of pizza-crazed, unwashed techie nerds"[7] gives an unflattering view of programmers most would not want to associate with. Nevertheless, I and my fellow programmers look past this view and remind ourselves of Lady Lovelace's famous comment: "Computers can only do what they are told to do." Further, to learn the lesson of Edward Yourdon: "Better coding techniques may do nothing more than help you arrive at a disaster sooner than before.[8]

The why of processing is found in programming languages. Yet programming isn't for everyone. Its history though is important in understanding computer development.

PROGRAMMING HISTORY

The ancient history of programming begins with Lady Lovelace while contemporary history begins with Dr. Grace Hopper. Early programming was based on mechanical logic and it bears little resemblance to digitally-based programming. Hence our jump to the 1950s.[Appendix 8]

Prior to this period computers were programmed in machine labguage with binary-coded numbers, letters, or symbols.[9] Working with ENIAC in the 1940s Mauchly and Eckert created short-order code. It was Dr. Hopper, writing in 1952 in the The Education of a Computer, who invented the idea of a compiler and created universal pseudo-code calling it Flowmatic.[10] Shortly thereafter IBM scientists, under the direction of Jim Backus, created FORTRAN(FORmula TRANslator) from assembler, compiler and interpreter research. IBM used it in its 1957 704 machine with research continuing until 1960 when

*ALGOL(*ALGOrithmic) was adopted as an improved scientific language.[11]

The commercial world wasn't impressed with scientific languages, wanting one specifically tailored for their use. The solution came from the Department of Defense with *COBOL(*COmmon Business Oriented Language) and according to experts its birth was trumatic.[12] It's employment in the microcomputer world will be examined later in the chapter.

MICROCOMPUTING LANGUAGES

1. BASIC

The first high-level microcomputer language we're concerning ourselves with is *BASIC(*Beginner's All-purpose Symbolic Instruction Code).[13] John Kemeny and Thomas Kurtz, two professors at Dartmouth College, created BASIC in 1964 as an adjunct to teaching students computer programming skills.[14] They continuously improved it until 1971 but it was in 1975 that Bill Gates invented $K BASIC, 'version 1' to run on the ALTAIR that popularized it. In rapid succession came 'version 2', 'version 3', 'version 4', 'version 4-extended' and finally 'version GW' - 'gee whiz BASIC.[15] [Used only in PC world.] The first commercial article on BASIC, called TinyBASIC, was published in <u>Dr. Dobb's Journal</u> in late 1975.[16] 8K BASIC, EXTENDED BASIC and DISK BASIC, also called BASIC-80 followed within 2 years. For the APPLE, COMMODORE and Radio Shack, Bill Gates of Microsoft wrote BASIC language interpreters.[17] This early era BASIC is referred to as 'Old Microsoft BASIC', ie. Applesoft BASIC, TRS-80 DISK BASIC, because "if you were to enter a BASIC phrase without giving it a line number, the parser would assume you are giving the system a direct order, and execute it immediately.[18]

Why is BASIC so popular? BASIC's syntax, ease-of-use, high readability and English-like command structure gives "in-experienced programmers no trouble following a program's logic.[19] Of course they're "programming purists who feel that BASIC corrupted the minds of budding programmers by encouraging bad habits.[20] This of course is not the fault of BASIC bit of programmers. If they're lazy, they're lazy. [Appendix 7]

BASIC according to its proponents is easier to debug. Yet Nilsson says its the end-user that counts: "Software bugs bedevil users and manufacturers alike but given the inevitable presence of bugs, what matters most in the end is the support a developer offers.[21] Meanwhile, Hofstadler says debugging software is different than error-detecting routines found in compilers and interpreters.[22] Witness the 1960s when programmers insisted that compilers generate assembly code so they could examine it for compactness and precision. Such a thing is unheard of today - well at least in the commercial world.[23]

One reason BASIC is so popular is that it 'imposes few structural constraints on the programmer...and lack of structure permits programmers to write tangled illogical 'spaghetti' code."[24] It is the infamous 'goto' statement that's much abused, with code leading "you into an opague tangle of spaghetti[25] virtually impossible to decode by another. Another reason is that BASIC is free-form: That is "you are free to insert extra lines and spaces just about anywhere you want."[26] Yet we programmers must be aware at all times of Lien's creeping elegance:

> Programs grow more elegant with the ego
> reinforcement of the programmer. This
> 'creeping elegance' increases the chance of
> silly errors. It's fun to let the mind wander
> and add some more program here and
> there, but it's also easy to lose sight of the
> program's purpose. It is at times like this
> when the flow-chart is ignored, and the
> trouble begins. Nuff said.[27]

2: C

C language is an adaptation of *CPL*(Combined Programming Language) developed at Cambridge and the University of London, in 1963; *BCPL*("Basic' Combined Programming Language) written by Martin Richards in 1967 at Cambridge, University; and *B*, written by Ken Thompson to run on a PDP-7 minicomputer in 1969.[28] All three versions came from the *ALGOL* language. In 1972 it was refined by Cambridge University and Bell Laboratories researcher Dennis Ritchie who designed it to run on IBM mainframes and DEC's PDP-11 mini-computers.[29]

Today's *C*, in standard version called *ANSI C*, was formulated in 1978 though *C* was seldom used in the 8-bit world. Nevertheless Dr. Dobb's Journal published a *Small C* compiler, *tiny-c One*(an interpreter) and *tiny-c Two*(a compiler) programs in May 1980. Other *C* interpreters and compilers were available by the mid 80s but never catching on in the 8-bit world due to high costs and memory requirements.[30]

3: COBOL

COBOL being a mainframe language is seldom employed by the 8-bit microcomputer because as an interpreted language it's very slow. Compilers on the other hand take up too much space, too much object-code generation time, thereby having limited appeal. Nonetheless Tandy has an excellent *COBOL* system for the TRS-80 Model III+ and later versions.

There is what some experts call Modular Construction Programming(MCP).[31] This style of programming, applying to all languages, loads in a shell and calls sub-programs or modules off the floppy or hard disk as required. It is particularly important for the early days when memory capacity was small. Today most programs use this method because of their large memory requirements - bloated software and all that.[32]

Now let's apply programming to applications.

Chapter Five

APPLICATIONS

No one is surprised more often by the dynamic
behavior of a program than its author.
- Russ Blake
Optimizing Windows NT

A: **APPLICATIONS**

The average computer user is not concerned
with process but results. He's not concerned
with how the computer arrives at the answer
as long as the 'solution' is correct or suitable
to his needs.
Computer processing is not important.
Human- processing - how he interacts with
the computer, described as user friendliness –
is.

To what use may we put microcomputers? As word
processors? Yet how much writing do average people do?[1]
In balancing our bank accounts with entering and manipulating
data being too much of a task and besides can it not be done faster
by pencil and calculator? What about income tax preparation?

Many programs exist, particularly in the public domain, but they're neither sophisticated nor simple enough. You can create a will and make multiple copies but how often do we write a will? Household inventory? Many uses here I'm sure. However does this challenge the real capacity of a home computer? I've found one that does - sorting and searching book, magazine and equine blood-line databases. This section traces the history of applications regardless of their importance or use.

1. WORD PROCESSING/CHARACTER STORAGE OR FORMATTING PROGRAMS

> Thanks to word-processing software, home
> Computers could become 'the most flexible
> electronic type-writer you've ever used'.
>   - Feb. 1992

This was the original use of the word processor.[2] The problem? Secretaries using constantly failing 'data-processing' equipment gave word processors a bad name.[3] As Andy Rooney remarks, "It may be more fun on a word processor and it looks neater when you're finished, but it's faster on paper, and I don't care whether it looks neater or not. I'm not a typist; I'm a writer."[4] Don Lancaster agrees, commenting on *Wordstar,:* "It should have been banned in all civilized nations of the world as cruel and inhuman punishment inflicted on a naïve secretary."[5] To get secretaries to use these computer programs companies referred to them as a Wang *Word Processor* or IBM *Displaywriter.*

Well what exactly is a word processor? The generally accepted definition is a computer program that "helps you write and edit sentences and paragraphs in a document that can be saved and /or printed.[6]

The first word processor for microcomputers was Michael Shrayer's *The Electric Pencil,* introduced in 1977, followed almost immediately by some 40 versions.[7] One of the first versions for the TRS-80 was quickly replaced by a Tandy clone called *Scripsit. Easywriter* another *Electric Pencil* look-a-like "was created for the *APPLE II*.[8] *Wordpro* from <u>Commodore International</u> is popular in its *PET* and *C-64*, while *Autoscribe II* is in use by <u>Heath/Zenith's</u> *H89*. For CP/M machines the <u>Magic Wand,</u> circa 1978, was an early favorite.[9] One of the best word processors ever, *Word Handler* from <u>Silicon Valley Systems</u>, ran on CP/M machines beginning around 1980. It's downfall was its expense. However, appearing on the horizon and casting doubt on all other word processors was *Wordstar* - originally known as *Wordmaster*.[10]

One area for word processing gaining prominence today is desktop publishing(DTP). Though they are stand-alone programs most people use word processors since they have many text and graphics formatting capabilities found in desktop publishers, i.e. WYSIWYG(What You See Is What You Get)being one of the most important. Yet early microcomputer DTP programs lacked these facilities but the best text editors had them, i.e. to those who could afford them. With today's more powerful processors integrated-software DTP is an industry in itself.[11]

2: **TEXT EDITING PROGRAMS**

Text editors have been around since the early days of computing.[12] Early programmers used them to write high-level code though back then they were only line editors. Text editing, moving the cursor from one line to another and editing at random, is the best tool for creating ASCII code: The only code programmers are interested in.[13]

3. **DATABASE, DATA DESCRIPTION PROGRAMS AND INFORMATION RETRIEVAL PROGRAMS**

According to Mike Lewis inputted data is separate and independent of the way programs store and retrieve information. This gives rise to three types of database approaches: relational, hierarchical and network. The standard database structure on microcomputers is relational or what Codd calls, true contents-accessible file systems.[14] Back in the late 60s Edgar Codd established 13 rules to determine whether a database manager was relational or not.[15]

The first microcomputer database program was invented by Wayne Ratliff, which he called *Vulcan* - a *JPL*(Job Control Language) program adopted to run under CP/M and S-100 bus.[16] George Tate bought the rights to *Vulcan* and called it *dBASE* - Assembly Language Relational *Database* System. It was released under *dBASE II* as a perfected version. As Marc Schnapp comments: dBASE II was the result of "creative design thinking and astute marketing."[17]

Additionally "there was no *dBASE I*, but calling it *dBASE II* lent a sense of maturity to the newborn package."[18] However, most 8-bit database programs were written in BASIC, Z-80 ASSEMBLY or MACHINE language not *dBASE.*[19]

One of the best information retrieval programs written, according to Russ Walter, was *PFS*(Personal Filing System).[20] APPLE Computer bought thousands of copies from Software Publishing Company to sell with its *APPLE II* for $100.00. Along with *PFS* it also sold *PFS Report* with other versions running on many 8-bit machines. For those with CP/M the best program available was *dBASE II*, if you had the $700.00 in your bank account to pay for it.[21]

4. SPREADSHEET OR MATRIX DESCRIPTION PROGRAMS

The first mass-marketed application for microcomputers was *VISICALC* - for visible calculator. It was invented by Harvard Business School graduate Dan Bricklin as an accounting project[22] with Bob Franston writing the program and marketed by Personal Software owner Dan Flystra. It sold in 1979 for $150.00 and within $2^{1/2}$ years had sold 150,000 copies. *Visicalc* was originally ported to the *APPLE II*, providing the impetus for APPLE

Computers' phenomenal growth.   Eventually <u>Radio Shack</u>, <u>Commodore</u>, <u>Atari</u>, <u>Hewelltt-Packard</u> and <u>IBM</u> machines ran *Visicalc*. For CP/M owners the most popular spreadsheet is *Supercalc*.[23]

5. GRAPHICS PROGRAMS

Graphics programs were limited in scope in early micro-machines. They were restricted by slow processors and small memory capacities. It wasn't until 1980 that microcomputers could draw reasonable real-life objects due to the 'invention' of *sprites*. Though restricted to minimal number of lines, columns and gray-scale levels early 80's attempts began to replicate minicomputer results.[24] With the arrival of the *IBM PC* in 1981 microcomputer graphics take off.[25]

6. GAME PROGRAMS

Spacewar implemented on CRTs in early 1960's minicomputers, by contrast started all graphics/animation with almost no text, is generally regarded as the first small computer game[26] -an original creation of MITs *Project MAC*, headed in 1961 by Steve Russell and his fellow hackers.[27] However, the first computer game and its science was invented many years prior by Willy Higinbotham.[28]

Paralleling computer games were video games, invented in 1966 by Ralph Baer of <u>Sanders Associates</u>, Nashua, New Hampshire.[29] It was Nolan Bushnell, Sanata Clara, Cal., in 1971 who invented the first microcomputer game *Computer Space*. It wasn't a commercial success. On the other hand his game *Pong* shipping in 1972 was an instant success. It turned <u>Atari</u> into the number one video game company of the 1980's.[30]

This almost concludes the section on applications. We have one vital part of programming left, the most important of all, the operating system. Without it, nothing happens.

7. **OPERATING SYSTEM PROGRAMS**

Hafner and Markoff give one of the best descriptions of an operating system I've come across: "Operating systems are programs that control a computer's task the way an orchestra conductor controls musicians. Operating systems start and stop programs and find and store files."[31]The most successful 8-bit operating system is CP/M.[32]

CP/M is a creation of Dr. Gary Kildall of Digital Research, Inc., while he was a software consultant for INTEL in 1973. He called his system *Control Program/Monitor* and offered it to DEC but they found it operated 'too slow' for their PDP-11 minicomputer. However, almost all microcomputer manufacturers of the S-100 variety and INTEL 8080 or Zilog Z-80 microprocessors included it with their systems for $75. "By 1980, CP/M 2.2 had become the defacto standard for microcomputer operating systems."[33] One reason for its success was that it had five basic built-in commands, with several more added by 1981.[34] Many transient(external) commands were added by individuals and corporate users. However, CP/M provides an interface between hardware and software so that different hardware would 'look the same' to the software enabling the operating system to be easily ported to many types of computers.[35] [For example, the FAA used Intertec *CompuStars*, Z-80 CP/M computers, in 1982 to monitor service and equipment outages at twenty-three small airports and report them to Washington.[36]] Yet David Ahl writes of their difficulties: "Operating systems and programs which run under them, compared to what they can be ten years from now, are 'user-hostile'".[37] Yet through it all CP/M was central to the marketing of 8-bit applications. [See Appendix 9 for an outline of the CP/M operating system.]

B: **MARKETING**

Software must be published and /or sold for the industry to flourish.[38] According to Bob Linstrom this is the process:
1) Write a program in BASIC or another language.
2) Answer the phone.
2) Take an order directly from a retail store clerk.
4) Mail a floppy in a Baggie along with a mimeographed documentation.
5) In 30 days, cash the check and collect your fortune.[39]

Very true in the earliest days.[40] T'is a pity it no monger is. Customers have come to demand legible manuals, bug-free programming, functional packaging and wider choice. Slowly, the software industry moved from funky to refined.[41] We can question, why wouldn't this happen? Who wants to pay $495 for a piece of software and not be able to use it properly? As John Weld asks: "Would you buy a shrink wrapped automobile?"[42] In the early days when you wrote your own application programs or bought a program for a few dollars money wasn't the limiting factor. Memory capacity and program input were.[43] [We all know what happens when mass-marketing and profitability enters the equation.[44] Yet without these two sisters of capitalism we'd probably still be running *Wordstar 1.0* on our CP/M computers.[45]]

Software companies that refuse to stand behind their products lose market share. Mike Wayne, in <u>PC Magazine</u> describes the microcomputer industry as agreed machine with many consumers agreeing with his assessment.[46]

Dan Gookin raises another contentious point about software publishing yet Lima states the case best: "Most computer manuals are as difficult to understand as a graduate-level course in quantum physics."[47] One only has to open a manual and be shocked at its complexity. No wonder non-computer people feel threatened. T'is a pity publishers haven't learn't the mechanism needed to ameliorate this problem. Yet should we not be surprised that this only amplifies techno-resistance in society, contributing to computerphobia with people throwing up their hands exclaiming: How can I possibly learn all this and why should I have to?

Chapter Six

HOME COMPUTING

A: **HOME COMPUTERS/PERSONAL COMPUTERS**

If you have ever imagined that some day you might possibly ponder the unlikely remote untoward improbability of the most minute illusionary consideration of your purchasing a computer...

-Editor Computer Now!
Sept. 1983

A writer used a teletype in his home to communicate with a mainframe on a time-share basis - then thought to be 'key to   the computer's future,' Personal computers, experts predicted, would never be affordable to individuals.

May 1967
(quoted in Popular Science/85

W hat is a home computer? Has it changed over time? Has it acquired a new definition? Why do people buy it?[1]

First of all who coined the term 'home computer'? From the available research it appears that Art Salsberg, in an editorial in Popular Electronics, January 1975, titled "*The Home Computer is Here!*, originated the term.[The term 'home computer console' was first used by J. R. C. Licklider in 1960.[1a]] Prior, it was known as a *personal minicomputer*. As far as the term 'personal computer' is concerned, it appears Nelson Winkless coined it in a newspaper article in 1976.[2] [I did find an earlier use of this phrase in Alvin Toffler's Future Schock, page 374. It seems Williamson was in error.]

In the early days of personal computing users defined the term as "personal access to and use of a computer, not a personal machine."[3] Though minicomputers were desktop in size by 1973 such as DEC's *PDP-8* they were far too expensive for the home. The reason: they were constructed from discrete transistors.[4] This changed with the microcomputers arrival in 1973. Its original form was probably Don Lancaster's '*TV Typewriter*', though it wasn't advertised as being a microcomputer, yet could be converted into one.[5] Dvorak and Solomon comment:

> A computer terminal for the time -sharing
> services, schools, and experimental uses.
> It's a comunications aide for the deaf. It's
> a teaching machine, particularly good for
> helping pre-schoolers learn the
> alphabet and words.[6]

However, the first home computers came in kit form and were offered to the public in 1974. For instance - the *Mark 8 Minicomputer*; *Scelbi-8b*; Martin Research *Mike-2* and *Mike -3;* and *RGS 008A*. Less well-known microcomputers were the *ELF Cosmac* from RCA; *JOLT*(Nationally advertised, Nov. 1975); *EBKA* and Ohio Scientific machines. These kits used the 8080, Z80 and 6502 microprocessors.[7] January 1975 saw the *ALTAIR*s, the most famous being the *8800* from MITS(Micro-instrumentation Telemetry Systems), IMSAIs, *SOL* and SWTP(Southwest Technical Products Computers). By 1977 mass-produced nationally-advertised personal computers such as the *APPLE II*, the Commodore *KIM-1* and the *TRS-80 Model 1/Level I* ended the era of kit microcomputing.[8] Even MITS began shipping assembled computers in 1977 - the *ALTAIR 8800b*.[9] In that year their were 120 companies manufacturing computer equipment with 60 making computers. [Appendix 10]

One of the best known microcomputers, created, manufactured and distributed by Tandy Inc. selling in Aug, 3, 1977 through its 7000 retail outlets in the U.S. and Canada, was the original *TRS-80 Model I, Level I*. It sold for $599.95. By 1979 the *Level II* was available, selling for $849. [Appendix 11] These two machines were the most popular microcomputers in schools across America. In 1980 Tandy came out with the *Model II* and in July with the *Model III* which took up residence in many schools, factories, businesses and homes. In 1983 came the *Model 4*, which used *CP/M* and Microsoft *BASIC 5.0*, which had the largest software availability of any computer to date.[10]

The 8-bit computer wasn't dead yet! "The most popular computer ever built was the Commodore *C-64*" introduced in 1982.[11] It sold uncounted millions around the world, yet the writing was on the wall. IBM's 'letters' were ready to crush the 8-bit opposition.

By 1978 users moved to the 8086 - the 'first' 16-bit microprocessor - with some arguing since then that we needn't go further:

> Apart from tinkering with word processors and spreadsheets, the industry has not really come up with a new application in years. Most of the products would hardly give an old 286 processor a headache. What is more, if the processor sat in anything like a half-decent hardware and / or software architecture, most applications would still run on a 8086 processor without taxing it.[12]

I agree with Banks. A home computer with an 8086 processor is all one needs. I still have my trusty *Tandy 1000,* with its 8086, and it still meets all my computing needs. (I'll go one step further. I still use my *ADAM* and it does essentially what my PC does. [Appendix 12] Its Z-80 microprocessor is all I really need.) It will run a $495 application program as well as a $25 shareware program.[12(a)] Mind you it's a bit slow but it gets the job done. More to the point - running communication programs on modem doesn't tax it. I need nothing faster.[13]

I believe it fair to conclude that the home computer is more powerful than ever yet available software makes such computers inefficient and much too expensive for most potential home users.

Russ Walter describes another potentially darker side to home computing - addiction. Computers like drugs, using the same terminology: you buy a computer from a *dealer*; once you begin computing you're a *user*, staying up most of the night waking up bleary-eyed, "eventually your boss suspects your computer habit, realizes that you're not giving full attention to your job, and fires you";[14] to support this habit you turn to writing programs, making you a *pusher*. Your friends become addicts joining your subculture of "computer phreaks".[15] When you become well-known, an establishment personality, then you're a *consultant* pushing young people into buying more computers, programs and accessories, etc.

Tom Lehrer's song sums it up best:

> He gives the kids free samples,
> Because he knows full well
> That today's young innocent faces
> Will be tomorrow's clientele.

Now maybe you can understand why APPLE Computer Company tried to make Congress pass a bill that (would) let APPLE give free samples to every school in the country - and get a tax write-off to boot.[16]

Some 'experts' argue that the home computer is a business or work computer in disguise. Ashton-Tate's Stanley Crane argues:

> I personally don't believe there's a home computer user out there. If there were, there would be a software program for the home that did something for the home that wasn't for the business. A lot of people have small businesses on the side at home but that's still a business. It's not that you have a home temperature program that turns the thermostat up and down, watches for burglars, and reminds you of when it's your anniversary.

Furthermore   Lewis   Levin   of   Microsoft comments:

> We, collectively - the industry of software and Hardware manufacturers - learned what the home market is. The home market is really a work-at-home market; it's people who bring work from their offices back home to do some more work, or it's people whose primary place of business is their home. Now the industry has realized that what this 'home' market really consists of is a large body of people who essentially want to do the same thing that office workers do, but they want to do it at home.[18]

There is more to micro-computing than having a computer on a desk. To get the most from a microcomputer one needs to contact others with commensurate interests. You do this through a modem to connect to bulletin boards; belonging to a user group and publishing newsletters for the other clubs; and attending specific-computer conventions, ie. ADAMcons.[19]

B: USER GROUPS, NEWSLETTERS, BBSs and CONVENTIONS

The early history of computer-user groups is rather murky. The available literature starts them circa 1973. However, Stephen B. Gray founded the <u>Amateur Computer Society</u> in 1966 who's goal was to build a digital computer as a hobby. These earliest groups were really nothing more than internal meetings of employees of computer or electronic firms, research establishments, secondary school electronic /computer clubs in Silicon Valley area, or university laboratories.[20] (One of the first magazines centered around one microcomputer was *Computer Notes* for the MITS *ALTAIR* **8800**, published by David Bunnel. [Appendix 13] To keep track of their meetings, agendas and discussions they published newsletters which are originally for group members but later made available to non-members.[21] In a short time these newsletters became associated with a certain type of, or a specific manufacturer's, computer, ie. The *ALTAIR Newsletter; the <u>SOL</u>* Newsletter or *TRS-80 Newsletter*. In the *ADAM* world, which I've been involved in for many years, there are many newsletter. For example: *Vancouver Island Senior ADAMphiles - <u>The ADVISA Newsletter; ADAM-LINK of Utah</u>* newsletter for the *ADAM* computer.[22]

The first microcomputer club was the *Homebrew Computer Club* in California's Silicon Valley, launched by Steve Wozniak and others.[23] By the late 70s user groups or clubs were well established yet "were mainly for engineers and hobbyists who banded together to talk jargon and exchange arcane information.[24] By the early 80s most clubs were for people interested in one computer and sharing information in a social setting.[25]

Many of the *ADAM* user-groups are going strong as are *APPLE*, *ATARI* and others.[26] This marks evidence that the 8-bit microcomputer is still alive and well thank you very much.[27]

Other computers have their conventions, particularly the *APPLE* and *ADAM*. What started it all though was the *Personal Computing '76* show, held on the weekend of August 28 in

Atlantic City, N.J. which Stan Veit says was the first big computer show ever held.[28]

The history of the telephone accessed, microcomputer-based BBS(Bulletin Board Service) goes back to Feb. 16, 1978 to Chicago, Ill. It was created by Ward Christensen and Randy Seuss. It's billed as "The world's first, and oldest micro based BBS catering to the more advanced, technical hobbyists."[29] This CBBS(Computerized Bulletin Board System) "emulated the functions of a cork bulletin board for information exchange" and is a message-only BBS. Today's BBSs are more interactive yet basically are only message-directed in nature.[30]

The home computer and its accessories or peripherals, either internal or external, are central to the early growth of 8-bit microcomputers.[31] It's now time to examine their societal impact and draw some conclusions.

Chapter Seven

COMPUTERS IN SOCIETY

As computers take over more and more of the work that human beings shouldn't be doing in the first place...there's going to be nothing left for human beings to do but the more creative types of endeavor.

_Issac Asimov
"World of Ideas"

For the most part historians haven't examined or documented the microcomputer revolution with regards to its structural and attitudinal impact on society nor considered the mental changes of computer scientists and programmers that give them the flexibility to do high-technology, experimental work. The precision of their thinking is enhanced by an analytical process because "computers are causing us to view the world with eyes that search for algorithms to describe the processes we see rather than words to describe the facts we see."[1] The microcomputer greatly expands the mental capacity of its user if he/she only engages it with this in mind. Our social institutions, particularly education, permit us to pass on knowledge to the next generation.[2] The impact of ideas, great magnified by the widespread implementation of computers, on reforming the structure and attitudes of society must be carefully examined and documented by historians.

What I've been elucidating in this paper is technological innovation in the computer industry across time, with concentration on the microcomputer. In other words, be it hardware or software they both drive the microcomputer industry. To see this at work let's first explore the past.

A: **LOOKING BACK**

> Computer makers haven't yet sold a PC that can be used
> by a novice - or produced a compelling reason to own one[3]

with Bill Machrone reporting in May 1993:

> With today's technology and a little imagination, we
> can personalize the world with our personal computers![4]

But this is not what the (personal) microcomputer world is all about? Could this statement not have been uttered 15 years ago? To have asked in 1993 seems to prove Michael Fereday right:

> Do you remember when,
> The K was King,
> And computers were
> The incoming thing?[5]

And perhaps Dvorak and Callahan summarize best why the microcomputer fails to live up to its expectations: "Don't expect PC productivity to truly skyrocket until PC products get a whole lot smarter",[6] doing things the non-computer way are faster, and "technology isn't always what it's cracked up to be".[7]

How true of early microcomputers. They were susceptible to brown-outs and voltage spikes 'caused' by your local electrical generator.[8] On more than one occasion my *ADAM* and PC have 'died' due to Ontario Hydro's electrical power adjustments.

Electricity gone? Silence![9] It reminds me of William Manchester's <u>A World Lit Only By Fire: The Medieval Mind and the Renaissance</u> - ... "an entirely different world ... virtually with no communications and magic and sorcery rule." Maybe the same ,may be said of the computer, micro or otherwise, as far as most people are concerned.[10]

B: **EDUCATION**

> Continued in their present patterns of fragmented unrelation, our school curricula will insure a citizenry unable to understand the cybernated world in which they live.
> _Marshall McLuhan (1964)

We see the microcomputerized classroom, or at least one view, as each student at a terminal - decreasing oral discussion with only a few students participating - keyboarding with nearly a 100% participation rate. With Kenner saying of this classroom situation: "It was eerie; all of them in the same room, looking not at one another but at monitors, and typing things they wouldn't venture to utter.[11] Is this learning or at least education?[12] We must keep in mind - "in the computer age the need to understand the difference between information and education is increasingly acute."[13] [Appendix 14]

Are we learning this lesson? Is their a fundamental difference between students now and then(1970s)? The statistics seem to point this way. SAT scores were 750 to 800 of which 2800 students had this score. Now only 1200 do. The microcomputer may solve this problem by moving education from a 'mass' system to a more 'individualized' system.[14] The central problem is that software for early microcomputers was truly awful. It's not much better today. As Jack Nimershein comments: "With few exceptions, they (software packages) represent an electronic echo of our past, rather than a harbinger of the bright future forecast at the beginning of the computer revolution".[15] These programs use flash cards and overly structured approaches that ignore academic skills of most students. The microcomputer industry may be changing these practices today, particularly with newer and less costly technology.

Yet it seems somewhat optimistic to me. As I write there are still "1$^{1/2}$ million *APPLE* IIs (circa 1977) in use"...(Moreover) "45% of hardware is 5 years old or more" and most "PCs cannot run WINDOWS".[16] And economic restraints will further extend the time. It's hardware we're talking here. Software is what's essential to computer-aided instruction (CAI) and most 'experts' agree that challenging software is many years off.

More to the point. "As commercial and educational applications for the computer multiply, a good many consumers succumbed to the sales' pitches for home computers have ended up with one industry analyst calls 'the $1000 doorstop'"[17]

Yet microcomputer growth in classrooms is dynamic, but is it benefiting education? Let's look at the numbers:
Computer Shopper, Jan. 1987, p. 108, gives the following statistics:

Ratio of students to computers in the Developed Countries:

Sept.	1983	125:1
Sept.	1993	16:1
Sept.	2005	1:1

(Projected by O.E.C.D., Paris)

By 1987, according to Stewart Brand, The Media Lab, the ratio was 50:1, i.e. 1,000,000 microcomputers to 50,000,000 students[18] while in Boston the ratio was 18:1. Probably less today. However the debate doesn't center around numbers. The debate, then and now, is between *computer-aided instruction* and *discovery-based learning*_also called *computer instruction*, i.e. programming. Students start programming from basics of BASIC or any other language and move to more structured complex methods, learning how computers work in the process, i.e. becoming computer literate, indeed understanding our cybernated world.[19] Or is Henry David Thoreau correct when he wondered about the importance of telegraphy when he said, Was it an 'improved means to an unimproved end.'[20] May we put education in the same boat?

Bringing computers to education is fraught with danger as most educators, professional or otherwise, don't know how best to accomplish goals, possibly because we don't know what the "best methods of teaching are".[21] Teaching machines of the 50s and 60s never caught on as they simply rewarded students for correct responses and punished for incorrect ones not permitting dynamic interchange.[22]

Whether one talks of C.A.I. or C.A.L. capitalism is only now making money from computers in classrooms.[23] With portable computers, bringing mainframe processing power to the average student, are we seeing 'intelligent' teaching machines with their value measured not in "what they teach as how they will go about it?[24] As a science of education emerges educational systems will use microcomputer-based tools to positive advantage one hopes.

C: **HOME COMPUTERS**

We must ask Why do hobbyists buy a personal computer?

Is it   1) to play games?
        2) for number crunching?
        3) to learn the inner workings of
           microcomputers/microprocessors?
           Or
        4) to control appliances in your
           home?

Early microcomputer manufacturers were not able to deliver what they promised.[25] With this in mind the Economist asks "So who really needs a personal computer at home?"[26] and concluding: "Computer makers haven't yet sold a PC that can be used by a novice - or produced a compelling reason to own one."[27]

All seem to forget Covvey's dictum: "A simple but adequate introduction to computer machinery and programming concepts to people who have no previous knowledge of the subject"[28] is all that most people want.

Now let's discover why one indeed would buy a home computer. There are two questions to answer?

1) To what use will you put a computer?
2) Which program will do the best job?

But first: Why is the microcomputer so dominant? Here are three explanations:

1) There is a plethora of interactive games. They offer immense sophistication and
    power offering intellectual stimulation of a
    kind not found in external world.[29]
2) There is a shift in education from public, group teaching in schools to home, private computer-based instruction.
3) In the 1980s and 90s there was an increase in social turbulence, discouraging travel, thereby making
     homes more attractive.[30]

Stanley Crane says that we want ever more powerful home computers to do ever more work concluding "the nature of being a human being has not significantly changed. I think it's all marketing trying to help people make decisions."[31] Hardware manufacturers have convinced us that we need more processing power while software producers supply more sophisticated programs that require this processing power.[32] The underlying "idea is to convince people to move from *Etch-a-Sketch* technology to the latest, high-speed, state-of-the-art doodad."[33] Yet for those contemplating moving from one technology to another they should heed the advice of Tim Albano:

> Keep in touch with the intended customers and avoid
> the pitfall of anaerobic isolation; do not nor assume
> that customers will pay any price to secure the latest
> computer technology; ease the way for customers to
> adopt a new standard by providing software and
> hardware bridges that help connect older machines to
> the new ones.[34]

And as far as microcomputers replacing books, a giant leap from
one technology to another, is concerned heeding the advice of
Edward P. Morgan is essential:

> A book is the only place in which you can examine a
> fragile thought without breaking it, or explore an
> explosive idea without fear it will go off in your face...
> It is one of the few havens remaining where a man's
> mind can get both provocation and privacy.[35]
>
>   Creativity in Action (No.
>   241, May 1994)

THE FUTURE AS PAST

> Even the future is not what it used to be.
>   _Paul Ambroise Valery
>   French poet and critic

   Man's growing dependence on computer technology is a
discussion moving beyond existential predicaments of the 50s and
60s to one of a growing concern highlighted by concrete example.
Science fiction writers, i.e. Asimov, Shelley, Capek, Willison and
Forester, if most were alive today would no doubt marvel, yet be
appalled, at the state of computer technology.[36] Yet we cannot
expect it to do marvelous things if we misuse its potential.[37]

CONCLUSION

As a nonhuman form of intelligence, the computer can help
overcome that most fundamental of human phobias
- the fear of the different.
-Arthur Gibson
World of the Unexpected

The danger of the past was that men became slaves.
The danger of the future is that men may become
robots.
_ Erich Fromm

Will the information rich get richer while the
information poor get poorer?
_ N. Negroponte, Wired

I believe if fair to conclude that hardware and software
play an equal role in driving micro-computing history
yet I concur with Jeff Evans summary of its very dynamic
development: "Where computers are concerned, it seems that
ancient history begins only moments before the present."[1]

For computers are "more than dumb receptacles of information
propagated by error-prone humans"[2] and still force us to enter

their world, not fitting into the human environment. But "to be effective, systems will have to be designed from the outside in. The terminal or console operator, instead of being a peripheral consideration, will become the tail that wags the whole dog."[3] And quite interesting: "A computer is a very useful tool, but if you don't use it, it will not do your work for you. And remember...A computer is only as good as its operator."[4]

The early micro-computing age was one of variety not uniformity. However IBM brought this to an end in 1981 with the PC. Rationality followed but innovation was somewhat stymied. Only inventions or discoveries that have commercial market viability are publicly released by large commercial software and hardware companies. Small, entrepreneurial firms have all but disappeared.

Over the years, since the late 70s at least, we've seen powerful programs evolved by software firms adding more features to applications.[5] Witness the fact that today they hardly give a 286 processor any problems. What's more, "if the processor sat in anything half-decent hardware and/or hardware architecture, most of the applications would still run on an 8086 processor without taxing it.[6] The reason applications won't run on early 1980s microcomputers is bloated software. Yet, it seems only small software companies are inventing anything new or daring, the not-discovered-here syndrome prevailing these days[7] at most large commercial software houses. Their interests lie in upgrading programs designed years earlier.

What may we conclude? In technical terms the evolution of computers marched hand-in-hand with the evolution of electronics - from vacuum tube(1940s) to VLSI(1980s) technology. As electronics advances so did computers - well hardware-wise anyway with software failing to keep pace. Programs and/or applications can't challenge the speed and sophistication of microprocessors. It was true in 1973, 1981 and today.[8]

The digital-technological revolution within its current infrastructure is now on an evolutionary track. What isn't happening is an accompanying social revolution, i.e. society isn't keeping up to the growth of science and technology of computers and digital information.[9] People haven't embraced the information highway let alone the computing revolution because they fear abuse by government and business of information gathered on them[10] A classic response to this, among some, is Ludditism while others raise legal challenges. For others they simply fall under the sway of 'experts' and analysts "who tell users what to buy, vendors what to sell, and journalist how to spin."[11] With a somewhat darker view is Robert Penn Warren-

> In the technetronic age...the boys who handle the
> post-computer mechanisms...will enevitably be in
> control...with a vast, functionless, pampered and
> ultimately powerless population of nonexperts
> living on free time, unemployed and unemployable.[12]

Then there's the "Faustian proposal that the experts make to us is to let them(the masses) lay their fallible hands on eternity..."[13] And finally, collecting and handling information in an open society is paramount to its success yet authoritarians may easily turn this process against us. Ethics and personal diligence are watchwords.[14]

For the future H. G. Well's, in <u>Things to Come</u>, asks 'What shall it be?' The answer appears either as an accelerating of computing technology or a "luddite movement who want to call a halt to scientific progress,"[15] i.e. end microcomputer development. Yet the English poetess Edith Nesbitt expounds: "It is wonderful how quickly you get used to things, even the most astonishing."[16] And as "someone one said the difficulty is not in creating new ideas but in breaking away from the old ones."[16(a) ,17]

Microcomputers had a "quirky beginning, consumer mistrust, excitement among the cognoscenti and of course, (the) bold claims for the future."[18] Furthermore, Jacques Leslie writes:

> One reason for the rise of computer-generated
> ambiguity is the newness of digital technology.
> Just as in the early years of electrification and
> the telephone, we're still trying to figure out
> what we want it to do for us, and in the
> meantime we're confused.[19]

Yet with all this, I for see continued technological development in the microcomputer industry, basing this conclusion on the history outlined in this paper. For across time the microcomputer has been transformed from a luxury item to a necessary evil[20] though I'm not a "Planglossian apologist for an unconvincing vision of the future"[21] as some writers are.

   As we've seen the micro-computing industry is dynamic with a history measured in two decades or so leaving insufficient time to definitively write its historical beginnings. Nevertheless, I've attempted to write its history. I hope to your satisfaction.

EPILOGUE

This book is an account of the earliest years of microcomputing as I have defined it. It essentially stops in 1981 with the IBM PC. 8-bit computing's days were numbered as far too many microcomputers, they weren't compatible but probably far more interesting to play /experiment with, were chasing customers that just weren't there. Cost being a major contributing factor. Nonetheless, what came before the PC era is an interesting story not historically speaking as too little time has past but if only for preservation sake. This edition includes the epilogue and cosmetic changes.

APPENDICES

APPENDIX ONE

COMPUTER TERMS DEFINED

A brief description of computer terms, a glossary you might say, follows:

BASIC: An acronym meaning "Beginner's All-purpose Symbolic Instruction Code. It's a high level language developed at Dartmouth College Hanover, New Hampshire) that is among the most popular languages in programming microcomputers. It's also one of the easiest to learn.

BIT: Binary Digit. The most elementary data representation in the computer. A 'bit" consists of a one or a zero and is used in a series to represent a single character or 'byte'. (Generally, 8 bits = 1 byte.)

BUG: A mistake, a malfunction, or a defect, in any part of the computer, program, or system.

BYTE: A consecutive group of 8 'bits' that are treated as a unit and are often used to represent one character.

CRT: Cathode Ray Tube. The 'television screen' monitor used to display information.

CURSOR: The character on the video display that indicates the next position at which a character will be inserted or deleted.

DEBUG: To remove errors from the program.

DISK: (or Diskette). Flat circular storage medium used to store programs, data and other information.

DATA PROCESSING[1]: Computers process data in four distinct ways:

1) Calculating - computers employ arithmetic to solve problems.

2) Sorting - the alphabetical, numerical, or logical ordering of data

3) Retrieval and 4) Storage - data flows in and out of program and external memory

MICROPROCESSORS - "The concept is essentially that of developing a device which can take instructions and operate upon them."[2] In other words, it employs logical circuits and registers to carry out instructions that a programmer writes.

RAM MEMORY or PROGRAM/INTERNAL MEMORY - The microprocessor reads and writes data to electronic devices that may be used immediately and/or stored frequently.

EXTERNAL MEMORY - The microprocessor reads and writes data to a tape, PCMCIA device, floppy disk, hard disk or electrooptic disc. This data is 'permanent' and not always directly or immediately available to the microprocessor.

[1] "The evolution of computers from data-processing machines to personal learning tools" is described with great clarity by Howard Rheingold, Tools for Thought(N.Y.: Simon & Schuster, 1985).

[2] Peter Ruber, "Anatomy of a Microchip", Computer Monthly March 1992: 52.

I hope this explains basic microcomputing terms and gives a clearer understanding of a microcomputer's inner workings.

APPENDIX TWO

ROLE OF ROBOTS AND INTELLIGENCE IN COMPUTING HISTORY

Karel Capec's play <u>R.U.R.</u> (Possum's Universal Robots) is a story of robots or androids. These robots or automated machines gave rise to cybernetics defined in 1947 by Norbert Wiener '"as the science of control and communication in the animal and the machine.'"[1]

To Weizenbaum it was socialization, "that is (robots) modified by its experiences with its world.[2] We know of Asimov's three <u>Laws of Robotics</u> that puts man first which was a natural consequence of people's view of robots in science fiction films and stories.[3] Yet the first computerized robot wasn't built until 1962 by Heinrich Ernst of MIT but it failed to live up to past images.[4]

Alan Turing's role in computer history is much more cerebral. Generally regarded as the discoverer of modern computing techniques and theory he outlined a concept called a 'methodist machine' in his classic paper <u>On Computable Numbers, with an Application to the Entscheidungsproblem</u>. In a second paper <u>Computing Machinery and Intelligence</u>[5] he argued that computers will "compete with men in purely intellectual pursuits"[6] and was the first concept of a stored-program computer.[7] This incidentally was the first publication of his famous test to determine whether a computer can think like a human - "a machine may be deemed intelligent when it can pass for a human being in a blind test."[8] He went further when he said computers could be taught abstract skills, be given sense organs, teach them chess and English, and "educate (them) the same way you'd educate a somewhat handicapped child."[9]   Finally, Turing went on to design the first electronic computer called *Colossus*.

[1] Walter, 25.

[2] Quoted in Fjermedal 134.

[3] Asimov

[4] Solomon 69.

[5] Turing

[6] Shipley 66.

[7] Hey 321.

[8] Turing

[9] Walter 253.

APPENDIX THREE

FIRST THREE GENERATIONS OF ELECTRONIC COMPUTERS

1: GENERATION ONE

> Modern computer knowledge was formulated by the following pioneers: Claude E. Shannon of MIT; Alan Turing; Konrad Zuse and Helmut Schreyer of the University of Berlin; Dr. Atanasoff; Dr. Howard Aiken of Harvard; Ivor Catt of Manchester, England; Drs. John Mauchley and J. Preper Eckert; Dr. John von Neumann and Norbert Wiener.

In 1937 Claude E. Shannon described the behavior of circuits using Boolean algebra which could use electronic circuits rather than analog ones to mimic reasoning. From his research came information theory, the foundation of today's computerized, electronic highway.[1] In 1936 Konrad Zuse and Helmut Schreyer used electro-magnetic relays and a punched-paper tape system to speed up computing power.[2] Later in the decade Schreyer wrote a paper describing electronic valves or tubes to build a high-speed digital computer but Evans says "with the coming of war this thesis found its way on to a library shelf and apparently had no influence whatsoever on the future development of computers".

  Burks and Burks argue that Atanasoff built the first electronic computer as outlined in his paper, Computing Machine for the Solution of Large Systems of Linear Algebraic Equations. In 1944 Dr. Howard Aiken built the first automatic computer at IBM that was externally programmable. It cost $250,000. Yet by early the 80's a $100 programmable hand-held calculator was many times more powerful. The MARK I was replaced by _ENIAC_ as the world's first modern, electronic computer. Drs. John Mauchley and J. Presper Eckert built the <u>Electronic Numerical Integrator and Computer</u> machine from 18000 vacuum tubes; 500,000 soldered joints; 10000 capacitors; 70000 resistors at the Univ. of Penn., that began operation on Feb. 15, 1946. ENIAC weighed 30 tons, occupied 1500 sq. ft. and could do 5000 calculations per second. With the construction of the Whirlwind, EDASAC and EDVAC in the late 40s stored-programming became possible.

The theoretical research laying the foundation for modern electronic computers was conducted by Dr. John von Neumann and Norbert Wiener. In his paper <u>Preliminary Discussion of the Logical Design of an Electronic Computing Instrument</u> he described random access memory,stored program characteristics and sequential operation known today as the von Neumann architecture. He created the foundation upon which today's computing superstructure is built. He's also famous for discovering the general theory of games along with Oskar Morgenstern. The other half of the equation, how man interacts with computers, was formulated by Wiener in his classic paper on cybernetics, a topic much discussed today.

2: GENERATION TWO

In generation two we witnessed the era of commercialization of computers. UNIVAC 1 was the first commercially 'mass-produced' computer sold to the U.S. Bureau of the Census. Yet it was in 1953 that "a typewriter company named IBM entered the computer marketplace". Most know of IBM's rise to power - beginning in 1890 as the Tabulating Machine Company, merging in 1911 with Computing Tabulating and Recording Company and finally in 1929 becoming International Business Machines Corporation. IBM's first computer the 701 was replaced by its 'workhorse' machine the 650 "with nearly 2000 of these machines eventually (being) produced".[3]

3: GENERATION THREE

Central to third generation computers is Bell Labs invention of the transistor in 1952.[4] However the first transistorized computers the TX-0 and TX-2 invented by Dr. Ivan Sutherland at MIT's Lincoln Labs began the era of discrete-transistor logic processing.[5] By the way Texas Instruments supplied these transistors at $16.00 apiece.

In the early 60's UNIVAC produced the 1004, a desk-sized , high-speed card tabulator destined to create the minicomputer industry. Minicomputers were "stripped down versions of large, general purpose computers" that accepted batch programs yet allowed individuals to program them.(DEC)[6] They were excellent as data acquisition systems but did more than just gather and print out data.They also manipulated the data, put it into a form more useful to the human operator and other machines".[7] By the late 60's Digital Equipment Corporation's PDP-6, with 16k of memory, became the standard. Later in the decade the PDP-8 was to be DEC's most successful computer.[8](DEC was challenged by Varian Data Systems, Xerox Data Systems and Wang Minicomputers.) All minicomputers could be used in laboratories, business offices or engineering centers. They needed a floor space of about 20 sq. ft., not quite desktopped in size. Computers were indeed shrinking though not computing power.

[1.] Claude E. Shannon is the founder of information theory. (Hsu\44). Marshall McLuhan coined the phrase "information processing" to explain what computers aer all about. (Bishop)The general theory of automata is postulated in John von Neumann's seminal work, The General Theory of Automata. Norbert Wiener's Cybernetics or Control and Communication in the Animal and Machine, 1948, is the generally acknowledged source for modern research in this   field. (See Hari Kunzru, "The Cyborg Ancestry", Wired Feb. 1997: 158+.)

[2.] The manufacturer of most paper-tape units was *Teletype*. It's throughput was 110 cps. Its prices in 1975 was $150.

3. Thomas\73.

4. For a history of the transistor and its inventors see <u>Silicon Valley Fever</u>, 37+.

5. IBM adopted hybrid solid-state technology in 1961. The first commercial computer using integrated circuits was announced in 1965.(Flamm]80) Large-scale integrated technology research was done at MIT, Berkeley and Stanford in the 1970s and 80s. *Project Lighting*, a U.S. government initiative from 1959-1962, spurred hardware and software computer development for the next decade.(TL-3]38)

6. *DEC* provided extensive software for all of its microcomputers. For instance: Benton Harbour(BASIC);

TED-8 (a text editor); HASL-8(an assembler); BUG-8(debug); PAM-8 (panel monitor). They were available on cassette tape or optionally on paper tape.

7. TL-3\38.

8. Digital Equipment Corporation(DEC), the largest manufacturer of minicomputers, was financed by venture capitalist Georges Doriot.

Here is an interesting sidenote:
"Why would anyone need a computer of their own?" With that question, posed as the 1970's wound to a close, *Digital Equipment Corp.*, president made one of the most astounding blunders in the history of business and missed the whole point of technology in the 1980s according to Geoffrey Rowan.

APPENDIX 4

PROCESSOR COMPARISONS

1973

CPU SPEED = 108 Khz. [8008]
MEMORY CAPACITY = 64 Kbytes
PROCESSOR CAPACITY = 50 KIPS
     (ThousandInstructions per second)

1983

CPU SPEED = 20 Mhz. [80286]
MEMORY CAPACITY = 16 Mbytes
PROCESSOR CAPACITY = 2.5 MIPS *
     (Million Instructions per second)

* A 50 fold increase in computing power in approximately 10 years. Computer experts from CPU manufacturers expect a 100 fold increase in computing power between now (2005) and 2015.

APPENDIX 5

FIRSTS IN MICROCOMPUTING INDUSTRY

1. Mike Cheiky - OSI(*Ohio Scientific Inc.*) -
   pioneer in use of multi-user, multi-processing
   microcomputers
   Built in *CHALLENGER 3* employed 3 CPUs
   -> 6502, 6800, Z-80 Operating System ->
   OS65/U

2. First small computer kit project advertised for sale was the *SCELBI-8H* First minicomputer(microcomputer) kit project advertised as a
   construction kit, ie. you had
   to purchase most/all of the components
   separately was *The Mark 8*(Jonathan Titus
   authored the project in Radio-Electronics,
   July 1974) A true die-hard hobbyist project.
   [Some argue that the first microcomputer kit
     was the Kanabek 1. Where/when or if it was
     advertised I haven't been able to ascertain.]

3. First widely available microcomputer kit *The ALTAIR 8800*
   Jan./Feb. 1975, Popular Electronics

4. The first personal/microcomputer retail store Arrowhead
   Computers: The Computer Store Dick Heiser and his wife Lois
   opened this store in Nov./Dec.? 1975.

   The second and most famous of the early
   computer stores was Stan Veit's, The
   Computer Mart of New York. It was opened
   in Feb. 1976.

5.   The 'first' microcomputer convention was <u>The Trenton (N.J.)Computer Show</u> held in early 1976. The computer show that established the foundation for all others that followed was *The Computer Show* in Atlantic City, N.J., held on August 27, 1976.

6.   The first microprocessor was the *4004* by <u>INTEL</u>. It was followed by the *8008* and *8080*, both 8-bit processors. The second microprocessor family is the <u>Motorola</u> *6800*; the third is <u>ZILOG</u> *Z80*.

7.   One of the first microcomputers to employ floppy disk drives was the <u>OSI</u> family of computers. The <u>OSI</u> *Challenger 3* was the first microcomputer to have a hard disk drive. It used the <u>Okidata</u> 14" - 84MB disk.

Sources: <u>History of the Personal Computer</u> by Stan Veit, other books, Internet and magazines, particularly <u>BYTE</u>.

APPENDIX 6

MICROCOMPUTER INFRASTRUCTURE AND ORGANIZATION

Diagram 1

MICROCOMPUTER INFRASTRUCTURE OR

ELECTRONIC LAYOUT OF THE MICROCOMPUTER

```
----------                    ----------
 CPU                           RAM
----------                    ----------
-----------------------------------------------------------

     B        U        S       S

-----------------------------------------------------------
----------  ---------  -----------  -----------
 VDT     FLOPPY   PRINTER   HARD
          DISK               DISK
```

BUSS - 8 or 16 or 32 bit data highway
CPU   - Central Processing Unit
RAM   - Random Access Memory (Internal Memory}
VDT   - Video Display Terminal (unit)

This is the inner workings of microcomputers. How it processes data, as outlined in <u>Family Computing</u>, Jan. 1985, 124,125, is as follows:

INPUT : *instructions and information, in the form of a program and data, are entered into the computer via keyboard, cassette tape recorder, disk drive, cartridge or modem.* Second.

PROCESSING: *the computer executes the steps of the program through the CPU.* Third.

OUTPUT: *the results of the computer's work are made visible and available to the user on a television, monitor or LCD(liquid display device) screen; printer or tape unit.* Fourth.

STORAGE: *results can be stored and saved on a tape, magnetic (hard or floppy) or optical disk.*

In its most simplistic form this is the structure of a microcomputer:

1. A CLOCK, to keep the operations moving smoothly, and in the proper order;

2. A small MEMORY, to save numbers needed immediately or frequently, (we will call the memory cells within the microprocessor, "REGISTERED", which name they have inherited from the days of mechanical calculators);

3. A group of LOGICAL CIRCUITS which have the capacity to read numbers from the "MEMORY" to the 'registers', and/or move them around from one 'register' to another, to add or subtract the contents of the various 'registers' to or from one another, etc., depending upon the capabilities of the particular microprocessor. It should also be noted that' the 'registers' can have their contents placed into any 'MEMORY' to which the microprocessor might be attached through electrical 'buss' lines.

Diagram 2 shows how modern microcomputers manipulate information:

Diagram 2
COMPUTER ORGANIZATION

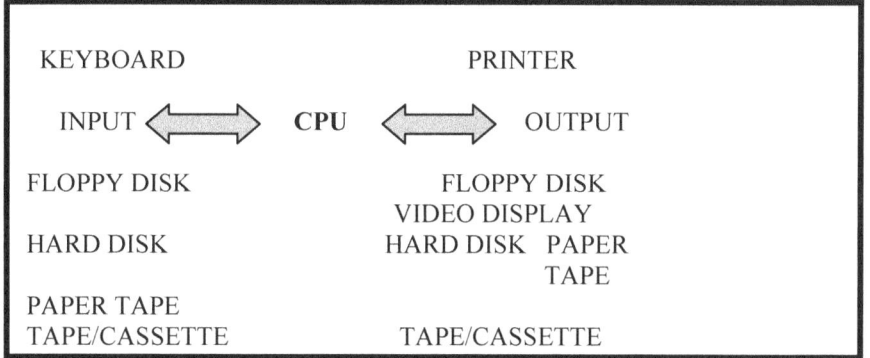

APPENDIX 7

PROGRAMMING ESSENTIALS

There are four essentials of programming:

1) *Ease of Learning - BASIC* is number one. Many have tried to duplicate it but have failed.

2) *Friendliness* - When programs seem to cooperate with the programmer.

3) *Compactness* - Permits shortened forms of commands.

4) *Readability* - A competent programmer can understand a program somebody else wrote.

The following is an outline of how to organize and write a program. It's simple yet complex.

Diagram 3

HOW TO WRITE A PROGRAM

To get work done on a computer do the following:

    I. Know what work is required.

    II. Organize

        A. Computer programs.
           To compose a computer program.
           1. Know the program's goal.
           2. Design the program.
           3. Write the program.

           To write a computer program.
           a) Comment
           b) Code
           c) Type
           d) Practice
    III. Set the organization to work.
    IV. Review the work.

APPENDIX 8

LANGUAGES

ANCIENT LANGUAGES FOR ENGINEERING

FORTRAN
APT

LANGUAGES FOR STATISTICS

SPSS - DATATEXT - EMPRESS
STATPACK

LANGUAGES FOR SIMULATION

SIMSCRIPT - GPSS - DYNAMO

LANGUAGES FOR STRUCTURED PROGRAMMING

ALGOL   SIMULA
PL/I

LANGUAGES FOR BUSINESS

COBOL - RPG
DIBOL   DATABUS
PASCAL   C

LANGUAGES FOR DATA BASES

>   ADA
>   SYSTEM 1022
>   DBASE 2

EXOTIC LANGUAGES – INTERACTIVE LANGUAGES –
LANGUAGES FOR BEGINNERS

LISP - COMIT

    BASIC - JOSS - APL
SNOBOL   VISICALC
    PILOT
FORTH

    EASY   FOCAL
    LOGO AID MUMPS

Source: <u>The Secret Guide to Computers, Vol. 2</u>,
        Russ Walter, 220.

MAINSTREAM LANGUAGES

NAME	WHAT THE NAME STANDS FOR	ORIGINAL USE	VERSION 1 AROSE AT	WHEN	NAME OF NEWEST VERSION
FORTRAN	FORmula TRANslating	sciences	IBM	1954-1957	FORTRAN 90
ALGOL	ALGOrithmic Language	sciences	International	1957-1958	ALGOL, BALGOL, ALGOL 60
COBOL	COmmon Business-Oriented Language	business	Defense Dept.	1959-1960	COBOL 85

NAME	WHAT THE NAME STANDS FOR	ORIGINAL USE	VERSION 1 AROSE AT	WHEN	NAME OF NEWEST VERSION
BASIC	Beginners All-purpose Symbolic Instruction Code	sciences	Dartmouth Coll.	1963-1964	Quick BASIC Turbo BASIC
PL/1	Programming Language	general	IBM	1963-1966	PL/1 (1)One Optimizer PL/C, ANSI PL/1
PASCAL	Blaise Pascal	general	Switzerland	1968-1970	Turbo PASCAL, Quick PASCAL
MODULA	MODULAr programming	systems	Switzerland	1975	MODULA-2

NAME	WHAT THE NAME STANDS FOR	ORIGINAL USE	VERSION 1 AROSE AT	WHEN	NAME OF NEWEST VERSION
C	C	system	Bell Telephone Labs	1970-1977	MS C Turbo C
ADA	ADA Lovelace	military equipment	France	1977-1980	ADA final version
DBASE	Data Base	database management	Jet Prop'n Lab & Ashton Tate	1978-1980	DBASE 4 FOXPRO 2 CLIPPER
EASY	EASY	general	Boston	1972-1982	EASY (R. Walter)

68   *History of the Microcomputer*

RADICAL LANGUAGES

NAME	WHAT THE NAME STANDS FOR	ORIGINAL USE	VERSION 1 AROSE AT	WHEN	NAME OF NEWEST VERSION
LISP	LISt Processing	artificial intelligence	MIT	1958-1960	Common LISP
SNOBOL	STrinG-Oriented symBOLic Langauge	string processing	Bell Telephone Labs	1962-1963	SNOBOL 4B
APL	A Programming Langauge	sciences	Harvard & IBM	1956-1966	APLSV APL PLUS
LOGO	LOGO	sciences	Bolt Beranek	1967	LCSI LOGO LOGO Writer

NAME	WHAT THE NAME STANDS FOR	ORIGINAL USE	VERSION 1 AROSE AT	WHEN	NAME OF NEWEST VERSION
FORTH	FOuRTH-generation	business & astronomy	Stanford Univ. & Mohasco MMS FORTH	1963-1968	FORTH83 FIG-FORTH
PILOT	Programmed Inquiry Learning or Teaching	tutoring kids	U. of Cal. At San Francisco	1968	Atari PILOT

SPECIALIZED LANGAUGES

NAME	WHAT THE NAME STANDS FOR	ORIGINAL USE	VERSION 1 AROSE AT	WHEN	NAME OF NEWEST VERSION
APT	Automatically Programmed Tools	cutting metal	MIT	1952-9157	APT 77
DYNAMO	DYNAmic MOdels	simulation	MIT	1959	DYNAMO 3 STELLA
GPSS	General-Purpose Simulation System	simulation	IBM	1961	GPSS 5
RPG	Report Program	business	IBM	1964	RPG 3

NAME	WHAT THE NAME STANDS FOR	ORIGINAL USE	VERSION 1 AROSE AT	WHEN	NAME OF NEWEST VERSION
SPSS	Statistical Package for the Social Sciences	statistics	Stanford Univ.	1965-1967	SPSS Release 4
PROLOG	PROgramming in LOGic	artificial intelligence	France	1972	Arity PROLOG, Turbo PROLOG

Source 1: The Secret Guide to Computers
Vol. 17, Russ Walter, 475.

Source 2: Byte, Sept. 1995, 121,122.

APPENDIX 9

CP/M OPERATING SYSTEM

Diagram 4

CP/M OPERATING SYSTEM HISTORY

CP/M 1.4

CP/M 2.2 - dominant system by 1981

CP/M 3.0 - used expanded memory in
                   IBM world

MP/M (multi-tasking, multi-user CP/M
              compatible – only specific 8-bit,
              bank-switched microcomputers used
              this operating system.

Walter's says this about CP/M:

The CP/M cartel is a group of small companies that have banded
together and have produced computers that resemble each other
and can share each other's programs.

APPENDIX 10

LIST OF 8-BIT MICROCOMPUTERS AVAILABLE IN TIME PERIOD

1. ACT "Sirius 1"
2. ACORN "Atom"
3. ACTRIX "Actrix Portable"
4. ALPHA DIGITAL SYSTEMS "ALPHA Z-80"
5. ALTOS & ALTOS[UK]
6. AMI "EVK 99" $133 (05/77)
7. APF "The Imagination Machine"
8. APPLE "I,II,III"
9. ARCOMP MICRO SYSTEMS "Zeus 2001, Super 400"
10. ASSOCIATE "Associate"
11. ATARI "400,800"
12. AVT SWITZERLAND "AVT Comp 2"
13. BASIS INC. "Basis 80"
14. BBC "Microcomputer"
15. BRITISH "Genius"
16. BYTE INC. "BYT-8"
17. CALIFORNIA COMPUTER SYSTEMS "S-100(Z-80), Expander"
18. CHEN ENTERPRISES "TK 8000"
19. CIFER "1800 Range, 2600 Range"
20. COLECO "ADAM"
21. COLUMBIA DATA SYSTEMS(CP/M)
22. COMART "Advantage"
23. COMMODORE "C-64, PET, VIC 20, 4032, 8032, 8096"
24. COMPUPRO "Z80,Compucolor 1&2, C-MOD 8 or MIL MOD 8, C-MOD 80"
25. CREATIVITY IN ACTION
26. CROMEMCO "MC 68000, Z-2, C-10, System One CS-1H" System 3, Z-2 $595 (08/77)

27. DAZZLER $215 (08/77)

28. DIGITAL RESEARCH COMPUTERS "Big Board"
29. DIGITAL EQUIPMENT CORP. "DEC VT 180 (Robin), Rainbow, Decmate 2, Digital Professional
30. DIGITAL SYSTEMS "DSC-2"
31. DRAGON DATA LTD. "Dragon 32"
32. DY-4 SYSTEMS, INC. "Orion 0412"
33. EBKA "Familiarizor"
34. ECD CORP. "The Pecos, MicroMind" $987.54 (07/77)
35. E&L INSTRUMENTS "min-Micro Designer" $500 (07/77)
36. ELECTRONIC TOOL COMPANY'S "ETC-1000"
37. ENCOTEL "Televideo TS80, System I, II, II[UK]"
38. EPA GROUP "Micro 68, 6800"
39. EPSON "MX80F/T, MX80F/T2, QX-10, HX-20 Notebook Computer"
40. EQUINOX "EQUINOX 100"
41. EURO MICRO[London] "DPS-1, EVK 99"
42. EXIDY "Sorcerer"
43. FLIGHT ELECTRONICS "Micro Professor"
44. FRANKIN "Franklin Ace 100, 500, 1000, 1200" APPLE Compatibles
45. FULCRUM "I-8080, I-8085, I-8025, I-8035, D, S& MDX Series"
46. GENERAL INSTRUMENT "GIMINI"
47. GENIE "I & II"
48. GODBOUT ELECTRONICS "Pace 16-bit"
49. GEMINI "Galaxy I, Gemini-68"
50. Gladstone Electronics "Micro 48"
51. GNAT Computers
52. HAL COMMUNICATIONS CORP. "MCEM-8080"
53. HATTORI-SEIKO COMPUTERS LTD. "Data-2000"
54. HEATH(KIT)/ZENITH "ET-100, H8, Z-159"

55. HEWLETT-PACKARD "HP 851, HP 86/87, HP 83/85"
56. HITECH COMPUTER SYSTEMS "Superbrain II Jr."
57. HITACHI "MB-6800"
58. IASIS "Compterbook" $450 (08/77)
59. IMS Inc. "IMSAI 8080, 8048, PCS-80/30, VDP 80 IVC-Integrated Video Computer" $599 (11/76)
60. INFINITE INC. "UC1800HK Hobbyist Kit, UC1800, Infinity 8800"
61. INTEL "SBC 80/10"
62. INTELLIGENT SYSTEMS CORP. "Intercolor 8001"
63. INTERSIL CORP. "Intercept Jr. 6100 Kit" $281 (08/77)
64. INTERTEC DATA SYSYTEM[UK] "Superbrain"
65. ITHACA COMPUTER SYTEMS
66. JAMES ELECTRONICS "Gemini-68"
67. JOLT "Jolt-1"
68. JC SYSTEMS "DCM*80*"
69. JUPITER CANTAB "Jupiter ACE"
70. KIM "Kim-1 6502 Kit" $245 (08/77)
71. KAYPRO "Kaypro 2-X, II, 4, 4 Plus 88, 10, Robie"
72. KONTRON "PSI-80[UK]"
73. LNW Research Ltd. "LNW80"
74. LSI "M3"
75. LANIER "EZ1"
76. LOBO DRIVE INTER. "MAX-80"
77. M&L "MMD-1"
78. M&R "Astral 2000"
79. MAGIC COMPUTERS
77. MARTIN RESEARCH "Mike 203A(8008), Mike 303A(8080)"
80. MATSUSHITA "The Link"
81. MIDWEST SCIENTIFIC INSTRUMENTS "MSI 6800"
82. MICRON "6502"

83. MITS "Altair 8800a/b, 680, 680b"
    Altair 8800-b $840 (11/76)
84. MORROW COMPUTERS "Micro Decision 3,
    MD3P, MD11"
85. MOT "MEK6800 D2" $235 (08/77)
86. MOTOROLA'S "Educator II, Microcomputer
    HEP"
87. MYCRO-TEK
88. MULTIFLEX "Multiflex CP/M"
89. MULTITECH IND. CORP. "Micro Professor,
    MPF III"
90. NABU "Nabu Personal"
91. NASCOM "1&2"
92. NATIONAL SEMICONDUCTOR "SC/MP –
    Microprocessor Kit" $95 (07/77); "BLC 90/10"
93. NATIONAL CASH REGISTER "NCR PC
    Computer"
94. NORTH STAR "Horizon-I, Horizon-II,
    Advantage, Advantage 8/16"
95. NEC "PC-8000"
96. NELMA DATA CORPORATION "Nelma
    Persona"
97. NETRONICS "Explorer/85, ELF-II"
98. NORTHSTAR "NorthStar Advantage, Horizon"
99. NSC "Scamp Kit" $99 (08/77)
100. OKI "IF800"
101. OLSON 8 COMPUTER "Mp-100"
102. OHIO SCIENTIFIC "Challenger II/IIP/III,
    Superboard II, C1P-MF, C3-B"
103. ORIC Computers[S.A.]
104. ORION ELECTRONICS "Winner"
105. OSBORNE COMPUTERS "Osborne 1,
    Executive"
106. PAIA "8700"
107. PANASONIC "HHC"
108. PARASITIC COMPUTERS
109. PEACH MICROSYSTEMS "Peach IV,
    Executive"
110. PEHACO Corporation
111. PCM Corporation

112. PIC "PIC-8 Priority" $125 (08/77)
113. POLYMORPHIC "Poly 88, 8813" $595
     (11/76)
114. PROCESSOR TECHNOLOGY "SOL-10, 20"
115. QCAL INTERNATIONAL "QCAL 500, 900,
     1000"
116. QUASAR DATA PRODUCTS "QDP-300"
117. RAIR "Black Box 3/30, 3/50"
118. RCA(Radio Corp. of America)
     "COSMAC(ELF) CDP1802" $92 (05/77)
119. RGS Ltd. "RGS-008A"
120. ROCKWELL "AIM 65, RM 65, PPS-4/2"
121. SAGE "Sage II[uk""
122. SANYO "MBC-1000, MBC-1100, 555"
123. SEALS "PUP"
124. SEMI-TECH MICROELECTRONICS "Pied
     Piper Professional"
125. SIGNETICS "2650"
126. SINCLAIR Research Ltd. "ZX80, ZX81" Kit
     $99.95 Assembled $149.95 (07/82)
127. SIRTON "Midas S-100, 1, 2, 3, 3HD, Ithaca-
     DPS 1"
128. SONY "Sony SMC-70"
129. SORD[UK] "M5(Z80A)"
130. SPECRAVIDEO "SV-318, SV-328"
131. SPHERE CORP. "Micro-Sphere 200"
132. SRI INDUSTRIES "SRI-500"
133. SHARP ELECTRONICS "MZ80, MZ-80B,
     MZ-80K, PC-1500"
134. STRATOS COMPUTERS[UK]
135. SUPERBRAIN[UK]
136. SWTPC (SOUTHWEST TECHNICAL
     PRODUCTS CORP.) "M6800, MF-68"
137. (TANDY) RADIO SHACK "TRS-80 MODEL
     1, 2, 3, 4, (PC-1, 2, 3, 4), MicroColor
     Computer(MC-10), Color Computer 2"
     [TANDY sold its microcomputer
     business to AST Research in 1994.]
138. TAVA CANADA Ltd. "TAVA PC"

139. TECHNICAL DESIGN LABS(TDL) "Xitan Z-80, The General, Alpha"
140. TECHNICO Inc. "SS-16"
141. TEI Inc. "MCS-112, MCS-122"
142. TELECON IND. Ltd. "Zorba"
142. TELEVIDEO "TPC1, TS802, TS803, TS1603"
144. TELETEX COMPUTERS[UK]
145. TEO COMPUTERS "Tiger 4000, TEO Personal, TPC 8300"
146. TEXAS INSTRUMENTS "TI-99/4, TI-994A, INTERTEC, TI Professional Computer"
147. TEI INC. "MCS-112/122"
148. THE DIGITAL GROUP "TVC-64"
149. THE PECOS
150. TIMEX SINCLAIR "ZX-80, XZ-81, Timex Sinclair(TS 1000, TS1500, TS 2068)"
151. TLF "MINI 12"
152. TOSHIBA "T-100, T-250"
153. UNITRON COMPUTER CORPORATION "Unitron"
154. UNIVERSAL RESEARCH "UR Portabrain"
155. VERSA "F8"
156. VECTOR GRAPHICS "S-100, S-4, Vector 1+"
157. VIASYB "Compupro"
158. VIDEO BRAIN

159. VIDEO TECHNOLOGY Ltd. "Laser 3000, VZ-200"
160. VIDEOGENIE "Genie 1&11"
161. WAVE MATE "Jupiter 11"
162. XEROX "820"
163. ZENITH "Z-100"
164. ZORBA COMPUTERS"

*1. ENERGY ELECTRONICS PRODUCTS "KX-33B"
   This microcomputer used Panasonic's 4-bit microprocessor.

This list I'm sure is not exhaustive. Please tell me if you know of any that may be added for the next edition. Strictly speaking some of the above were not 8-bit computers; some were 8/16-bit machines.

Here's the breakdown of the type of microprocessor used in the above computers:

Microprocessor Type	# of Manufacturers Using It
8080	21
6502	12
Z-80	12
6800	7
1802	5
SC/MP	2
LSI-11	1

8-bit microcomputers to my knowledge are no longer manufactured though 8-bit microprocessors for embedded purposes are.

APPENDIX 11

COMPARATIVE PRICES - EARLY YEARS

RAM MEMORY

	1973	1974	1977	1979
8225 64 bit		4.95	2.75	
1101 256 bit	4.00	1.75	.69	
1103 1024 bit	4.95	.69		
2102 1024 bit Static Ram	1.49			
2112 1024 bit Static Ram		3.95		
2101-1 2048 bit		3.95		
P1103A 1024 Dynamic RAM		.42		
4116 4096 bit				10.95
2117 16 Kbit				9.95
16 KB SIMM				79.50
MK4200 P-11 4096 bits		10.95		
C5101-3 Static RAM			3.95	

MICROPROCESSORS

TYPE	1973	1976	1977	1979
8008 8-bit		19.95	16.95	
8080 super 8-bit		295.95	129.95	
8080A advanced 8-bit		37.95	19.95	8.95
MC6800 8-bit		129.95		17.50
Z80A		17.95		
6502		12.50		
8085		19.95		

KEYBOARDS

		1979
Keyboard 56 key ASCII	67.50	
Keyboard only kit		29.95
KB-1 Keyboard	55.00 (1973)	
UNIVAC Kbd/encoder	35.00 (1973)	

S-100 BUS(S)

                                        1979 prices

8k static RAM kit   Godbout Electronics   135.00
32K dynamic RAM kit   "   "   310.00

Motherboard   39.00

FLOPPY DISK DRIVES

          1979

5 ¼ " Vista   395.00
    Shugart   295.00

8" Shugart   495.00

FLOPPY INTERFACE CONTROLLER $229.00

ACOUSTIC MODEM 300 baud $198.00

MINI CORE MEMORY

180 words of 18 bits each $24.95

  Hobbyists ported core memory to their microcomputers using instructions found in 50 page manuals. This type of memory was never used extensively in the microcomputer industry as it was far too 'expensive' and not compatible with RAM memory.

Sources for Appendix 11: Radio-Electronics, Popular
                Electronics, Byte.

APPENDIX TWELVE

HISTORY OF THE ADAM MICROCOMPUTER

The *ADAM* microcomputer was released with great fanfare in June 1983. Arthur Dent, in <u>The First Book of ADAM the Computer</u>, has this to say about it:

History will report that the era of affordable personal computing power began in the mid-70s with the advent of the integrated-circuit processor(sometimes called 'the computer on a chip'.)

However, the true debut of the era of home computing may well be traced to a June 1983 announcement that took the computer industry and the general public by surprise, raising a lot of eyebrows in the press and in the investment community along the way. The location was the huge Chicago Consumer Electronics Show, a gathering place for both the giants and aspiring giants of the home electronics manufacturing industry and buyers for the nation's large electronics distributors and retailers. Making the announcement was <u>Coleco Industries, Inc.</u>, a Connecticut- based manufacturer of products for family recreation and entertainment.

Coleco took wraps off a daring price tag.

- *ADAM, the ColecoVision Family Computer System.*[1]

Following these same lines Richard Clee, writing in <u>ADVISA</u>, gives his opinion on the *ADAM*'s success:

The digital data drive was Coleco's ingenious answer to the problem of providing their home computer with a data storage method that didn't impose the infuriating delays of the tape recorders used by the *TI 99/4A*, *APPLE*,*C64* and similar competitors, but still avoided the prohibitively high costs (at that time) of the disc drive on computers aimed at business users.

Reliability was a concern; it's worth noting that even today after many years of technological progress, businesses that can't afford data loss often use glorified equivalents of ADAM's tape drive to do an automatic running backup of their hard or floppy discs.[2] Furthermore.

ADAMneta sophisticated data bus not seen until the 80386, allowed the ADAM to connect with peripherals that other micros didn't have.[3]

With Richard Dent concluding:

In 1983, Coleco and AT&T announced that they would be participating in a joint development that would lead to expanded home entertainment offerings through the use of telephone lines, video games, and home computers. No doubt, more surprises are on the way.[4]

How prophetic Dent was. The surprise however was by mid '84 ADAM was orphaned. The IBM *PC JUNIOR* destroyed its support base in the personal computer industry, or maybe not!

Rich Clee writes:

If there is one product that has undergone incredibly speedy technological change in the last few years, it's computers. A computer that was introduced in 1983 was so full of bugs it went through 80 revisions to get it working right, then as far as the manufacturer was concerned went down in flames with a thundering crash within a year of its introduction.[5]

Russ Walter's agrees:

But Coleco's main problem is its reputation. Because of first ADAMs shipped were defective and because Coleco made many statements that turned out to be false, many people are still afraid to buy the ADAM, and many software companies are afraid that Coleco might go bankrupt. Therefore, the major software companies aren't developing any software for the ADAM yet.[And never did.] [6]

To sum it up Russ Walter's quote says it all:

Because of Coleco's problems, cruel jokes became popular.
    Here they are...
    1. To pronounce 'ADAM Computer' correctly, put the accent on the second syllable: it's 'A DAMN computer;
    2. The ADAM computer is made by Coleco, which also makes the Cabbage Patch doll. If your ADAM doesn't work, put a wig on it and sell it as a 'Cabbage Patch computer.';

3. Each ADAM has its own peculiar defect. In fact, ADAM computers are like Cabbage Patch dolls: no two are alike.[7]My favorite computer ridiculed, laughed at, trashed! Oh, well, such is life.

[1] Arthur Dent, <u>The First Book of ADAM the Computer</u>, p. 1.
[2] Richard Clee, <u>ADVISA</u>, p. 7.
[3] Ibid., I, p.9.
[4] Richard Dent, <u>The First Book of ADAM the Computer</u>, p. 10.
[5] Rich Clee, B, p.12.
[6] Russ Walter, IV, p. 37.
[7] Ibid.

APPENDIX 14

AN INEXPENSIVE
SCHOOL COMPUTER

(ANN) Alex Sweitzer is a frequent caller to the Southwest ADAM User's Group's SFAUG) BBS. One day, he left a message describing how he uses his ADAM in elementary school teaching. I asked him if he would prepare an article for the ADAM News Network. The follow-ing is his product. I gave him an A+ on the assignment and told him he could play a game of his choice on his

ADAM (read on and see why). If you would like to communicate with Alex, please leave a message for him on the SFAUG BBS (813-473-2905).

Bob Blair

I teach elementary school at the third grade level, and I have an inexpensive computer for school use. The name of the computer is ADAM.

Our school is one of the poorest within Pennsylvania so, needless to say, we do not have many computers. Several years ago the district purchased APPLE//GS computers and printers. Each system cost around $1800. The APPLE is a good computer but not cost effective when compared with an ADAM.

Before using the ADAM I was using another very cost effective computer in my classroom, the TIMEX 1000! The *TIMEX 1000* is a good computer; but for classroom use the color, sound and the daisy wheel printer of the ADAM is much better.

The ADAM is a perfect computer for the students. It is simple enough, with the SMART KEYS, for them to learn word processing. Don't even think of teach-ing an entire third grade class how to use *Word Perfect, Word for Windows,* or *Microsoft Works*, etc.! The students can print their short stories on the ADAM printer, and then draw and color a picture to go along with their article.

I give each student fifteen minutes on the ADAM to complete their article.

Other than *Smart-Writer* the next best educational software is *FlashCard Maker*. With this program I have taught, or should I say, ADAM has taught, the students their math tables which are very important to students in third and fourth grades. Each math problem is placed on a separate card and flashed on the television (I have at least two connected to the ADAM) and on the lCD overhead projector. Incidentally all I had to do to connect the ADAM with the LCD projector was to use an RCA wire - no expensive interface! The students write the factors and the product on their papers. After the last problem we take turns going around the room reading the factors and the products. Since you can set time limits with FlashCard Maker, sometimes orally drill the math tables using the timing feature.

One of my students is a very poor reader, and the ADAM has helped him in the following way. I entered into Flash-Card Maker the first 300 sight words and all the vocabulary words from the first grade reader. The student then has so say the word before it disappears from the screen - I usually set the time limit at one second. I also set FlashCard Maker to save the missed questions, so if the student cannot identify the word then I mark it incorrect and the word will come up again for him to say.

This drill has helped him read better.

FlashCard Maker also is used in Science, Social Studies, and Reading Class as an introduction to the new vocabulary, and as a review/drill tool.

If I am not using the ADAM with *SmartWriter* or *FLashCard Maker*, then I may be using *SmartFiler*. I use *SmartFiler* to keep track of discipline problems. When a student does some-thing inappropriate I enter the student's name, the date and the

inappropriate behavior. This is a great help when it comes time to indicate to the principal or the student's parents why the student is having a problem. I am even surprised at how many times certain students are in trouble for the same inappropriate behavior.

The program *ADAMCALC* is used to keep track of all the grades for each student. Our school is using the Whole Language Approach now and we have twelve areas that we must track for each student. The ADAM computes all the averages. Also the hardcopy of the grades looks much more impressive than a handwritten copy when you show them to the principal or parent.

With my slow 300 baud modem we can connect the ADAM to our local college where we can access their library using the card catalog.

I am also inter-ested in using *BASIC* on the ADAM and have written a few simple programs. In class we also used some BASIC programs that I have acquired recently.

Our school district now requires detailed lesson plans. ADAM has helped solved the extra, and very time consuming work of writing the plans for each subject weekly.

Several sections of each lesson plan are identical, so I use *SmartWriter*'s copy feature. I have saved to tape all of the plans (with backups), so next year all I have to do is search for the correct plan and print it out again. I have calculated there are almost 10,000 lines of lesson plans!

The ADAM is also used as an award for receiving an A+ on important tests.

Source: **ADVISA**, Sept/Oct 1993: p. 19.

APPENDIX FIFTEEN

A LOOK AT FOUR SOCIETAL ISSUES OF MICROCOMPUTING

1. COMPUTING ADDICTION & TECHNOBABBLE

The computer enthusiast or hacker(they are not one in the same) isn't a social animal except in relations to his peers and only then in conversing in technobabble.[1] Hardware has associated with it 'techno-aroma' - the smell of raw electronics associatedwith running machinery inhaled by the hacker like a drug.[2] And Gookin writes:

The biggest problem is that there are still a lot of dorks in computing. They're the kind of people who were in chess clubs in high school - real bright, but wound up in their self-centered little technical world, and they can't communicate with other people.[3]

They can't write for novices either. Try reading their instruction manuals. Is language the problem?

2. LANGUAGE

As John Dickinson writes in <u>PC/Computing</u>, "the words may be familiar; the meanings are purposely obscure"[4], we're forced to ask, Is microcomputing lingo deflecting honest debate? Personal computer people shy away from criticism of their industry through a vocabulary that's impossible for average people to comprehend or as Kittredge states:

Wonks speak out - "I delight in freaking out the service and training people by diving into the system at kernel level and playing games with the utilities - they're not real happy to discover that a doctor can be a wonk, too."[5]

What makes wonks computer literate are special applications called mentor programs.

3. MENTOR PROGRAMS

Don Lancaster says that "what makes or breaks any particular brand of computer"[7] is software called a mentor (or tormentor, depending on your point of view) program. For APPLE II it was *Integer BASIC*, "with its stunning advances in color game animation; *Visicalc* for the APPLE II+; *Wordstar* for the CP/M world[8] and for IBMers it was *Lotus 1-2-3*.[9] Yet are these programs worthy of the name? "Is an application good or bad, does it perform a useful and or entertaining service or is it just another UCR(Useless Computer Routine)?"[10] according to Ervin Bobo.

The importance of *Visicalc* cannot be over-estimated.[11] This spreadsheet (accounting) program gave computer users an application which didn't require any programming skills.[12] Besides, here is an application that actually did something useful, balancing your checkbook for example. *Visicalc* is the first microcomputer application that reached the mass consumer market making APPLE Computer number one in the late 70s.[13]

Mentor programs have led to user authoring.[14] It permits users to add questions, answers and information to commercial applications without having programming skills.[15] This concept was pioneered by *Advanced Ideas(AI)* in 1981 though hackers and computer devotees were doing it back in the 60s (on minicomputers) and 70s (on microcomputers.)[16]

Mentor programs were essential to the industry as Phoebe Hoban says in Omni: "The average Joe Public is never going to learn BASIC. You have to program the computer to be people-literat."[17] Since user authoring permits innovation one may individualize applications or programs. Therefore it's most suitable for education and entertainment purposes.

4. ENTERTAINMENT

For pure entertainment microcomputers excel. It's their forte. For instance, *The National Film Board of Canada*' Hunger (or Faim). This ten minute color film traces the descension of an individual into hell. As the film progresses he's mandated such a place because of his penchant for food, becoming "increasingly fat, lustful, slothful, and miserable."[18]

As he enters hell he falls prey to starving, naked children who consume him. This film as Russ Walter's says, "combines computer art and left-wing humanitarian politics, to create an unforgettable message."[19] Hunger is much like Running Cola is Africa. Both demonstrate the power of graphical manipulation by microcomputers, thereby so thoroughly entertaining us.

Equally so computers in the movies. For instance in films since the 50s like Demon Seed, Dr. Strangelove, 2001 A Space Odyessy, and The Hitch-Hiker's Guide to the Galaxy we find computer-controlled robots running amok. HAL in 2001 is probably the most famous - a computer who had to have his ROMs removed. [For home robotists who wanted to discover the 'real world' of robotics, Hero 1 and Hero II, Topo and Unicorn 1,[20] etc. were robots you could build and hoped they worked. These early machines were not much more advanced then children's wind-up robots of the 50s and 60s. They just blinked incessantly.]

[1] Ritter p. A22.
[2] Ibid.
[3] Gookin, p. A18.
[4] John Dickinson, p. 112.
[5] Kitteredge, p. 43.
[6] mentor progs
[7] Don Lancaster, p. 241.
[8] Friedman, p. 84.
[9] Nimershein, p. 72.
[10] Ervin Bobo.
[11] Bishop, p. 29.
[12] Licklider, p. 324; Barron, pps. 326-328.
[13] APPLE Computer.
[14] Authoring languages are outlined in Microsoft Encarta '95.
[15] Connife, p. 14.
[16] Richardson, p. 578.
[17] Phoebe Hoban, p. 24.
[18] Walter, d, p. 41.; ibid.; Stan Veit, ee p.638; Volkonmir, p. 71
[19] Ibid.
[20] Stan Viet; ee p. 638; Volkonmir p. 71.

APPENDIX SIXTEEN

GENERAL HISTORY OF MICROCOMPUTING(SOURCES)

1. A general historic review of the entire microcomputing industry, ie. software, hardware and people, is to be found in <u>Byte</u>, Sept. 1995, More information is contained in this volume than is to be found in most history texts on the subject.

2. Fred Moody, <u>I Sing the Body Electronic </u>(N.Y.: Viking, 1995) 51, has one of the best descriptions of the microcomputer I've come across:
   For all its apparently miraculous powers, the personal computer is little more than a mathematical jukebox, a Wurlitzer of digits. It repeatedly fetches sets of the same two numbers, one and zero, from where they are stored in the computer's memory, and moves them onto a microprocessor chip - a rectangle piece of silicon as small as a postage stamp on some computers, slightly less than an inch square on others - where they are used to, turn the chip's tiny switches, or transistors, on or off. These switches, which are linked on a chip by intricate pathways $1/100^{th}$ the width of a human hair, are turned off, or closed, if the number assigned to them is one. Electrical signals flow through the microprocessor along routes shaped by the pattern of open and close switches. The resulting pattern of signals eventually translates into words, decimal numbers, colors, and sounds.

3. There is a series of articles in <u>Byte</u>, July 1978:
    a) *The First Ten Years of Amateur Computing* by Sol Libes.
    b) *A Short History of Computing* by Keith S. Reid-Green.
    c) *How to Choose a Microprocessor* by Lou Frenzel.

APPENDIX 17

THE HEATH H-8, MOUSE and D. Englebart

[1(a).] The *Heath H-8* came with an impressive software package for its time: BH (Benton Harbor) BASIC; expanded BH BASIC, TED-8 (text editor); HASL-8 (an assembler);

BUG -8 (debug); PAM-8 (Panel Monitor). The more powerful Heath H11 had an equally powerful package: PTS BASIC-11; 8K FOCAL-11 (a high level langauge); 4K FOCAL-11; LINK-11 (tie-in for DEC's PDP-11 mini-computers) and PAL-11S. This microcomputer employed DEC's LSI-11 microprocessor used in the PDP-11 mini-computer. (Radio-Electronics Aug. 1977:44)

"The primary reason is that it has taken almost three decades to develop a different view of what computing machines are good for. The original notion that they are good for serving as glorified clerks and adding machines is shifting. Now (finally), thanks in no small measure to Englebart himself, we view computers as tools that should, indeed, amplify human creativity,   thinking, and planning. (Russell Lipton, Multimedia Toolkit: Build Your Own Solutions with DocuSource (NY.: Random House Electronic Publishing, 1992) 70)

[1(b).] The mouse and chord keyset were first demonstrated publicly at the Fall Joint Computer Conference, San Francisco, in 1968. (TL-3\62).

If you had asked the 'computer experts' in 1965 what the future of computing would be in 1985, they would invariably have said, 'There will be huge main-frame computers and they will have databases filled with everything! People will use smart terminals and access them via telephone lines.' Their idea of a smart terminal was one with editing functions and perhaps a   built-in 300-baud modem - the world of personal computers was not even a gleam in their yes.'"

(Stan Viet, "What Ever Happened To...Time-sharing, Multiuser Personal Computers," Computer Shopper Sept. 1992: 743).

[1][©] Douglas Englebart[d] is famous for creating the mouse which he patented in 1964. (Byte Sept. 1005: 95).

[1][(d)] The *Augment Project* of Doug Englebart is covered in Wired Nov. 1993: 18.

APPENDIX 18

EDUCATIONAL ISSUES & SOURCES IN MICROCOMPUTING WORLD

[1(a).] One of the earliest microcomputer educational programs called *Tymon's Tutor(TT)* ran on the Trash 80(A user's term of endearment for the first widely available home computer, the amazingly capable Model 1 Radio Shack TRS-80).(Tymon/43)

[1(b).] Compute!'s *Computing Together* is a "parent's and teacher's guide to using computers with young children." One of the best early attempts to help 'adults' understand microcomputers and how to make them work in the educational field.

[1©.] In a controversial article, "Academic Piracy: Software Costs & Education", Hal Nieberg raises the question of why particular pieces of software are successful and others not. According to Nieberg it is because they are 'pirated' by professors, students, and computer science department 'users'. He concludes: "In short, the college campus is the best promotional tool   invented for future and long term sales of all kinds of products."(208) Bob Wallace, of Buttonware fame, author of PC-Write learned this lesson and created the PC shareware industry in the early 1980s.

[1(d).] Here are two *Letters To The Editor*, The Globe & Mail, September 9, 1995, p. D7, that closely examine the role computers play in education or don't:

"As a computer review editor, I have trouble deciding which is the bigger obscenity, the Microsoft banner hung on the CN Tower or Gerry Blackwell's amphigory article, *Back-*

To-School Tools To Make The High-Tech Grade, in the Sept. 2 *Report on Business*. Both are aimed at selling people something they don't really need. I found the lack of understanding in Mr. Blackwell's article to be unacceptable. Why would a high-school student, with a computer, need a programmable calculator? A hand scanner may save on photocopy charges, but has he not recommended using it to violate international copyright laws?

Does he really think your own copy of an encyclopedia can replace visiting a well-equipped   library with real books instead of video terminals? Why would ne insist upon a "brand name" for a family's first computer? My "clone" has worked flawlessly for 12 to 18 hours a day for several years. It appears that Mr. Blackwell is trying to get people to buy, buy, buy instead of think, think, think. The role of the computer is to facilitate and enhance a student's ability to transfer thoughts to paper. For this, most of the hardware and software discussed is overkill. The teacher must judge the assignment that is submitted - and Mr. Blackwell has not discussed the need for a good printer.

There is no doubt that this generation of students will run computers at an earlier age than their parents, but if they don't learn to operate pen and paper first, it is highly likely that they will be unable to function if a fuse blows - and Mr.Blackwell did not recommend a battery-operated uninterruptable power supply.
                          -Marvin Silbert

The back-to-school column in *Personal Affairs* lists tools to buy your kids as they go back to school. For elementary students, it suggests personal computers at more than $2,000 a shot, as well as a $95 electronic organizer and hundreds of dollars in software and CD-ROMs. For high-school, it is more of the same, but with more power and more cost. And, of course, every student must have a pager - "One way for families to stay in touch." Are these really necessary? The article says, "Hey, you want to succeed, don't you?" As I read this, I couldn't help but think about the some one million Canadian children who live in poverty. Their families can't even afford the old-fashioned school supplies and a good lunch every day. Yes, we have a serious deficit problem in this country. It is a social deficit made worse every year as some students get the high-tech, high-cost benefits, while others live in families whose already inadequate welfare cheques are being cut to provide tax breaks for those who can afford pagers for their kids.
                          _Larry Kuehen

[1(e).] Jerry Pournelle says this about microcomputers, technology and education: "A major issue in education technology is distance learning. Studies by the Danish Ministry of Education   conclude that the critical cost factor is how to make low-paid people - such as students - do the work formerly done by high-paid people. Danish and other studies also indicate that the general result of applying technology to education is to increase educational quality, but at increased costs; it's rare when high-tech education saves money. That's a big disappointment in this era of falling education budgets".(Byte, Sept. 1995: 275)

[1(f).] Burton Hillis in C. Evans, comments: "I'm not surprised that kids today have no sense of history. Burt, Jr., campaigning for a new printer for our home computer, calls our present three year old model a 'Stone Age relic'".(204)

[1(g).] "The computer coupled to a printer converts every schoolchild into a publisher and reinforces the notion of writing as a communications activity rather than a dreadful and empty school exercise".(R. K. Logan) And paraphrasing Deming, the greatest waste in America is failure to use peoples' abilities(Ferguson\3). Education cannot afford this, especially as it introduces next-generation microcomputers.

[1(h).] "Microcomputers perform the same function as larger computers and offer a tremendous variety of architectures. The availability of complete working systems for a few hundred dollars means that even small schools can afford to give their students a range of computer experience."(Leventhal\11)

[1(i).]. Here are 1995 microcomputer statistics concerning the North York Board of Education, Toronto, Ontario:

Total 7158 microcomputers in schools

Ratio of 8.5 : 1
Breakdown as follows:
a) 1200 Apple IIs
b) 300 Dos-based systems(all over 10 years
                        old)
c) 3000 almost 10 years old(PCs and
                        MacIntoshs)

To buy all new microcomputers, ie. to run up-to-date software and hardware(mostly multimedia), would cost almost $15 million. A sum not available under current economic conditions. (Globe&Mail[White] Sept. 09,1995: E5)

APPENDIX 19

TECHNOLOGY AND SOCIETAL ISSUES

[1(a)] Canada Online - CBC News Sept. 1995. This program dealt with high-tech haves and have-nots. More and more will become marginalized and reality will be replaced by virtual reality, ie. people not going to museums and decline of books will become the norm as they're replaced by virtual museums and books.

[1(b)] See Suneel Ratan's article in TIME, Spring 1995. "Computers in general are marginalizing the rural/urban poor.[c] Their access to computing technology descreases as industrial/ communication combines control more and more of the entertainment and educational networks.   They are seeking profit and are not in the business of promoting social policy.

[1©] Is technology leaving the poor behind?[d] According to Statscan[Statistics Canada] it is. (Bruce Little, "Poor left behind in computer revolution", Toronto Star 15 Jan. 1996: B11.

[1(d)] "Those who have access to technology can particpate in a technocracy while those who don't can't." (Tim M. Anderson, "The Future", ECOAUG (Vol. 1, No. 2,3) 1995: 6.

[1(e)] David Buerger, "Power Pundit", Wired March 1995: 123.

APPENDIX 20

TECHNOLOGICAL   ISSUES   RAISED   BY MICROCOMPUTERS

[1(a)] "A recent study commissioned by a group of organizations including Kodak and the U.S. Internal Revenue Service says that computers can be a waste of time. The study results indicate that productivity may actually have declined after the dawn of the information age. One theory is that the computer has introduced as many non-productive tasks as it has time-serving ones. (Globe & Mail, Oct. 12, 1993: A18).

[12b)] Kirkpatrick Sale in Rebels Against the Future: The Luddites and Their War on the Industrial Revolution - Lessons for the Computer Age, encapsulates the modern Luddite movement[c] - the war on the techno-sphere.[d] (UTNE READER\37) William Gibson argues this in his novels - are computers dangerous or destructive to today's ecology and social framework? See also Bob Ickes, "Die, Computer, Die: First we kill all the computers", New York 24 July 1995: 24.[e]

[1©] Wendell Berry according to Russell Lipton "is a throw-back to an American tradition: the workingman who comments literately and critically on the darker side of our culture. Though he might wince, Berry follows in the tradition of Thoreau." (Lipton, 173)

[1(d)] "Machines were once an amazement and they were both admired and feared. Reformers preached the dawn of a new freedom, but the workmen threw their wooden shoes into the cogwheel. (Scientific American Reader: 491)

[1(e)] "If people's lives are governed by the unelected controllers of technology, the freedom granted by democratic vote are totally undermined." (M. Shallis, The Silicon Idol. Toronto: Oxford Univ. Press: 151). For expansion of this theme and an opposite view see Michael A. Arbib's, "Democracy in the Computer Age" in Computers & The Cybernetic Society. Orlando: Academic Press, 1984: 373-386.)

[1(f).] Ted Nelson in <u>Computer Lib</u> gives a layman's view of computing as the personification of computers or personal expressions of our humanity not through "the cold and inhuman monsters of the traditional stereo-types" but "the color and excitement of this newest of art forms, the computer application." (Quoted in <u>Byte</u> July 1976: 102).

[1(g).] :The primary reason is that it has taken almost three decades to develop a different view of what computing machines are good for. The original notion that they are good for serving as glorified clerks and adding machines is shifting. Now (finally), thanks in no small measure to Englebart himself, we view computers as tools that should, indeed, amplify human creativity,   thinking, and planning." (Russell Lipton, <u>Multimedia Toolkit: Build Your Own Solutions with DocuSource</u> NY.: Random House Electronic Publishing, 1992: 70).

[1(h).] "If you had asked the 'computer experts' in 1965 what the future of computing would be in 1985, they would invariably have said, 'There will be huge main-frame computers and they will have databases filled with everything! People will use smart terminals and access them via telephone lines.' Their ideas of a smart terminal was one with editing functions and perhaps a   built-in 300-baud modem - the world of personal computers was not even a gleam in their yes.'"

(Stan Veit, What Ever Happened To...Time-sharing, Multiuser Personal Computers", <u>Computer Shopper</u> Sept. 1992: 743.)

APPENDIX 21

10 COMMANDMENTS OF COMPUTER ETHICS

1. Thou shalt not use a computer to harm other people.
2. Thou shalt not interfere with other people's computer work.
3. Thou shalt not snoop around in other people's computer files.
4. Thou shalt not use a computer to steal.
5. Thou shalt not use a computer to bear false witness.
6. Thou shalt not copy or use proprietary software for which you have not paid.
7. Thou shalt not use other people's computer resources without authorization or proper compensation.
8. Thou shalt not appropriate other people's intellectual output.
9. Thou shalt think about the social consequences of the program you are writing or the system you are designing.
10. Thou shalt always use a computer in ways that ensure consideration and respect for your fellow humans.

Source: Available on the Net.

APPENDIX 22

ARE YOU COMPUTER COMPULSIVE? (Quiz yourself!)

by P. J. Herrington (One of the really great ADAMphiles. We truly miss you. May God bless.)

1. I GET MOST OF MY NEWS BY:
    a)   Watching the morning, evening, and late-night news broadcasts on TV.
    b)   Listening to hourly radio spots and scanning the headlines in the newspaper.
    c)   Electronic bulletin board systems, ADAM newsletters, and A.N.N. disks.

2. MY IDEA OF RELAXATION IS:
    a)   Nine holes of golf.
    b)   A long soak in a hot tub while reading a user's manual.
    c) Debugging a program.

3. THE FOLLOWING BEST DESCRIBES MY COMPUTER AREA:
    a)   I have my ADAM set up neatly in a corner; I have a place for everything, and everything in its place.
    b)   My computer gear is threatening to overflow my living room, but I sometimes remember to use dust covers.
    c)   My computer equipment fills three or more rooms, but I can still spend six weeks looking for a favorite program.

4. ON MY DAY OFF, I USUALLY:
    a)   Work around the house, run a few errands, and relax in the evening with a rented movie
    b)   Check out the local bulletin boards and play a quick game of Dragon's Lair in the evening.
    c)   Play ADDICTUS for 24 hours or until my eyes look like Monte's did at the convention.

5. MY PET IS:
   a) An Afghan who needs frequent walks and eats only sauteed
       calves liver prepared by my own hand.
   b) A Labrador retriever who sits quietly at my feet
       when I am busy at the computer.
   c) 32 turtles. (I had a cat once, but I gave her away the last time she
       strolled across the
       keyboard.)

6. THE FOLLOWING BEST DESCRIBES MY POLITICAL
INVOLVEMENT:
   a) I vote judiciously, only after a careful study of the
       candidates & the issues.
   b) I occasionally send a Congressgram via
       Compuserve.
   d) I feel that if God had wanted us to vote, he would have made
       polling booths accessible by
       modem.

APPENDIX 23

LITTLE ADAM ORPHAN

The Adam is one of the best loved orphans in town. Toronto area aficionados of the machine that Coleco abandoned in 1984 have become expert at upgrading and renovating their favorite PC. One of the reasons for the machines unparalled staying power is the flexibility of its design. "Coleco designed the Adam to be a very open-ended machine. It was advertised as the expandable computer" said Richard Clee, president of the Metro Toronto Adam Group (MTAG).

Orphans are typically the victims of creeping obsolescence, as parts and peripherals become hard to find and repair shops refuse to fix machines too unorthodox for their staff. Clee cited friendliness and functionality as the features that have kept Adam users interested in maintaining their machines. "It's head and shoulders above the Commodore 64. You can view it as a really great word processing typewriter with a video game for the kids and an honest to god computer on the side," Clee said. "You can just sit down, turn it on, and everything is so obvious you can just work straight through." Clee said the Adam survives because of a sub-culture of programmers and hackers who have remained loyal Adam users. Clee himself collects old Adams and uses the parts for repairs on other machines. "There's still a good amount of parts around," said Clee. "An outfit in New Jersey bought a huge inventory which they have sold profitably ever since. But the local tightwads have ideas of their own."

Syd Carter, a Toronto tinkerer and MTAG member has developed a number of products to bring the ADAM UP TO DATE. Among these is a 100 per cent Hayes compatible modem. Carter has also developed a tape formatter that allows a regular cassette tape to be used in the computer. "The tape drive was set up so that you couldn't use ordinary tapes," said Carter. "They claimed that the factory version had a superior shell and a higher resistance to heat. With my formatter you can make your own tapes for everyday stuff, and for the data that needs ultimate protectability, use the Coleco tapes." Carter has sold his formatter to sources in England, Australia and the U.S., and he has put it through four design changes. He's also experienced at all kinds of repairs on the Adam.

Gary Bowser, another local, has expanded the Adam's drive capability. The Adam came from the factory with a 160K 5 1/4 inch tape drive. Bowser designed a 3 1/2 inch 720K drive which can be installed in the original case, or used in tandem with the original drive. Other Toronto Adam specialists include John Lindgrow who developed an improved hard drive, and Tony Moreham who rewrote the Adam operating system.

Toronto Computes by Norman Ravvin; May 1989.

APPENDIX 24

DATABASE PROGRAM IN 'BASIC' LANGUAGE

```
100  WIDTH 40: KEY OFF
110  ON ERROR GOTO 140
115  REM  FIELD ARRAYS
120   DIM AU$(99),TI$(99),PR$(99),CO$(99),TE$(99)
130  TNC = 1
140  COLOR 2
145  REM CLEAR SCREEN
150  CLS
160  A$-INKEY$
170  CNT = 0
175  REM DRAW SCREEN BOX
180  AA=1:BB=1
190  FOR  X = 1 TO 39
200  LOCATE AA,BB: PRINT CHR$(178);
210  BB=BB+1
220  NEXT
230  FOR X = 1 TO 24
240  LOCATE AA,BB:PRINT CHR$(178);
250  AA=AA+1
260  NEXT
270  AA=1:BB=1
280  FOR X = 1 TO 24
290  LOCATE AA,BB: PRINT CHR$(178);
300  AA =AA+1
310  NEXT
320  A=24:BB=1
330  FOR X = 1 TO 39
340  LOCATE AA,BB: PRINT CHR$(178);
350  BB=BB+1
360  NEXT
370  IF REP = 1 THEN RETURN
380  COLOR 15
390  X=23: Y=5: O=X
400  FL=0
405  _REM GLOBAL VARIABLES
410  I=20: P=20: Q=5: R=15
420   A=5: B=5: C=2: D=4: E=6: F=8: G=10: H=12:
     II=14: JJ=16
```

```
430  X=23:Y=5
435  REM DISPLAY SCREEN MENU
440  LOCATE A,B: PRINT "INPUT INFO";"  1";
450  LOCATE (A+C),B: PRINT "PRINT INFO ";
     "  2";
460  LOCATE (A+D),b: PRINT "SORT RECS,";
     "   3";
470  LOCATE (A+E),B: PRINT "SAVE/LOAD";
     "   4";
480  LOCATE (A+F),B: PRINT "EDIT";"       5";
490  LOCATE (A+G),B: PRINT "PRINTER";
     "      6";
500  LOCATE (A+H),B: PRINT "SEARCH";
     "       7";
510  LOCATE (A+II),B; PRINT "SCREEN #2";
     "   8";
520  LOCATE (A+JJ),B; PRINT "END";"       9";
530  COLOR 14: LOCATE X,Y: PRINT "SELECT
     # 1 TO  9 "; :COLOR 15
540  NN=VAL(INKEY$): MN=0
550  ON NN GOTO
     670,910,2180,1710,1420,1310,1990,2140,660
560  GOTO 520
570  FOR AA = 2 TO 23
580  FOR AB = 2 TO 38
590  LOCATE AA,AB: PRINT " ";
600  NEXT: NEXT: RETURN
610  A=5: B=5: LOCATE A,B: PRINT
     "AUTHOUR";
620  LOCATE (A+C),B: PRINT "TITLE";
630  LOCATE (A+D),B: PRINT "PUBLISHER";
640  LOCATE (A+E),B: PRINT "COST";
650  LOCATE (A+F),B: PRINT "DATE";
660  RETURN
670  CLS: WIDTH 80: END
680  PRINT NN;: CLS: REP = 1: GOSUB 140:
     GOSUB 610
685  REM INPUT FIELD NAMES
690  CNT = CNT+1: LOCATE 20,5: PRINT CNT
700  LOCATE A,R: COLOR 9: INPUT "
     ",AU$(CNT): COLOR 15:  GOSUB 770
710  COLOR 9: INPUT " ",TI$(CNT): COLOR 15:
     GOSUB 770
```

```
720  COLOR 9: INPUT " ",PR$(CNT): COLOR 15:
     GOSUB 770
730  COLOR 9: INPUT " ",CO$(CNT): COLOR 15:
     GOSUB 770
740  COLOR 9: INPUT " ",TE$(CNT): COLOR 15:
     GOSUB 770
750  GOSUB 780
760  GOSUB 560: GOTO 420
770  A = A+2: LOCATE A,R: RETURN
780  LOCATE (A+3),B: PRINT "TO CONT. INPUT
     '1' "
790  LOCATE (A+4),B: PRINT "TO END INPUT
     '2' "
800  MM = VAL(INKEY$)
810  ON MM GOTO 830,910
820  GOTO 780
830  GOSUB 610
840  A=5: R=15
850  FOR SD= 2 TO 15
860  FOR DS = R TO 38
870  LOCATE SD,DS: PRINT " ";
880  NEXT: NEXT
890  IF RT = 1 THEN RETURN
900  GOTO 690
910  GOSUB 570: GOTO 420
920  GOSUB 570: GOSUB 610: TP=1
930  FOR PT = 1 TO CNT
940  COLOR 2
945  REM PRINT FIELDS ON SCREEN
950  IF NT = 1 THEN PT= PT+1
960  LOCATE 22,5: PRINT PT
970  LOCATE A,R: PRINT AU$(PT)
980  LOCATE (A+C),R: PRINT TI$(PT)
990  LOCATE (A+D),R: PRINT PR$(PT)
1000 LOCATE (A+E),R: PRINT CO$(PT)
1010 LOCATE (A+F),R: PRINT TE$(PT)
1020 COLOR 15
1030 IF NT = 1 THEN RETURN
1040 FOR TM=1 TO 3500: NEXT
1050 GOSUB 2160
1060 NEXT PT
1070 IF MN = 0 THEN LOCATE 20,20: INPUT
     "CONT.",B$
1080 IF MN = 0 THEN GOSUB 570: GOTO 420
```

```
1090 RETURN
1100 GT=1:DD=1
1110 CLS
1120 DD=DD*2
1130 LOCATE 3,10: PRINT DD;
1140 IF DD <= CNT THEN 1120
1150 DD = INT((DD-1)/2)
1160 IF DD=0 THEN 1290
1170 LOCATE 3,20: PRINT DD: LOCATE 3,25:
     PRINT CNT
1180 FOR II= 1 TO CNT-DD
1190 JJ=II
1200 LL=JJ+DD
1210 LOCATE 10,5: PRINT LL
1220 GOTO 1310
1230 A1$=AU$(JJ): A2$=TI$(JJ): A3$=PR$(JJ):
     A4$=CO$(JJ):  A5$=TE$(JJ)
1240 AU$(LL)=A1$: TI$(LL)=A2$: PR$(LL)=A3$:
     CO$(LL)=A4$: TE$(LL)=A5$
1250 JJ=JJ-DD
1260 IF JJ>0 THEN 1200
1270 NEXT II
1280 GOTO 1150
1290 GOSUB 570: GOSUB 610: GOSUB 930
1300 GOSUB 570: GOTO 420
1310 IF AU$(LL) <+ AU$(JJ) THEN 1230
1320 GOTO 1270
1330 GOSUB 4720
1340 GOTO 1430
1345 REM PRINT FIELDS ON PRINTER
1350 LPRINT: LPRINT "AUTHOUR   TITLE
     PUBLISHER   COST   DATE"
1360 FOR YY= 1 TO CNT
1370 LPRINT AU$(YY);" ";
1380 LPRINT TI$(YY);" ";
1390 LPRINT PR$(YY);" ";
1400 LPRINT CO$(YY);" ";
1410 LPRINT CO$(YY);" "; LPRINT: LPRINT
1420 NEXT
1430 GOTO 530
1440 GOSUB 570
1445 REM FIELD # TO EDIT
1450 ED=1
1460 LOCATE 3,5: INPUT "RECORD # TO EDIT ", RC
```

```
1470 IF GT=1 THEN GOSUB 2870
1480 LOCATE 8,5: PRINT "#"
1490 LOCATE 10,5: PRINT "1";"AUTHOUR
     ";AU$(RC)
1500 LOCATE 12,5: PRINT "2";"TITLE
     ";TI$(RC)
1510 LOCATE 14,5: PRINT "3";"PUBLISHER
     ";PR$(RC)
1520 LOCATE 16,5: PRINT "4";"COST
     ";CO$(RC)
1530 LOCATE 18,5: PRINT "5";"DATE
     ";TE$(RC)
1540 LOCATE 20,5: PRINT "ENTER FIELD # TO
     EDIT 1 TO  6",FD
1550 BEEP
1560 GOTO 4050
1570 ON FD GOTO 1580,1640,1660,1700,1600
1580 LOCATE 10,16: INPUT " ",AU$(RC)
1590 GOTO 1540
1600 PRINT
1605 REM ENTER NEW FIELD NAMES
1610 IF ED=1 THEN 2930
1620 IF SB=1 THEN LOCATE 23,5: PRINT "
     ": GOTO 2100
1630 GOSUB 570: GOTO 390
1640 LOCATE 12,16: INPUT " ",TI$(RC)
1650 GOTO 1590
1660 LOCATE 14,16: INPUT " ",PR$(RC)
1670 GOTO 1590
1680 LOCATE 16,16: INPUT " ",CO$(RC)
1690 GOTO 1590
1700 LOCATE 18,18: INPUT " ",TE$(RC)
1710 GOTO 1590
1720 GOTO 1600
1730 GOSUB 570
1735 REM SAVE/LOAD FILE ROUTINE
1740 COLOR 9
1750 LOCATE 5,5: PRINT " PRESS 's' TO SAVE"
1760 LOCATE 7,5: PRINT " PRESS 'l' TO LOAD"
1770 LOCATE 9,5: PRINT "ENTER s/l";SL$
1780 IF SL$="S" THEN 1790 ELSE 1890
1790 LOCATE 11,5: PRINT "SAVE";
1800 OPEN "O",#1,"DBM"
1810 WRITE#1,CNT
```

```
1820 FOR X = 1 TO CNT
1830 WRITE#1,AU$(X),TI$(X),PR$(X),
     CO$(X),TE$(X)
1840 NEXT
1850 COLOR 15
1860 CLOSE
1870 LOCATE 15,5: PRINT "SAVE
     COMPLETED";
1880 GOSUB 570: GOTO 420
1890 LOCATE 11,5: PRINT " LOAD";
1900 OPEN "I",#1,"DBM"
1910 INPUT#1,CNT
1920 FOR X = 1 TO CNT
1930 INPUT#1,AU$(X),TI$(X),PR$(X),
     CO$(X),TE$(X)
1940 NEXT X
1950 CLOSE
1960 COLOR 15
1970 LOCATE 15,5: PRINT "LOAD COMPLETED"
1980 LOCATE 17,5: INPUT "TO CONT. PRESS
     'ENTER' ",FT$
1990 NT=0
2000 GOSUB 570: GOTO 420
2010 GOSUB 570
2005 REM GLOBAL SEARCH ROUTINE
2020 LOCATE 3,5: INPUT "GLOBAL SEARCH
     y/n ",GS$
2030 IF GS$= "y" THEN 3120 ELSE 2040
2040 LOCATE 5,5: INPUT "RECORD # TO
     SEARCH ",RC
2050 CT=1: SB=1
2060 AZ=1: NT=1: PT=FS: GOSUB 2130:
     GOSUB 1480
2070 AZ=0: SB=1
2080 LOCATE 23,5: INPUT "TO EDIT THIS FILE
     PRESS y/n ",YN$
2090 IF YN$="y" GOTO 2120
2100 LOCATE 23,5: INPUT "ANOTHER SEARCH
     y/n ",SA$
2110 IF SA$="n" THEN GOSUB 570: GOTO 390
2120 GOSUB 2870: GOTO 2040
2130 FOR SS = 2 TO 5: FOR ST = 2 TO 39
2140 LOCATE SS,ST: PRINT " ";
2150 NEXT: NEXT: RETURN
```

```
2160 RT=1
2170 IF PT=CNT THEN RETURN
2180 GOSUB 840: RT=0
2190 RETURN
2200 GOSUB 570
2205 REM SORT ROUTINES
2210 LOCATE 5,5: PRINT "SORT ON"
2220 LOCATE 7,8: PRINT "AUTHOUR   1 ";:
     LOCATE  9.8:  PRINT "TITLE    2 ";:
     LOCATE 11,8: PRINT "PUBLISHER  3 ";:
     LOCATE 13,8: PRINT "COST
     4 ";: LOCATE 15,8:  PRINT  "DATE     5 ";
2230 LOCATE 18,5: INPUT "#  1,2,3,4,5 ", NM
2240 ON NM GOTO 2250,2390,2510,2630,2750
2250 LOCATE 20,5: PRINT "SORTING ON
     'AUTHOUR' "
2260 FOR FF = 1 TO CNT-1
2270 FOR SS = FF+1 TO CNT
2280 IF AU$(FF) <= AU$(SS) THEN 2340
2290 SWAP AU$(FF),AU$(SS)
2300 SWAP TI$(FF),TI$(SS)
2310 SWAP PR$(FF),PR$(SS)
2320 SWAP CO$(FF),CO$(SS)
2330 SWAP TE$(FF),TE$(SS)
2340 NEXT SS
2350 NEXT FF
2360 LOCATE 22,5: PRINT "CONT.";
2370 INPUT "";IP$
2380 GOSUB 570: GOTO 440
2390 LOCATE 20,5: PRINT "SORTING ON
     'TITLE' "
2400 FOR FF = 1 TO CNT-1
2410 FOR SS = FF+1 TO CNT
2420 IF TI$(FF) <= TI$(SS) THEN 2480
2430 SWAP AU$(FF),AU$(SS)
2440 SWAP TI$(FF),TI$(SS)
2450 SWAP PR$(FF),PR$(SS)
2460 SWAP CO$(FF),CO$(SS)
2470 SWAP TE$(FF),TE$(SS)
2480 NEXT SS
2490 NEXT FF
2500 GOTO 530
2510 LOCATE 20,5: PRINT "SORTING ON
     'PUBLISHER' "
```

```
2520 FOR FF = 1 TO CNT-1
2530 FOR SS = FF+1 TO CNT
2540 OF PR$(FF) <= PR$(SS) THEN 2600
2550 SWAP AU$(FF),AU$(SS)
2560 SWAP TI$(FF),TI$(SS)
2570 SWAP PR$(FF),PR$(SS)
2580 SWAP CO$(FF),CO$(SS)
2590 SWAP TE$(FF),TE$(SS)
2600 NEXT SS
2610 NEXT FF
2620 GOTO 530
2630 LOCATE 20,5: PRINT "SORTING ON
     'COST' "
2640 FOR FF = 1 TO CNT-1
2650 FOR SS = FF+1 TO CNT
2660 OF PR$(FF) <= PR$(SS) THEN 2720
2670 SWAP AU$(FF),AU$(SS)
2580 SWAP TI$(FF),TI$(SS)
2690 SWAP PR$(FF),PR$(SS)
2700 SWAP CO$(FF),CO$(SS)
2710 SWAP TE$(FF),TE$(SS)
2720 NEXT SS
2730 NEXT FF
2740 GOTO 530
2750 LOCATE 20,5: PRINT "SORTING ON
     'DATE' "
2760 FOR FF = 1 TO CNT-1
2770 FOR SS = FF+1 TO CNT
2780 OF PR$(FF) <= PR$(SS) THEN 2720
2790 SWAP AU$(FF),AU$(SS)
2800 SWAP TI$(FF),TI$(SS)
2810 SWAP PR$(FF),PR$(SS)
2820 SWAP CO$(FF),CO$(SS)
2830 SWAP TE$(FF),TE$(SS)
2840 NEXT SS
2850 NEXT FF
2860 GOTO 530
2870 FOR FR = 5 TO 18
2880 FOR RO = 17 TO 30
2890 LOCATE FR,RO: PRINT " ";
2900 NEXT RO
2910 NEXT FR
2920 RETURN
```

```
2930 LOCATE 3.5: INPUT "ANOTHER RECORD
     TO EDIT  y/n",AE$
2940 IF AE$="y" THEN LOCATE 4,5: INPUT
     "RECORD # ",RC ELSE 1630
2950 GT=1: GOTO 1470
2960 LOCATE 5,5: PRINT "RECORDS TO
     SEARCH"
2970 LOCATE 7,5: INPUT "FIRST RECORD",FI
2980 LOCATE 9,5: INPUT "LAST RECORD",LA
2990 GOSUB 570: GOSUB 610: FL=1
3000 GOSUB 3020
3010 FL=0: GOTO 420
3020 FOR PT = FI TO LA
3030 LOCATE A,R: PRINT AU$(PT)
3040 LOCATE (A+C),R: PRINT TI$(PT)
3050 LOCATE (A+D),R: PRINT PR$(PT)
3060 LOCATE (A+E),R: PRINT CO$(PT)
3070 LOCATE (A+F),R: PRINT TE$(PT)
3080 GOSUB 2160
3090 LOCATE 15,5: PRINT PT
3100 NEXT
3110 RETURN
3115 REM FIELD SEARCH ROUTINE
3120 LOCATE 7,5: PRINT "FIELD TO SEARCH"
3130 LOCATE 9,5: PRINT " AUTHOUR    1"
3140 LOCATE 11,5: PRINT " TITLE     2"
3150 LOCATE 13,5: PRINT " PUBLISHER  3"
3160 LOCATE 15,5: PRINT " COST      4"
3170 LOCATE 17,5: PRINT " DATE      5"
3180 LOCATE 19,5: INPUT " #1,2,3,4,5 ",TU
3190 FOR X = 7 TO 23
3200 FOR Y = 2 TO 38
3210 LOCATE X,Y: PRINT " ";
3220 NEXT Y,X
3230 AZ=1
3240 AR$=""
3250 ON TU GOTO 3260,3280,3300,3320,3340
3260 LOCATE 5,5: PRINT " SEARCHING ON
     'AUTHOUR' "
3270 LOCATE 7,5: INPUT " AUTHOUR ", AR$:
     GOTO 3360
3280 LOCATE 5,5: PRINT " SEARCHING ON
     'TITLE' "
```

```
3290 LOCATE 7,5: INPUT " TITLE ',AR$: GOTO
     3360
3300 LOCATE 5,5: PRINT " SEARCHING ON
     'PUBLISHER' "
3310 LOCATE 7,5: INPUT " PUBLISHER ", AR$:
     GOTO 3360
3320 LOCATE 5,5: PRINT " SEARCHING ON
     'COST' "
3330 LOCATE 7,5: INPUT " COST ",AR$: GOTO
     3360
3340 LOCATE 5,5: PRINT " SEARCHING ON
     'DATE' "
3350 LOCATE 7,5: INPUT " DATE ";AR$
3360 FOR X = 1 TO CNT
3370 ON TU GOTO  3380,3390,3400,3410,3420
3380 IF AU$(X)=AR$ THEN 3580 ELSE
     AZ=AZ+1: GOTO  3430
3390 IF TI$(X)=AR$ THEN 3580 ELSE AZ=AZ+1:
     GOTO  3430
3400 IF PR$(X)=AR$ THEN 3580 ELSE AZ=AZ+1:
     GOTO  3430
3410 IF CO$(X)=AR$ THEN 3580 ELSE
     AZ=AZ+1: GOTO  3430
3420 IF TE$(X)=AR$ THEN 3580 ELSE AZ=AZ+1:
     GOTO  3430
3430 NEXT X
3440 ON TU GOTO 3450,3460,3470,3480,3490
3450 LOCATE 9,5: PRINT "AUTHOUR NOT ON
     FILE ":  GOTO  3500
3460 LOCATE 9,5: PRINT "TITLE NOT ON ":
     GOTO 3500
3470 LOCATE 9,5: PRINT "PUBLISHER NOT ON
     FILE ":  GOTO  3500
3480 LOCATE 9,5: PRINT "COST NOT ON FILE
     ": GOTO  3500
3490 LOCATE 9,5: PRINT "DATE NOT ON FILE
     ":  GOTO  3500
3500 LOCATE 19,5: INPUT " ANOTHER SEARCH
     y/n ",SA$
3510 IF SA$="y" THEN ELSE 3570
3520 FOR MM = 6 TO 20
3530 FOR OO = 2 TO 38
3540 LOCATE MM,OO: PRINT " ";
3550 NEXT OO,MM
```

```
3560 GOTO 3120
3570 FOR N = 1 TO LEN(CO$(RC))
3580 LOCATE 9,5: PRINT " AUTHOUR
     ;AU$(AZ)
3590 LOCATE 11,5: PRINT " TITLE    ";TI$(AZ)
3600 LOCATE 13,5: PRINT " PUBLISHER
     ";PR$(AZ)
3610 LOCATE 15,5: PRINT " COST   ";CO$(AZ)
3620 LOCATE 17,5: PRINT " DATE   ";TE$(AZ)
3630 GOTO 3500
3640 GOSUB 570
3650 LOCATE 5,5: PRINT "PRESS 's' TO SAVE"
3660 LOCATE 7,5: PRINT "PRESS 'l' TO LOAD"
3670 LOCATE 9,5: PRINT "ENTER s/l ", SL$
3680 LOCATE 10,5: PRINT "cnt= ";CNT
3690 IF SL$="s" THEN 3700 ELSE 3830
3700 LOCATE 11,5: PRINT "SAVE"
3710 GOSUB 3940
3720 LOCATE 12,5: PRINT "tnc= ";TNC
3730 LOCATE 14,5: PRINT "cont",OC$
3735 REM APPEND FILE ROUTINE
3740 OPEN "DBFILE" FOR APPEND AS 1
3750 FOR X = TNC TO CNT
3760 WRITE#1,AU$(X),TI$(X),PR$(X),CO$(X),
     TE$(X)
3770 NEXT X
3780 TNC = CNT
3790 CLOSE
3800 LOCATE 11,5: PRINT "SAVE COMPLETED"
3810 LOCATE 10,5: PRINT "  ";CNT; "  ";TNC
3820 GOSUB 570: GOTO 420
3830 GOSUB 3990
3840 OPEN "DBFILE" FOR INPUT AS 1
3850 FOR X = 1 TO CNT
3860 IF EOF(1) THEN 3900
3870 INPUT#1,AU$(X),TI$(X),PR$(X),CO$(X),
     TE$(X)
3880 NEXT X
3890 CNT = X-1
3900 CLOSE
3910 LOCATE 10,5: PRINT "cnt= ";CNT
3920 LOCATE 11,5: PRINT "LOAD
     COMPLETED"
3930 GOSUB 570: GOTO 420
```

```
3940 OPEN "O",#1,"COUNTER"
3950 WRITE#1,CNT
3960 CLOSE
3970 LOCATE 13,5: PRINT  "cnt= ",CNT
3980 RETURN
3990 OPEN "I",#1,"COUNTER"
4000 INPUT#1,CNT
4010 CLOSE
4020 LOCATE 13,5: PRINT  "cnt= ";CNT
4030 LOCATE 14,5: INPUT "CONT",OC$
4040 RETURN
4045 REM EDIT FIELD ROUTINES
4050 ON FD GOTO 4060,4200,4330,4460,4590
4060 YY=17: XX=0
4070 UA$(RC)=""
4080 LOCATE 10,YY
4090 INPUT "",AA$
4100 XX=XX+1
4110 YY=YY+1: IF XX=LEN(AU$(RC)+1 THEN 4180 ELSE  LOCATE
     10,YY
4120 IF AA$ >= CHR$(48) AND AA$ <=
     CHR$(122) GOTO  4140
4130 GOTO 4090
4140 FOR N = 1 TO LEN(AU$(RC))
4150 IF N=XX THEN UA$(RC) = UA$(RC)+AA$:
     GOTO  4170
4160 UA$(RC)=UA$(RC)+MID$(AU$(RC),N,1)
4170 NEXT N
4180 AU$(RC)=UA$(RC)
4190 LOCATE 22,5: INPUT "MORE CHANGES y/n
     ",HG$: IF HG$="y" THEN  1460 ELSE GOSUB
     570: GOTO 390
4200 YY=17: XX=0
4210 UA$(RC)="": LOCATE 12,YY
4220 INPUT "",AA$
4230 XX=XX+1: YY=YY+1
4240 IF XX=LEN(TI$(RC))+1 THEN 4310 ELSE
     LOCATE  12,YY
4250 IF AA$ >= CHR$(48) AND AA$ <=
     CHR$(122) GOTO 4270
4260 GOTO 4350
4270 FOR N = 1 TO LEN(TI$(RC))
4280 IF N = XX THEN UA$(RC)=UA$(RC)+AA$:
     GOTO 4300
```

```
4290 UA$(RC)=UA$(RC)+MID(TI$(RC),N,1)
4300 NEXT N
4310 TI$(RC)=UA$(RC)
4320 LOCATE 22,5: INPUT "MORE CHANGES
     y/n ", HG$: IF  HG$="y" THEN 1460 ELSE
     GOSUB 570: GOTO 390
4330 YY=17: XX=0
4340 UA$(RC)="": LOCATE 14,YY
4350 INPUT "",AA$
4360 XX=XX+1: YY=YY+1
4370 IF XX=LEN(PR$(RC))+1 THEN 4440 ELSE
     LOCATE  14,YY
4380 IF AA$ >= CHR$(48) AND AA$ <=
     CHR$(122) GOTO 4400
4390 GOTO 4350
4400 FOR N = 1 TO LEN(TI$(RC))
4410 IF N = XX THEN UA$(RC)=UA$(RC)+AA$:
     GOTO 4300
4420 UA$(RC)=UA$(RC)+MID(TI$(RC),N,1)
4430 NEXT N
4440 PR$(RC)=UA$(RC)
4450 LOCATE 22,5: INPUT "MORE CHANGES
     y/n ", HG$:  IF  HG$="y" THEN 1460 ELSE
     GOSUB 570: GOTO 390
4460 YY=17: XX=0
4470 UA$(RC)="": LOCATE 16,YY
4480 INPUT "",AA$
4490 XX=XX+1: YY=YY+1
4500 IF XX=LEN(CO$(RC))+1 THEN 4440 ELSE
     LOCATE  16,YY
4510 IF AA$ >= CHR$(48) AND AA$ <=
     CHR$(122) GOTO 4530
4520 GOTO 4480
4530 FOR N = 1 TO LEN(CO$(RC))
4540 IF N = XX THEN UA$(RC)=UA$(RC)+AA$:
     GOTO 4560
4550 UA$(RC)=UA$(RC)+MID(CO$(RC),N,1)
4560 NEXT N
4570 CO$(RC)=UA$(RC)
4580 LOCATE 22,5: INPUT "MORE CHANGES
     y/n ", HG$: IF  HG$="y"  THEN 1460
     ELSE GOSUB 570: GOTO 390
4590 YY=17: XX=0
4600 UA$(RC)="": LOCATE 18,YY
```

```
4610 INPUT "",AA$
4620 XX=XX+1: YY=YY+1
4630 IF XX=LEN(TE$(RC))+1 THEN 4440 ELSE
     LOCATE 18,YY
4640 IF AA$ >= CHR$(48) AND AA$ <= CHR$(122)
     GOTO 4660
4650 GOTO 4610
4660 FOR N = 1 TO LEN(TE$(RC))
4670 IF N = XX THEN UA$(RC)=UA$(RC)+AA$:
     GOTO 4690
4680 UA$(RC)=UA$(RC)+MID(TE$(RC),N,1)
4690 NEXT N
4700 TE$(RC)=UA$(RC)
4710 LOCATE 22,5: INPUT "MORE CHANGES
     y/n ",  HG$: IF HG$ = "y"  THEN 1460
     ELSE GOSUB 570: GOTO 390
4715 REM PRINT RECORDS ON PRINTER IN
     FORMATTED FORM
4720 FOR RR = 1 TO CNT
4730 LPRINT "  RECORD ";RR;: LPRINT TAB
     "RECORD";RR+1
4740 LPRINT
4750 LPRINT "AUTHOUR     ";" ";AU$(RR);:
     LPRINT  TAB(40) "AUTHOUR    ";"
     ;AU$(RR+1)
4760 LPRINT "TITLE       ";" ";TI$(RR);: LPRINT
     TAB(40) "TITLE      ";" ";TI$(RR+1)
4770 LPRINT "PUBLISHER   ";" ";PR$(RR);:
     LPRINT  TAB(40) "PUBLISHER  ";"
     ";PR$(RR+1)
4780 LPRINT "COST        ";" ";CO$(RR);:
     LPRINT  TAB(40) "COST       ";"
     ";CO$(RR+1)
4790 LPRINT "DATE        ";" ";TE$(RR);:
     LPRINT  TAB(40) "DATE       ";"
     ";TE$(RR+1)
4800 LPRINT: LPRINT
4810 RR=RR+1
4820 LPRINT:LPRINT:LPRINT:LPRINT
4840 RETURN
```

APPENDIX 25

DATABASE PROGRAM IN 'C' LANGUAGE

```c
#include "stdio.h"        /*LIBRARY & HELP FILES*/
#include "dos.h"
#include "stdlib.h"
#include "conio.h"
#define REVERSE "\x1B[7m"  /*ANSI FUNCTIONS*/
#define NORMAL  "\x1B[0m"
#define U_ARRO 72       /*EXTENDED-KEY
                            FUNCTIONS DEFINED*/
#define D_ARRO  80
#define INS    82
#define STOPBIT 0x20
#define CURSIZE 1
#define VIDEO   0x10
#define HOME    71
#define R_ARRO  77
#define BK_SPC  8
#define F1     59
#define F2     60
#define CTRL F1 94
#define CF10   103
#define END     79
#define LEFT   2       /*SCREEN-WINDOW
                          DIMENSIONS DEFINED*/
#define TOP    3
#define RIGHT 80
#define BOT   22
#define HEIGHT (BOT-TOP+1)
#define WIDTH  (RIGHT-LEFT+1)
#define LT     40      /*POP-UP/FLOATING-WINDOWS
                          DEFINED*/
#define TP     8
#define RT     70
#define BT     12
#define HT    (BT-TP+1)
#define WH    (RT-LT+1)
#define LLT    15
#define TTP    5
#define RRT    58
```

```
#define BBT    18
#define HHT    (BBT-TTP+1)
#define WWH    (RRT-LLT+1)
#define LE     5
#define OP     5
#define RGH    35
#define TOB    20
#define WE     5      /*POP-UP/FLOATING-WINDOWS
                          DEFINED*/
#define WX     5
#define WG     30
#define WB     14
#define FT     10
#define TPX    5
#define GHT    40
#define BTX    15
#define TFL    5
#define POT    9
#define TGR    45
#define MTB    15
#define FT1    11
#define TPX1   6
#define GHT1   38
#define BXT1   14
#define LF     10
#define PO     5
#define RIG    50
#define BM     20
#define LF1    11
#define PO1    6
#define RIG1   49
#define BM1    17
#define LTL    10
#define TPT    10
#define RTR    40
#define BMB    20
#define MMM    20
#define NNN    4
#define OOO    35
#define PPP    4
#define AAA    2
#define BBB    2
#define CCC    80
#define DDD    2
```

```c
#define FFF    30
#define GGG     5
#define HHH    60
#define III    20
#define RRR    31
#define SSS     6
#define TTT    59
#define UUU    19
typedef struct personnel    /*STRUCTURAL ELEMENTS
                                DEFINED*/
{                   /*FIXED-LENGTH FIELDS*/
 char authour [40];
 char title [40];
 char publisher [40];
 double cost;
 char date [8];
 char ccost [10];
}personnel;
struct personnel record[50];
int n = 1;         /*GLOBALLY DEFINED VARIABLES*/
int count = 0;
int line;
int cols;
int rws;
int rcr;
int cnt = 1;
char d11() = "AUTHOUR";
char d12() = "TITLE";
char d13() = "PUBLISHER";
char d14() = "COST";
char d15() = "DATE";
char box;
int curpos = 3;

main()             /*MAIN ROUTINE*/
{
 int left, top, right, bot;
 window(LEFT,TOP,RIGHT,BOT);
 clrscr();
 textcolor(WHITE);
 textbackground(BLUE);
 clrscr();
 dr_b();
 menu1();
```

```
control();
}
control()          /*CURSOR CONTROL*/
{
 char ch;
 int cp = 5;
 int code;
 int n;
 ch = 'a';

 BBX();
 while( ch != 'z' )
  {
  menu1();
  gotoxy(cp,curpos);
  printf("%s%d",REVERSE,cnt);
  rcn(cnt);
  curoff();
  code = getcode();
  switch (code)
    {
    case U_ARRO:
          curpos = curpos - 1;
          --cnt;
          gotoxy(cp,curpos);
          cprintf("%s%d%s",REVERSE,cnt,NORMAL);
      break;
    case D_ARRO:
          curpos = curpos + 1;
          ++cnt;
      gotoxy(cp,curpos);
          cprintf("%s%d%s", REVERSE,cnt,NORMAL);
          break;
    case R_ARRO:
      action(cnt);
          break;
    case F2:    /*DATE & TIME*/
      dte();
          break;
    case F1:    /*EXIT KEY*/
          exit(1);
    case HOME:    /*CURSOR TO TOP OF MENU*/
      hm();
          break;
```

```
     case END:      /*CURSOR TO BOTTOM OF
                         MENU*/
               dne();
            break;
      case CF10:
               cf10();
            break;
    }
  }
}

action(cnt)           /*MENU CONTROL ROUTINES*/
{
 char ch;
 switch (cnt)
  {
 case 1: BBC(); bbxc(); boxc(); qfile(); BBX(); break;
 case 2: daf(); rfile(); clrscr(); BBX(); break;
 case 3: dag(); wfile(); clrscr(); BBX(); break;
 case 4: BBC(); box2(); newrec(); BBX(); BBD(); break;
 case 5: BBC(); prtbx2(); prtrecs(); BBD(); break;
 case 6: BBC(); box20(); box21(); break;
 case 7: BBC(); BBX(); search(); BBX(); break;
 case 8: BBC(); box48(); break;
 case 9:  dte(); break;
 case 10: rstruct_srt(); BBD(); break;
 case 11: BBC(); box35(); box20(); box21(); chrec(); box26();
box27(); box36(); BBX(); break;
 case 12: BBC(); box15(); box12(); prtfields(); box40(); BBX();
break;
  }
}
hm()               /*CURSOR DISPLAY*/
{
 cnt = 1;
 gotoxy(5,3); printf("%s%d%s",REVERSE,cnt,NORMAL);
 gotoxy(8,3); printf("%sQUIT",REVERSE,NORMAL);
 curpos = 3; }
dne()
{
 cnt = 12;
 gotoxy(5,14); printf("%s%d%s",REVERSE,cnt,NORMAL);
 gotoxy(8,14); printf("%sPRINT FIELDS",REVERSE,NORMAL);
 curpos = 14;
```

```
}
cf10()
{
 cnt = 10;
 gotoxy(5,12); printf("%s%d%s",REVERSE,cnt,NORMAL);
 gotoxy(8,12); printf("%sSORT RECORDS",REVERSE,NORMAL);
 curpos = 12;
 }
prtfields()          /*PRINT FIELDS OF DATABASE*/
{
char sp[5];
char ra[5];
int ch = 'a';
int j;
int sph;
float dd,yy,xx;
char arn;
int ct = 0;
int p;
 while ( ch != 'n' )
 {
  prr();
  prll();
  gotoxy(2,8); cprintf("ENTER FIELD #");
  gotoxy(2,9); cprintf("TO DISPLAY ");
  gets(sp);
  sph = atoi(sp);
  gotoxy(13,9); cprintf("%d",sph);
  prr();
  switch ( sph )
  {
  case 1:
        if (n<=0)
          { prr(); gotoxy(3,3); cprintf("EMPTY LIST."); }

        for ( j=1; j<n; j++ )
           {
     gotoxy(3,3); cprintf("PRINTING %s", d11);
           gotoxy(3,j+3); cprintf("[%d] %s
                 ",j,record[j].authour);
 }
        break;
 }
  gotoxy(3,7); cprintf("TO PRINT ANOTHER FIELD");
```

```
    gotoxy(3,8); cprintf("<y> or <n> ");
    ch = getche();
  }
}
prll()              /*FIELD NAMES DISPLAYED*/
{
  gotoxy(3,2); cprintf(" # 1 %s", d11);
  gotoxy(3,3); cprintf(" # 2 %s", d12);
  gotoxy(3,4); cprintf(" # 3 %s", d13);
  gotoxy(3,5); cprintf(" # 4 %s", d14);
  gotoxy(3,6); cprintf(" # 5 %s", d15);
}
prr()
{
  int mm;
  int mm1;
  line = 255;
  for (mm = 2; mm < 10; mm++)
    for (mm1 = 2; mm1 < 30; mm1++)
      {gotoxy(mm1,mm); cprintf("%c", line);};
}
box10()              /*ROUTINES TO DRAW WINDOWS*/
{
  int ft,tpx,ght,bxt;
  window(FT,TPX,GHT,BTX);
  clrscr();
  textcolor(WHITE);
  textbackground(RED);
  clrscr();
  wbx();
}
box11()
{
  int ft,tpx,ght,bxt;
  window(FT,TPX,GHT,BTX);
  clrscr();
  textcolor(WHITE);
  textbackground(GREEN);
  clrscr();
  wbx();

}
box12()
{
```

```
 int ft1,tpx1,ght1,bxt1;
 window(FT1,TPX1,GHT1,BXT1);
 clrscr();
 textcolor(WHITE);
 textbackground(RED);
 clrscr();
}
box15()
{
 int ft,tpx,ght,btx;
 window(FT,TPX,GHT,BTX);
 clrscr();
 textcolor(WHITE);
 textbackground(BLUE);
 clrscr();
 wbx();
}
wbx()                /*BORDERS DRAWN AROUND
                        WINDOWS*/
{
  line = 220;
  for ( cols = 1; cols < 30; cols++ )
    cprintf("%c", line);
  line = 218;
    gotoxy(1,1); cprintf("%c", line);
  line = 222;
    for ( rws = 2; rws < 11; rws++ )
    {gotoxy(1,rws); cprintf("%c", line);};
  line = 221;
    for ( rws = 2; rws < 11; rws++ )
    {gotoxy(30,rws); cprintf("%c", line);};
  line = 191;
    gotoxy(30,1); cprintf("%c", line);
  line = 223;
    for ( cols = 2; cols < 30; cols++ )
    {gotoxy(cols,11); cprintf("%c", line);};
  line = 192;
    gotoxy(1,11); cprintf("%c", line);
  line = 217;
    gotoxy(30,11); cprintf("%c", line);
 }
box39()
{
 int tfl,pot,tgr,mtb;
```

```
  window(TFL,POT,TGR,MTB);
  clrscr();
  textcolor(WHITE);
  textbackground(RED);
  clrscr();
  getch();
}
box40()
{
  int ft,tpx,ght,btx;
  window(FT,TPX,GHT,BTX);
  clrscr();
  textcolor(WHITE);
  textbackground(BLUE);
  clrscr();
}
wbx1() {
  line = 220;
  for ( cols = 10; cols < 60; cols++ )
    { gotoxy(cols,4); cprintf("%c", line); };
  line = 218;
    gotoxy(9,4); cprintf("%c", line);
  line = 179;
    for ( rws = 5; rws < 17; rws++ )
    {gotoxy(9,rws); cprintf("%c", line);};
  line = 179;
    for ( rws = 5; rws < 17; rws++ )
          {gotoxy(45,rws); cprintf("%c", line);};
  line = 191;
    gotoxy(45,4); cprintf("%c", line);
  line = 217;
    gotoxy(45,16); cprintf("%c", line);
  line = 192;
    gotoxy(9,16); cprintf("%c", line);
  line = 223;
    for ( cols = 10; cols < 60; cols++ )
    {gotoxy(cols,17); cprintf("%c", line);};
  getch();
 }

prtrecs()              _/*PRINT RECORDS ON SCREEN*/  {
  int j;
  if (n<0)
   {gotoxy(2,2);cprintf("EMPTY LIST."); }
```

```
    for (j=1; j<n; j++)
      {
         gotoxy(3,12); cprintf(" Record # is %d", j);
         gotoxy(3,2); cprintf("AUTHOUR:  %s", record[j].authour);
         gotoxy(3,4); cprintf("TITLE:    %s", record[j].title);
         gotoxy(3,6); cprintf("PUBLISHER: %s",
record[j].publisher);
         gotoxy(3,8); cprintf("COST:    %4.2f", record[j].cost);
         gotoxy(3,10); cprintf("DATE:    %s", record[j].date);
         getch();  } }
boxc() {
 int we,wx,wg,wb;
 window(WE,WX,WG,WB);
 clrscr();
 textcolor(WHITE);
 textbackground(RED);
 clrscr();
 bbxc(); }
bbxc() {
 line  = 220;
 for (cols = 1; cols < 26; cols++)
   {gotoxy(cols,1); cprintf("%c", line);};
 line = 221;
   for( rws = 2; rws < 10; rws++)
   {gotoxy(1,rws); cprintf("%c",line );};
 line = 222;
   for( rws = 2; rws < 10; rws++)
   {gotoxy(25,rws); cprintf("%c", line);};
 line = 223;
   for(cols =1; cols < 26; cols++)
   {gotoxy(cols,10); cprintf("%c", line);}; }
qfile()          /*QUIT OR END ROUTINE*/ {
  char ch;
  gotoxy(2,3); cprintf("TO END PRESS <q>.");
  gotoxy(2,5); cprintf("OTHERWISE PRESS");
  gotoxy(2,6); cprintf("ANY KEY.");
  ch = getche();
  if ( ch == 'q' )
    exit(1); }

search()          /*SEARCH RECORDS BY FIELDS*/ {
  char name [40];
  int d;
  int enter = 0;
```

```
int nme;
int jk = 'a';
float cst,tsc;
int count;
int lne = 95;
line = 255;
 while ( jk != 'n' )
 {
 gotoxy(3,3); cprintf("SEARCH ON  (a) AUTHOUR ");
 gotoxy(3,4); cprintf("         (t) TITLE   ");
 gotoxy(3,5); cprintf("         (p) PUBLISHER");
 gotoxy(3,6); cprintf("         (c) COST    ");
 gotoxy(3,7); cprintf("         (d) DATE    ");
 gotoxy(25,9); cprintf(" ");
 gotoxy(25,9); cprintf("%c",lne);
 gotoxy(3,9); cprintf("Select < a t p c d > ");
 nme = getche();
 textcolor(WHITE);
  switch( nme )
   {
        case 'a':
      gotoxy(3,11); cprintf("AUTHOUR");
      gotoxy(11,11);
      gets(name);
             gotoxy(11,11); cprintf("%s", name);
          for(d=1; d<n; d++)
    if(strcmp(record[d].authour,name) == 0)
               {enter=1; gotoxy(3,12);
     cprintf("AUTHOUR MATCH =
             %s",record[d].authour);}
                 if ( enter == 1 )
                    {gotoxy(3,13); cprintf(""); }
    else
                    {gotoxy(3,13); cprintf("NO MATCH"); }
      break;
 }
    textcolor(WHITE+BLINK);
    gotoxy(3,14); cprintf("Press <n> or <y> ");
            jk = getche();
    textcolor(WHITE);
    gotoxy(3,14); cprintf("Press <n> or <y> ");
    sch();
 } }
sch()
```

```
{
  int yy;
  line = 255;
  for( yy=11; yy < 30; yy++)
  {gotoxy(yy,11); cprintf("%c",line);};
}
wfile()            /*WRITE TO DISK ROUTINE*/ {
 FILE *fp;
  if(n < 1)
    {gotoxy(2,2); cprintf("Can't write empty list.");}
  if( (fp=fopen("RECD.TXT","wb")) == NULL )
    {gotoxy(2,2); cprintf("Can't open file RECD.TXT"); }
  else
    {
    fwrite(record, sizeof(record[0]), n, fp);
    fclose(fp);
    gotoxy(4,2);
    cprintf("File of %d", n);
    gotoxy(4,3); cprintf("records written.");
    }
  getch(); }
rfile()            /*READ DISK ROUTINE*/ {
 FILE *fp;
  if((fp=fopen("RECD.TXT","rb")) == NULL )
    {gotoxy(2,2); cprintf("Can't open file RECD.TXT. "); }
  else
    {
    while( fread(&record[n],sizeof(record[n]),1,fp)==1 )        n++;
    fclose(fp);
    gotoxy(2,2);
    cprintf("File read. Total agents");
    gotoxy(2,3); cprintf("is now %d.",n );
    }
  getch(); }
rstruct_srt()        /*SORT ROUTINES ACCORDING TO FIELDS*/  {
  int in,out;
  int count = n;
  char ta[50],ti[50],tu[50],td[50];
  float tc;
  char fd[10];
  char fd1;
  char f11[] = "AUTHOUR";
  char f12[] = "TITLE";
  char f13[] = "PUBLISHER";
```

```
char f14[] = "COST";
char f15[] = "DATE";
int st;
BBX();
gotoxy(3,2); cprintf("SORTING FILE");    /*SORT ROUTINES*/
gotoxy(3,4); cprintf("Press < a t p c d > ");
st = getche();
gotoxy(3,6); cprintf("SORTING ON ");
while ( st != 'n' )
{
  switch(st)
  {
  case 'a':
  textcolor(YELLOW);
  gotoxy(14,6); cprintf("%s", f11);
  textcolor(WHITE);
  for(out=1;out<count-1;out++)
       for(in=out+1;in<count;in++)
        if(strcmp(record[out].authour,record[in].authour)
        > 0 )
          {
            strcpy(ta,record[in].authour);
      strcpy(ti,record[in].authour);
      strcpy(tu,record[in].title);
            strcpy(tc,record[in].publisher);
            strcpy(td,record[in].cost);
      strcpy(record[in].authour,record[out].authour);
      strcpy(record[in].title,record[out].title);
      strcpy(record[in].publisher,record[out].publisher);
      strcpy(record[in].cost,record[out].cost);
      strcpy(record[in].date,record[out].date);
      strcpy(record[out].authour,ta);
      strcpy(record[out].title,ti);
      strcpy(record[out].publisher,tu);
      strcpy(record[out].cost,tc);
      strcpy(record[out].date,td);
          }
  }
  getche();
  break;
 } }
BBX()               /*WINDOW-DRAWING ROUTINES*/  {
 int le,op,rgh,tob;
 window(LE,OP,RGH,TOB);
```

```
 clrscr();
 textcolor(WHITE);
 textbackground(RED);
 clrscr();
 bb_x(); }
BBC() {
 int le,op,rgh,tob;
 window(LE,OP,RGH,TOB);
 clrscr();
 textcolor(WHITE);
 textbackground(BLUE);
 clrscr(); }
bb_x() {
 line = 205;
    for (cols = 1; cols < 30; cols++)
    cprintf("%c", line);
 line = 201;
    gotoxy(1,1); cprintf("%c", line);
 line = 186;
    for (rws = 2; rws < 16; rws++)
     {gotoxy(1,rws); cprintf("%c", line);};
    for (rws = 2; rws < 16; rws++)
     {gotoxy(30,rws); cprintf("%c", line);};
  line = 187;
    gotoxy(30,1); cprintf("%c", line);
  line = 205;
    for (cols = 2; cols < 30; cols++)
    {gotoxy(cols,16); cprintf("%c", line);};
  line = 200;
    gotoxy(1,16); cprintf("%c", line);
  line = 188;
    gotoxy(30,16); cprintf("%c", line); }
getcode()          /*GET EXTENDED-KEYBOARD CONTROL KEYS*/  {
 int key;
 while( getch() != 0 )
  ;
 return( getch() ); }
curoff()           /*TURNS CURSOR OFF*/  {
 union REGS regs;
 regs.h.ch = STOPBIT;
 regs.h.ah = CURSIZE;
 int86(VIDEO, &regs, &regs); }
newrec()           /*INPUT NEW RECORD*/  {
   char ch;
```

```
char numstr[81];
int rec;
ch = 'a';
while ( ch != 'n' )
 {
 gotoxy(3,12);
 cprintf("RECORD #        ");
 gotoxy(3,12);
 cprintf("RECORD # %d",n);
 gotoxy(3,13);
 cprintf("ANOTHER y/n     ");
 le();
 cur();
 gotoxy(15,2);
 gets(record[n].authour);
 gotoxy(15,2);
 cputs(record[n].authour);
 cnt = 1;
 cur();
 gotoxy(15,4);
 gets(record[n].title);
 gotoxy(15,4);
 cputs(record[n].title);
 cnt = 2;              /*INPUT NEW RECORD*/
 cur();
 gotoxy(15,6);
 gets(record[n].publisher);
 gotoxy(15,6);
 cputs(record[n].publisher);
 cnt = 3;
 cur();
 gotoxy(15,8);
 gets(record[n].ccost);
 record[n].cost = atof(record[n].ccost);
 gotoxy(15,8);
 cprintf("%4.2f", record[n].cost);
 cnt = 4;
 cur();
 gotoxy(15,10);
 gets(record[n].date);
 gotoxy(15,10);
 cputs(record[n].date);
 n++;
 textcolor(WHITE+BLINK);
```

```
  gotoxy(3,13);
  cprintf("ANOTHER y/n ");
  ch = getche();
  textcolor(WHITE);
  count = 0;
  } }
cur()               /*ACTIVATES AND DISPLAYS CURSOR*/ {
 count = count +2;
 line = 95;
 gotoxy(15,count);
 cprintf("%c", line); }
le()                /*BLANKS LINE IN A RECORD*/ {
 int dd;
 line = 255;
  for(count=2; count<14; count++)
   for(dd=15; dd< 43; dd++)
     {gotoxy( dd,count); cprintf("%c", line);};
  count = 0; }
rcn(cnt)            /*DISPLAYS CURSOR IN REVERSE FORM*/ {
 int x;
 switch (cnt)
 {
  case 1:
    gotoxy(8,3);
    printf("%sQUIT",REVERSE,NORMAL);
    line = 255;
    for (x = 8; x < 16; x++)
              cprintf("%c",line);
    break;
   case 2:
    gotoxy(8,4);
    printf("%sREAD RECORDS",REVERSE,NORMAL);
    break;
  case 3:
    gotoxy(8,5);
    printf("%sWRITE RECORDS",REVERSE,NORMAL);
    break;
  case 4:
    gotoxy(8,6);
    printf("%sENTER RECORDS",REVERSE,NORMAL);
    break;
  case 5:
    gotoxy(8,7);
    printf("%sPRINT RECORDS",REVERSE,NORMAL);
```

```
        break;
    case 6:
      gotoxy(8,8);
      printf("%sCHANGE A REC.",REVERSE,NORMAL);
      break;
    case 7:
      gotoxy(8,9);
      printf("%sSEARCH RECORDS",REVERSE,NORMAL);
      break;
    case 8:
      gotoxy(8,10);
      printf("%sPRINTER OUTPUT",REVERSE,NORMAL);
      break;
    case 9:
      gotoxy(8,11);
      printf("%sTODAY'S DATE",REVERSE,NORMAL);
      break;
    case 10:
      gotoxy(8,12);
      printf("%sSORT RECORDS",REVERSE,NORMAL);
      break;
    case 11:
      gotoxy(8,13);
      printf("%sPRINT A REC.",REVERSE,NORMAL);
      break;
    case 12:
      gotoxy(8,14);
      printf("%sPRINT FIELDS",REVERSE,NORMAL);
      break;
}}
dte()              /*DISPLAYS DATE AND TIME*/  {
  struct date today;
  struct time now;
  dae();
  getdate(&today);
   gotoxy(2,2);
   cprintf("Today's date is %d %d %d ", today.da_mon,
today.da_day, today.da_year);
  gettime(&now);
   gotoxy(2,3);
   cprintf("Today's time is %02d:%02d:%02d\n", now.ti_hour,
now.ti_min, now.ti_sec);
  getch();
  clrscr();
```

```
 BBX();
 }
dae() {
 box1();            /*REDRAWS MAIN WINDOW*/ }
dr_b() {
 line = 205;
   for (cols =1; cols <79; cols++)
      cprintf("%c", line);
 line = 201;
   gotoxy(1,1); cprintf("%c", line);
 line = 186;
    for (rws= 2; rws < 20; rws++)
     { gotoxy(1,rws); cprintf("%c",line);};
    for (rws = 2; rws < 20; rws++)
     { gotoxy(79,rws); cprintf("%c", line);};
 line = 187;
   gotoxy(79,1); cprintf("%c", line);
 line = 205;
   for( cols=2; cols < 79; cols++)
     { gotoxy(cols,19);  cprintf("%c", line);};
 line = 200;
   gotoxy(1,19); cprintf("%c",line);
 line = 188;
   gotoxy(79,19); cprintf("%c", line);
 }
box1() {
 int lt,tp,rt,bt;
 char name;
 window(LT,TP,RT,BT);
 clrscr();
 textcolor(WHITE);
 textbackground(BLUE);
 clrscr();
 b_1(); }
b_1()               /*REDRAWS INTERNAL WINDOW*/ {
 int x;
 clrscr();
 textcolor(YELLOW);
 line = 205;
   for (cols = 1; cols < 11; cols++)
     cprintf("%c", line);
     gotoxy(12,1); cprintf("%s", "TIME");
   for (cols = 16; cols < 30; cols++)
     cprintf("%c",line);
```

```
  line = 201;
    gotoxy(1,1); cprintf("%c", line);
  line = 187;
    gotoxy(29,1); cprintf("%c", line);
  line = 186;
    for (rws= 2; rws < 4; rws++)
      { gotoxy(1,rws); cprintf("%c",line);};
    for (rws = 2; rws < 4; rws++)
      { gotoxy(29,rws); cprintf("%c", line);};
  line = 205;
    for (cols= 2; cols < 30; cols++)
      {gotoxy(cols,4); cprintf("%c",line);};
  line = 200;
    gotoxy(1,4); cprintf("%c", line);
  line = 188;
    gotoxy(29,4); cprintf("%c", line);
  textcolor(WHITE); }
daf() {
 box4(); }
dr_c()                /*REDRAWS INTERNAL WINDOW*/  {
  line = 205;
    for (cols =1; cols <79; cols++)
        cprintf("%c", line);
  line = 201;
    gotoxy(1,1); cprintf("%c", line);
  line = 186;
    for (rws= 2; rws < 20; rws++)
      { gotoxy(1,rws); cprintf("%c",line);};
    for (rws = 2; rws < 20; rws++)
      { gotoxy(79,rws); cprintf("%c", line);};
  line = 187;
    gotoxy(79,1); cprintf("%c", line);
  line = 205;
    for( cols=2; cols < 79; cols++)
      { gotoxy(cols,19);  cprintf("%c", line);};
  line = 200;
    gotoxy(1,19); cprintf("%c",line);
  line = 188;
    gotoxy(79,19); cprintf("%c", line);
}
box4() {
 int lt,tp,rt,bt;
 char name;
 window(LT,TP,RT,BT);
```

```
clrscr();
textcolor(WHITE);
textbackground(BLUE);
clrscr();
b_5(); }
b_5() {
 int x;
 clrscr();
 textcolor(YELLOW);
 line = 205;
   for (cols = 1; cols < 9; cols++)
     cprintf("%c", line);
     gotoxy(9,1); cprintf("%s", "READING FILE");
   for (cols = 22; cols < 30; cols++)
     cprintf("%c",line);
 line = 201;
   gotoxy(1,1); cprintf("%c", line);
 line = 187;
   gotoxy(29,1); cprintf("%c", line);
 line = 186;
   for (rws= 2; rws < 4; rws++)
          { gotoxy(1,rws); cprintf("%c",line);};
     for (rws = 2; rws < 4; rws++)
     { gotoxy(29,rws); cprintf("%c", line);};
 line = 205;
   for (cols= 2; cols < 30; cols++)
     {gotoxy(cols,4); cprintf("%c",line);};
 line = 200;
   gotoxy(1,4); cprintf("%c", line);

 line = 188;
   gotoxy(29,4); cprintf("%c", line);
 textcolor(WHITE); }
dag() {
 box6(); }
dr_d() {
 line = 205;
   for (cols =1; cols <79; cols++)
       cprintf("%c", line);
 line = 201;
   gotoxy(1,1); cprintf("%c", line);
 line = 186;
     for (rws= 2; rws < 20; rws++)
       { gotoxy(1,rws); cprintf("%c",line);};
```

```
    for (rws = 2; rws < 20; rws++)
      { gotoxy(79,rws); cprintf("%c", line);};
  line = 187;
    gotoxy(79,1); cprintf("%c", line);
  line = 205;
    for( cols=2; cols < 79; cols++)
        { gotoxy(cols,19);  cprintf("%c", line);};
  line = 200;
    gotoxy(1,19); cprintf("%c",line);
  line = 188;
    gotoxy(79,19); cprintf("%c", line);
  }
box6() {
 int lt,tp,rt,bt;
 char name;
 window(LT,TP,RT,BT);
 clrscr();
 textcolor(WHITE);
 textbackground(BLUE);
 clrscr();
 b_6(); }
b_6() {
 int x;
 clrscr();
 textcolor(YELLOW);
 line = 205;
   for (cols = 1; cols < 9; cols++)
     cprintf("%c", line);
     gotoxy(9,1); cprintf("%s", "WRITING FILE");
   for (cols = 22; cols < 30; cols++)
     cprintf("%c",line);
  line = 201;
    gotoxy(1,1); cprintf("%c", line);
  line = 187;
    gotoxy(29,1); cprintf("%c", line);


  line = 186;
    for (rws= 2; rws < 4; rws++)
        { gotoxy(1,rws); cprintf("%c",line);};
    for (rws = 2; rws < 4; rws++)
      { gotoxy(29,rws); cprintf("%c", line);};
  line = 205;
   for (cols= 2; cols < 30; cols++)
```

```
    {gotoxy(cols,4); cprintf("%c",line);};
 line = 200;
   gotoxy(1,4); cprintf("%c", line);
 line = 188;
   gotoxy(29,4); cprintf("%c", line);
 textcolor(WHITE); }
menu1()            /*DISPLAY MENU ITEMS*/ {
 textcolor(WHITE);
 gotoxy(5,3);
 cputs("1  QUIT");
 gotoxy(5,4);
 cputs("2  READ RECORDS");
 gotoxy(5,5);
 cputs("3  WRITE RECORDS");
 gotoxy(5,6);
 cputs("4  ENTER RECORDS");
 gotoxy(5,7);
 cputs("5  PRINT RECORDS");
 gotoxy(5,8);
 cputs("6  CHANGE A REC.");
 gotoxy(5,9);
 cputs("7  SEARCH RECORDS");
 gotoxy(5,10);
 cputs("8  PRINTER OUTPUT");
 gotoxy(5,11);
 cputs("9  TODAY'S DATE");
 gotoxy(5,12);
 cputs("10 SORT RECORDS");
 gotoxy(5,13);
 cputs("11 PRINT A REC.");
 gotoxy(5,14);
 cputs("12 PRINT FIELDS"); }
menu2()            /*DISPLAY INPUT RECORD
                     ITEMS*/ {
 int n;
 textcolor(WHITE);
 gotoxy(3,12);
 cprintf("RECORD # %d",n+1);
 gotoxy(3,2);
 cprintf("1 AUTHOUR");
 gotoxy(3,4);
 cprintf("2 TITLE");
 gotoxy(3,6);
 cprintf("3 PUBLISHER");
```

```
 gotoxy(3,8);
 cprintf("4 COST");
 gotoxy(3,10);
 cprintf("5 DATE"); }
menu22(rcr)        /*DISPLAY MENU ITEMS ON
                     INPUT SCREEN*/ {
 textcolor(WHITE);
 gotoxy(3,10);
 cprintf("RECORD # %d",rcr);
 gotoxy(3,3);
 cprintf("1 AUTHOUR");
 gotoxy(3,4);
 cprintf("2 TITLE");
 gotoxy(3,5);
 cprintf("3 PUBLISHER");
 gotoxy(3,6);
 cprintf("4 COST");
 gotoxy(3,7);
 cprintf("5 DATE"); }
box2()            /*RE-DRAWS BORDERS*/ {
  int llt,ttp,rrt,bbt;
  char name;
  window(LLT,TTP,RRT,BBT);
  clrscr();
  textcolor(WHITE);
  textbackground(RED);
  clrscr();
  b_3();
  menu2();
  getch(); }
prtbx2()             /*RE-DRAWS BORDERS*/ {
  int llt,ttp,rrt,bbt;
  char name;
  window(LLT,TTP,RRT,BBT);
  clrscr();
  textcolor(WHITE);
  textbackground(RED);
  clrscr();
  bx_2(); }
b_3() {
 int x;
 clrscr();
 line = 205;
  for (cols = 1; cols < 15; cols++)
```

```
    cprintf("%c", line);
    cprintf("%s", "INPUT BOX");
  for (cols = 25; cols < 44; cols++)
    cprintf("%c", line);
 line = 201;
  gotoxy(1,1); cprintf("%c", line);
 line = 187;
  gotoxy(43,1); cprintf("%c", line);
 line = 186;
   for (rws= 2; rws < 15; rws++)
        { gotoxy(1,rws); cprintf("%c",line);};
   for (rws = 2; rws < 15; rws++)
     { gotoxy(43,rws); cprintf("%c", line);};
 line = 205;
  for (cols= 2; cols < 43; cols++)
     {gotoxy(cols,14); cprintf("%c",line);};
 line = 200;
  gotoxy(1,14); cprintf("%c", line);
 line = 188;
  gotoxy(43,14); cprintf("%c", line); }
bx_2() {
 int x;
 clrscr();
 line = 205;
  for (cols = 1; cols < 10; cols++)
    cprintf("%c", line);
  cprintf("%s", "PRINTING RECORDS");
  for (cols = 28; cols < 45; cols++)
    cprintf("%c", line);
 line = 201;
  gotoxy(1,1); cprintf("%c", line);
 line = 187;
  gotoxy(43,1); cprintf("%c", line);
 line = 186;
   for (rws= 2; rws < 15; rws++)
        { gotoxy(1,rws); cprintf("%c",line);};
   for (rws = 2; rws < 15; rws++)
     { gotoxy(43,rws); cprintf("%c", line);};
 line = 205;
  for (cols= 2; cols < 43; cols++)
     {gotoxy(cols,14); cprintf("%c",line);};
 line = 200;
  gotoxy(1,14); cprintf("%c", line);
 line = 188;
```

```
   gotoxy(43,14); cprintf("%c", line); }
BBD() {
  int llt,ttp,rrt,bbt;
  char name;
  window(LLT,TTP,RRT,BBT);
  clrscr();
  textcolor(WHITE);
  textbackground(BLUE);
  clrscr();
  BBX(); }
menu5()              /*MAIN-MENU SCREEN DISPLAY*/  {
  textcolor(WHITE);
  gotoxy(30,8);
  cputs("1  ");
  gotoxy(35,9);
  cputs("2  ");
  gotoxy(35,10);
  cputs("3  ");
  gotoxy(35,11);
  cputs("4  ");
  gotoxy(30,12);
  cputs("5  ");
  gotoxy(25,13);
  cputs("6  ");
  gotoxy(20,12);
  cputs("7  ");
  gotoxy(15,11);
  cputs("8  ");
  gotoxy(15,10);
  cputs("9  ");
  gotoxy(15,9);
  cputs("10 ");
  gotoxy(20,8);
  cputs("11 ");
  gotoxy(25,7);
  cputs("12 "); }

menu15()            /*MAIN-MENU SCREEN ITEMS
                        DEFINED*/  {
  textcolor(WHITE);
  gotoxy(50,5);
  cputs("1  QUIT");
  gotoxy(50,6);
  cputs("2  READ RECORDS");
```

```
gotoxy(50,7);
cputs("3  WRITE RECORDS");
gotoxy(50,8);
cputs("4  ENTER RECORDS");
gotoxy(50,9);
cputs("5  PRINT RECORDS");
gotoxy(50,10);
cputs("6  CHANGE A REC.");
gotoxy(50,11);
cputs("7  SEARCH RECORDS");
gotoxy(50,12);
cputs("8  PRINTER OUTPUT");
gotoxy(50,13);
cputs("9  TODAY'S DATE");
gotoxy(50,14);
cputs("10 SORT RECORDS");
gotoxy(50,15);
cputs("11 PRINT A REC.");
gotoxy(50,16);
cputs("12 PRINT FIELDS"); }
cnr(cnt)            /*DISPLAY MENU CONTROL
                    ITEMS*/ {
 int x;
 switch (cnt)
 {
  case 1:
    gotoxy(30,8);
    printf("%s%d%s",REVERSE,cnt,NORMAL);
    break;
  case 2:
    gotoxy(35,9);
    printf("%s%d%s",REVERSE,cnt,NORMAL);
    break;
  case 3:
    gotoxy(35,10);
    printf("%s%d%s",REVERSE,cnt,NORMAL);
    break;
  case 4:
    gotoxy(35,11);
    printf("%s%d%s",REVERSE,cnt,NORMAL);
    break;
  case 5:
    gotoxy(30,12);
    printf("%s%d%s",REVERSE,cnt,NORMAL);
```

```
    break;
  case 6:
    gotoxy(25,13);
    printf("%s%d%s",REVERSE,cnt,NORMAL);
    break;
  case 7:
    gotoxy(8,9);
    printf("%sSEARCH RECORDS",REVERSE,NORMAL);
    break;
  case 8:
    gotoxy(8,10);
    printf("%sPRINTER OUTPUT",REVERSE,NORMAL);
    break;
  case 9:
    gotoxy(8,11);
    printf("%sTODAY'S DATE",REVERSE,NORMAL);
    break;
  case 10:
    gotoxy(8,12);
    printf("%sSORT RECORDS",REVERSE,NORMAL);
    break;
  case 11:
    gotoxy(8,13);
    printf("%sPRINT A REC.",REVERSE,NORMAL);
    break;
  case 12:
    gotoxy(8,14);
    printf("%sPRINT FIELDS",REVERSE,NORMAL);
    break;
} }
conrol()              /*ROUTINE CONTROLS CURSOR DISPLAY*/  {
  char ch;
  int cp = 30;
  int cnt = 1;
  int curpos = 8;
  int code;
  int n;
  ch = 'a';
  while( ch != 'z' )
   {
   menu5();
   cnr(cnt);
   curoff();
   code = getcode();
```

```
switch (code)
  {
   case U_ARRO:
        curpos = curpos - 1;
        --cnt;
        cnr(cnt);
        break;
   case D_ARRO:
        curpos = curpos + 1;
        ++cnt;
      cnr(cnt);
        break;
   case R_ARRO:
      action(cnt);
        break;
   case HOME:

      dte();
        break;
   }
} }

box20() {
 int lf,po,rig,bm;
 window(LF,PO,RIG,BM);
 clrscr();
 textcolor(WHITE);
 textbackground(BLUE);
 clrscr();
 wind(); }
box21() {
 int lf1,po1,rig1,bm1;
 window(LF1,PO1,RIG1,BM1);
 clrscr();
 textcolor(WHITE);
 textbackground(GREEN);
 clrscr(); }
wind() {
  line = 220;
  for ( cols = 1; cols < 41; cols++ )
    cprintf("%c", line);
  line = 218;
    gotoxy(1,1); cprintf("%c", line);
  line = 222;
```

```
   for ( rws = 2; rws < 14; rws++ )
     {gotoxy(1,rws); cprintf("%c", line);};
  line = 221;
    for ( rws = 2; rws < 14; rws++ )
           {gotoxy(41,rws); cprintf("%c", line);};
  line = 191;
    gotoxy(41,1); cprintf("%c", line);
  line = 223;
    for ( cols = 2; cols < 41; cols++ )
     {gotoxy(cols,14); cprintf("%c", line);};
   line = 192;
    gotoxy(1,14); cprintf("%c", line);
   line = 217;
    gotoxy(41,14); cprintf("%c", line);
 }
prtarec()              /*PRINT A RECORD ON THE
                        SCREEN*/  {
 char ky[5];
 int j,rcr;
 gotoxy(2,2);
 cprintf("Enter record # to print: ");
 gets(ky);
 rcr = atoi(ky);
 gotoxy(2,10);
 cprintf("%d",rcr);
 clrscr();
 menu22(rcr);
 gotoxy(16,3); cprintf("%s",record[rcr].authour);
 gotoxy(16,4); cprintf("%s",record[rcr].title);
 return(rcr); }
chrec()              /*CHANGE A RECORD ROUTINE*/
 {
  int cr,rc,rcc,j,dr;
  char nrt[5];
  int fg = 'a';
  int lee;
  lee = (line = 95);
   while ( fg != 'n' )
     {
     clrscr();
     dr = prtarec();
     line = 95;
     gotoxy(2,10); cprintf("Record # Changing: %d",dr);
     gotoxy(2,11); cprintf("Field # to Change: ");
```

```
      textcolor(WHITE+BLINK);
      gotoxy(20,11); cprintf("%c",line);
      gets(nrt);
      textcolor(WHITE);
      cr = atoi(nrt);
      gotoxy(21,11); cprintf("%d",cr);
      line = 255;
      gotoxy(20,11); cprintf("%c", line);
    switch ( cr )
      {
      case 1:
        textcolor(BLACK);
           gotoxy(2,8); cprintf("ENTER AUTHOUR: ");
        gets( record[dr].authour);
        textcolor(WHITE);
        gotoxy(16,3); cprintf("                ");
           gotoxy(16,3); cprintf("%s", record[dr].authour);
        gotoxy(2,11); cprintf("                ");
        textcolor(WHITE+BLINK);
           gotoxy(2,11); cprintf("Press <n> or <y> ");
        textcolor(WHITE);
           break;
           }
      fg=getche();
  } }
BBY() {
 textbackground(BLUE); }
box26() {
 int lf,po,rig,bm;
 window(LF,PO,RIG,BM);
 clrscr();
 textcolor(WHITE);
 textbackground(BLUE);
 clrscr(); }


box27() {
 int lf1,po1,rig1,bm1;
 window(LF1,PO1,RIG1,BM1);
 clrscr();
 textcolor(WHITE);
 textbackground(BLUE);
 clrscr(); }
box35() {
```

```
 int mmm,nnn,ooo,ppp;
 window(MMM,NNN,OOO,PPP);
 clrscr();
 textcolor(WHITE);
 textbackground(RED);
 clrscr();
 gotoxy(1,3); cprintf("Change-a-rec."); }
box36() {
 int mmm,nnn,ooo,ppp;
 window(MMM,NNN,OOO,PPP);
 clrscr();
 textcolor(WHITE);
 textbackground(BLUE);
 clrscr(); }
box55() {
  int aaa,bbb,ccc,ddd;
  window(AAA,BBB,CCC,DDD);
  clrscr();
  textcolor(WHITE);
  textbackground(BLACK);
  clrscr();
  gotoxy(1,1);
  printf("QUIT READ WRITE ENTER PRINT CHANGE
       SEARCH PRINTER DATE SORT P-A-REC PRT
       FIELDS");
 }
tcon()              /*CURSOR CONTROL FOR MAIN MENU*/
 {
 int x;
 switch (cnt)
   {
   case 1:
     gotoxy(1,1);
     printf("%sQUIT",REVERSE,NORMAL);
     break;
   case 2:
     gotoxy(6,1);
     printf("%sREAD",REVERSE,NORMAL);
     break;
   case 3:
     gotoxy(11,1);
     printf("%sWRITE",REVERSE,NORMAL);
     break;
   case 4:
```

```
      gotoxy(17,1);
      printf("%sENTER",REVERSE,NORMAL);
      break;
    case 5:
      gotoxy(22,1);
      printf("%sPRINT",REVERSE,NORMAL);
      break;
    case 6:
      gotoxy(28,1);
      printf("%sCHANGE",REVERSE,NORMAL);
      break;
    case 7:
      gotoxy(35,1);
      printf("%sSEARCH",REVERSE,NORMAL);
      break;
    case 8:
      gotoxy(42,1);
      printf("%sPRINTER",REVERSE,NORMAL);
      break;
    case 9:
      gotoxy(50,1);
      printf("%sDATE",REVERSE,NORMAL);
      break;
    case 10:
      gotoxy(55,1);
      printf("%sSORT",REVERSE,NORMAL);
      break;
    case 11:
      gotoxy(60,1);
      printf("%sP-A-REC.",REVERSE,NORMAL);
      break;
    case 12:
      gotoxy(68,1);
      printf("%sPRT FIELDS",REVERSE,NORMAL);
      break;
  } }
box56() {
  int aaa,bbb,ccc,ddd;
  window(AAA,BBB,CCC,DDD);
  clrscr();
  textcolor(WHITE);
  textbackground(BLACK);
  clrscr();
```

```
  gotoxy(1,1); printf("QUIT READ WRITE ENTER PRINT CHANGE
SEARCH
PRINTER DATE SORT P-A-REC PRT FIELDS");
  tcon();
  }
box48() {
 int fff,ggg,hhh,iii;
 window(FFF,GGG,HHH,III);
 clrscr();
 textcolor(WHITE);
 textbackground(BLUE);
 clrscr();
 wibx();
 getch();
 box49();
 exit(1); }
 box49()
 {
  int rrr,sss,ttt,uuu;
  window(RRR,SSS,TTT,UUU);
  clrscr();
  textcolor(WHITE);
  textbackground(GREEN);
  clrscr();
 }
wibx()              /*RE-DRAWS MAIN WINDOW*/  {
 line = 220;
   for ( cols = 1; cols < 30; cols++ )
   cprintf("%c", line);
 line = 218;
   gotoxy(1,1); cprintf("%c", line);
 line = 222;
   for ( rws = 2; rws < 14; rws++ )
   {gotoxy(1,rws); cprintf("%c", line);};
 line  = 221;
   for ( rws = 2; rws < 14; rws++ )
   {gotoxy(61,rws); cprintf("%c", line);};
 line = 191;
   gotoxy(61,1); cprintf("%c", line);
 line = 223;
   for ( cols = 2; cols < 30; cols++ )
   {gotoxy(cols,14); cprintf("%c", line);};
 line = 192;
   gotoxy(1,14); cprintf("%c", line);
```

```
 line = 217;
   gotoxy(61,14); cprintf("%c", line);
}
```

NOTES:

1. This is not a *MICROSOFT WINDOWS* program.
2. To run this program ANSI.SYS file, in DOS directory,
   must be installed in your CONFIG.SYS file on your hard
   disk's root directory.
   [DEVICE = ANSI.SYS in CONFIG.SYS]
   [Example: DEVICE=C:\DOS\ANSI.SYS]

[1.] "Comments in a program are English language statements that tell the reader
what the programmer meant to do with the code. Some programmers use a lot
of comments, and others use very few. There is no consensus on how many
comments a program should have. Program documentation consists of separate
volumes of notes, charts, and operating instructions. Some programmers
maintain documentation rigorously. Others are not so
conscientious."(Stevens\40)

ENDNOTES

INTRODUCTION

[1.] M. Allaby. <u>Inventing Tomorrow</u>. (Abacus: London, 1977: 28.)
   In <u>The Limits to Growth</u> we saw the beginnings of the
acceptance of computers as predictors of human behavior. The
problem is trying to limit and define the number of factors
computers must consider in their analysis which determines the
degree of sophistication of human behavior computers can predict.

[1(a).] The advancement of computer technology is remarkable yet
computer power particularly since the arrival of microcomputers
is dramatically increasing. However, this must be kept in
perspective. For instance the comparison with the human brain is
hardly fair since its evolution is across millenia while the
computer's is at the most across 200 years.(C. Helmers, "What is
this Phenomenon Personal Computing?" <u>Byte</u> Jan. 1978: 6+.

CHAPTER ONE

[1.] D. F. Scott, "The Next Operating System: Some New Ideas,"
<u>Computer Shopper</u>,   Oct. 1987:191.

[2.] Treon Verdery, "Future Clean: Isotopically Pure
Semiconductors," <u>Wired</u> March 1995: 70.

[2(a).] Here is how John Titus, Peter Rony, and David Larsen define
software: The programs and routines used to extend the
capabilities of computers, such as compilers, assemblers,
narrators, routines and subroutines; and hardware: The
mechanical, magnetic, electronic, electromechanical, and
electrical devices from which a system is fabricated.("Komputer
Korner: Substituting microcomputer software for hardware,"
<u>Radio-Electronics</u>, Sept. 1976: 22.)

[3.] Milan Kundera, <u>Slowness</u>,(New York: Harpercollins, 1996).

[4.] Otto Friedrich, "Glork! A Glossary for Gweep: Even users should gork this cuspy sampler of computerese," TIME, 3 Jan. 1983: 24.

[5.] Edward Yourdon, Decline and Fall of the American Programmer (Englewood, NJ.: PTR Prentic-Hall, 1992).

[6.] The technological elite[a] are defined by Michael Walzer, "The New Masters", The New York Review of Books, March 20, 1980. It is best said by Jack Tramiel, founder of Commodore, in establishing the foundation for the microcomputing industry and ending elitism's control of computer technology, with his slogan - "Computers for the masses, not the classes."

[6(a).] Michael Shallis, The Silicon Idol (Toronto, Oxford Univ. Press) 151, writes the following on technological elites: "If people's lives are governed by the unelected controllers of technology, the freedoms granted by democratic vote are totally undermined." For an expansion of this theme and an opposite view see Michael A. Arbib, Computers and the Cybernetic Society (Orlando, FL.: Academic Press, 1984) 373.[b]

[6(b)] Wired 03 1995: 84.

[7.] "Electronics: Buzzwords - Paging the Digerati," [a] Popular Electronics, Aug. 1992: 43.

[7(a).] Paul Keegan writes of "The Digerati´in the New York Times Magazine May 21 1995.[b]

[7(b).] Suneel Ratan, "A New Divide Between Haves and Have-Nots,´ TIME, Spring 1995(Special Issue): 25.

[7©.] Bruce Little, "Poor left behind in computer revolution," Toronto Star 15 Jan. 1996: B11, has an excellent article on this issue.

CHAPTER TWO

[1.] Russ Walter, The Secret Guide to Computers Vol. 1 (Boston: Birkhauser Boston Inc. Russ Walter, 1984) 250. [See Appendix 16]

[2.] A sophisticated device was discovered in 1900 near Rhodes, Greece. This device is known as the *Antikythera mechanism.* It is a calendrical computer "showing the position of the sun and moon and of the rising of the most important stars." Martin James, The Computerized Society (N.Y.: Prentice-Hall, 1970), 123). Some experts regard this as the first mechanical/analog computer.

[2.] Russ Walter, The Secret Guide to Computers Vol. 1 (Boston: Birkhauser Boston Inc. Russ Walter, 1984) 250.

[3(a).] Fred D'Ignazio, "The World Inside the Computer: The Talking Head", Compute! 09 1982: 78. For Canadian readers, Electronics Today, Sept. 1977 - Mar. 1978 ran a series of articles for microcomputer beginners:

   1) *Data transmission before microcomputers*
   2) *The Microcomputer*
   3) *Roads of access*
   4) *I/O techniques*
   5) *Memory*
   6) *A microcomputer and software*

[4.] Mickey Williamson. Artificial Intelligence for Microcomputers: The Guide for Business Decisionmakers (N.Y.: Simon & Schuster, 1985) 5.
     A 'new' human-like function for microcomputers is *artificial life.* "The seeds of artificial life were sown when programmers realized that they could induce surprisingly organic-like behavior in computers, the prime example being a program called *Life* developed in the 1970s by an academic researcher called John Conway. *Life* chops the computer

screen into a grid and applies very simple rules to dots or cells on the screen – certain arrangements of cells breed new cells, and certain other arrangements of cause existing cells to die. Although very simple, populating the initial screen with certain patterns can eventually breed a state of equilibrium in which the resulting cell population seems to be self-sustaining, and the resulting pattern mimics one of the recurring patterns seen in natural life." Edge, Oct. 1996, 60.

[5.] Stephen Strauss, "Mind & Matter", Globe & Mail 7 Jan. 1995: D8.

[6.] David H. Ahl, Getting Started in Classroom Computing Maynard, MA.:Digital Equipment Corporation, 1974) 69.

[7.] John C. Dvorak, "What Ever Happened to...Burroughs, The Seventh Dwarf," Computer Shopper, Oct. 1997: 594.

[8.] Mel Ostler, 10.

[9.] Joel Shurkin, Engines of the Mind.

[10.] Russ Walter, The Guide to Computers Vol. 2 (Boston: Birkhauser Boston Inc., 1984) 364.

[11.] She is famous for her Objection: "The Analytical Engine has no pretensions to *originate* anything. It can do whatever we know how to order it to perform."

[12.] David H. Ahl, 70.

[13.] Vannevar Bush's work precedes today's *knowledge augmentation* created by computer pioneer Doug Englebart.(Lipton/69.)

[14.] Shirley Thomas, 59.

[15.] According to Fred D'Ignazio in Compute Oct. 1990: G-18, "We are in an age of   rampant miniaturization extending into the world of mechanical engineering as well. A new generation of *nano-*

technologists are attempting to shrink gears, electric motors, and pumps to microscopic size. They've achieved some remarkable successes."

Opposite this:

"Originally, digital computers were somewhat ponderous and unreliable, using many thousands of thermionic valves, kiloamps of heater current, were built in large racks and housed in air-conditioned rooms to prevent them from dying of heat exhaustion."

(Waddington, Wireless World Oct.
1975: 550).

CHAPTER 3

[1.] David Suzuki, "Science", Farewell to the 70's, Anna Porter & Marjorie Harris, eds. (Toronto: Thomas Nelson & Sons, 1979).

[2.] "INTEL labeled this first microprocessor chip the '4004'['four thousand four']. The four thousand number mean't that it was a custom product, designed for Busicom.
     The final number four designated the 4004[a] as the fourth custom chip made by INTEL."(Everett Rogers and Judith K. Larsen, Silicon Valley Fever: Growth of High-Technology Culture.(New York: McGraw-Hill Basic Books, Inc., 1984.)

[2(a).] The 4004 was first advertised in Electronic News magazine in 1971.

[2(b).] Who invented the single-chip processor? According to a 1990 U.S. patent it was "Gilbert Hyatt, a 52-year-old engineer".(Douglas E. Kilarski, "Editorial - Who Invented the Single-Chip Computer?" Computer Monthly Nov. 1990:2.)The patent was issued to him for inventing a computer-on-a-chip design in 1968. As we see it was an over 20-year struggle to obtain ownership of the idea.

An excellent article entitled, *Micro, Micro: Who Invented the Micro?*, <u>Byte</u>, Jan. 1991: 305+ says that Hyatt trademarked the term *microcomputer* in 1968.

[The history of micro-chip manufacturing is best described in Peter Ruber's series in <u>Computer Shopper</u> (Sept. 1987); for a layman's, technical description of the microprocessor see <u>Byte</u>(May 1988: 239); Rogers & Larsen, <u>Silicon Valley Fever</u>, 111-121, have Silicon Valley's and INTEL's view of microprocessor history.

[2©.] Frederico Faggin gives the history of the microprocessor in a March 1992 article in <u>Byte</u> - "The Birth of the Microprocessor".

[3.] The best, concise history of the microprocessor can be found in Rogers and Larsen, <u>Silicon Valley Fever</u>, 103-111.

To learn about specific microprocessors see *Microbiography* in <u>Electronics Today</u>:

    The 8008/8080 - Oct. 1977
    The 8085 and Z80 - Nov. 1977
    The 6800 and 6500 - Dec. 1977
    The 1802 - Jan. 1978
    The 2650 - Mar. 1978

[3(a).] A more detailed history of the microprocessor is found in Russ Walter, <u>The Secret Guide to Computers, Vol. 1</u>.

[4.] Prior to 8-bit code there was 6-bit code. "for years the 6-bit code was a default industry standard and the default character set was the 48 characters available on the IBM model 026 keypunch. When IBM introduced the 360 computer they went to a model 029 keypunch with 64 characters. The computer, however, used an 8-bit character code."(Eugene H. Mitchell, "In's and Out's of Computers for Beginners," <u>Popular Electronics</u> June 1976:48.)

[5.] Rogers and Larsen, <u>Silicon Valley Fever: Growth of High - Technology Culture</u>, 10.

[6.] Phil Lemmons, "Chuck Peddle: Chief Designer of the *Victor 9000*", interview, <u>Byte</u> Nov. 1982: 256.

[7.] Roy Coles, "The 44 million chip question", <u>Practical Computing</u> May 1983: 39.

8. Zilog was created by Dr. Frederico Faggin, Ralph Ungerman and four other INTEL engineers in 1974. "The Zilog Company took took as its symbol a superhero named 'Captain Zilog', who wore a flashing Z on his chest. The Z-80 became the most popular CPU chip ever built."(Stan Veit,   "What Ever Happened to...Zilog?"   <u>Computer Shopper</u> May 1993:648. Today Zilog builds embedded processors for the
computer and consumer electronics industry.

[9.]   Rogers and Larsen in <u>Silicon Valley Fever</u> 277, say this of Ed Roberts and MITS:
    "The Altair 8800, the first microcomputer to be sold, in December 1974, was produced by MITS[Micro Instrumentation and Telemetry Systems]of Albuquerque.
The *Altair* was built around the INTEL 8080A microprocessor. [b c]
Ed Roberts, the principal at MITS, intended to sell 800 of the *Altair 8800*s during 1975, but after Les Solomon featured the machine on the cover of the Junuary issue of <u>Popular Electronics,</u> *MITS* sold all that it could manufacture, about 2,000 in 1975. In 1977, *MITS* was acquired by <u>Pertec</u> for $6 million."

[9(a).] There were courses on cassettes that explained how microprocessors worked. They were from <u>SYBEX</u>: [S1 - *Introduction to Microprocessors* and S2 - *Programming Microprocessors*].

[9(b)]. An excellent article in July 1976, <u>Radio-Electronics</u>, describes how this microprocessor chip works. <u>Scientific American</u>, Sept. 1977, has an excellent series on the history of microelectronics. The 11 articles are:

1) <u>Microelectronics</u> by Robert N. Noyce.
2) <u>Microelectronic Circuit Elements</u> by James D. Meindl
3) <u>The Large-Scale Integration of Microelectronic Circuits</u> by William C. Holton.
4) <u>The Fabrication fo Microelectronic Circuits</u> by William C. Holton.
5) <u>Microelectronic Memories</u> by David A hodges.
6) <u>Microprocessors</u> by Hoo-Min D. Toong.
7) <u>The Role of Microelectronics in Data Processing</u> by Lewis M. Terman.
8) <u>The Role of Microelectronics in Instrumentation and Control</u> by Bernard M. Oliver.
9) <u>The Role of Microelectronics in Communication</u> by John S. Mayo.
10) <u>Microelectronics and Computer Science</u> by Ivan E. Sutherland and Carver A. Mead.
11) <u>Microelectronics and the Personal Computer</u> by Alan C. Kay.

[9(c)]. A direct competitor for the 8080 was <u>MOS Technology</u>'s *MCS6501*.

[10]. John C. Dvorak, "The First Personal Computer?", <u>Computer Shopper</u> June 1992: 720.[a]

[10(a)] According to Joel Shurkin, <u>Engines of the Past</u> (N.Y.: W. W. Norton & Comp., 1984) 311, "engineers at *IBM*s Palo Alto lab,led by Paul Freidl, had in 1971 produced a working table-model microcomputer with a crude micro-processor."

11. CP/M became the de facto standard, meaning, "it's not the best operating system conceivable, but Gary Kildall, who wrote it in 1973, got to the market place first, and now everybody's got it, so you'd better get it too"." (Chris Bidmead, "The Big Memory Machine," Electronics & Computing April 1982: 26).

The standard system operating CP/M was the S-100 buss discovered by Ed Roberts in 1974/75.(Stan Veit, "What Ever Happened To...The S-100 Bus,"(Computer Shopper, Oct. 1993:595.)

CP/M did not run on the original TRS-80. Tandy made this task impossible.(Stan Veit, Stan Veit's History of the Personal Computer(Asheville, NC.: WorldComm, 1993: 166).

12. The most successful of S-100 computers, defined by longevity, was Polymorphic Systems, *Poly 88*. It was manufactured between 1976 and 1989. The original *Poly-88* was followed by *Systems 8810, 8813,88M/S* and *Two-Tier System 88*. These microcomputers used either a single-sided, single-density(SSSD) or double-sided, double density(DSDD) floppy disk drives. They were ahead of there time according to Preston ("How it Works: Floppy Disk Drives," Microcomputer Printout Oct. 1982: 36) with Kenyon commenting: "There were things the *Poly* did in 1976 that still aren't done on micrcomputers and many others have only recently been implemented". (Stan Viet, "The Rise and Fall of Polymorphic Systems," Computer Shopper Dec. 1989: 764.)

13. Stan Veit, "Rashomon or the First PC," Computer Shopper Jan. 1989: 29.)

14. Ibid, Stan Veit's History of the Personal Computer, 34.

15. Ibid.

16. Ibid, "*IMSAI*: The Foundation," Computer Shopper Feb. 1989: 84.

17. Ibid, "What Ever Happened To...Kit Computers?" <u>Computer Shopper</u> April 1994: 595.

18. Ibid, "What Ever Happened To...Time-Sharing, Multiuser Personal Computers." <u>Computer Shopper</u> Sept. 1992: 743.

19. *TDL* sold a display terminal called ASCIISCOPE in 1976/77 capable of displaying 80x25 characters, the standard today. (Stan Veit, "How DO You Make a Company Disappear?" <u>Computer Shopper</u> Dec. 1989: 300.)

19(a). "A monitor, or Executive program which included an assembler for assembly language was needed. To use it you have to have a teletype with a tape reader. First you used the front panel keys to load in a bootstrap loader program. Then you could load the executive program from the tape. Then you could use the keyboard on the teletype to write an assembly language program and assemble it. The object code was stored in RAM and if you had enough memory you could then run your program. If everything ran OK, you could then save your source code and object code punching a new paper tape with the punch on your teletype. The next time you wanted to run the program, you could load the object code tape and there you were, simple!" (Stan Veit, *IMSAI*: The Foundation." <u>Computer Shopper</u> Feb. 1989: 85) also see Stephen B. Gray's article "Building a Computer of Your Own." <u>The Best of Creative Computing</u>: 107-108. Don Lancaster's articles in <u>Radio-Electronics</u> and <u>Popular Electronics</u> pioneered the design of microcomputer peripherals.

19(b). Sol Libes wrote an article in <u>Byte</u> Jan. 1978: 162, called "Notes on Bringing up a Microcomputer" that tells how to build a homebrew machine or how to build a kit in a logical fashion, debugging in a step-by-step fashion, saving time and money.

[20.] Robert's and Yate's articles in <u>Popular Electronics</u> early 1975 showed how to build the *Altair 8800* minicomputer. [Early articles, particularly in the mass media, did not refer to these machines as microcomputers.]

[20(a).] Leor Zolman wrote <u>BDS C</u> the first C compiler targeted exculsively for personal computers in the early 80s.

[20(b).] Here is what John C. Dvorak has to say about this language: "Remember this thing?

It was the first universal OS and language. Just as it was starting to become popular, the state-funded University of California was anxious about it making money and forced it outside the University, where it lost its aura and died." ("Technologies (of the past)?" <u>PC Magazine</u> Nov.1995: 89)

[21.] The story of <u>Polymorphic Systems</u>, *Poly-88* by Ralph Kenyon, is the history of microcomputers in a microcosm. It began with three experimenters, Brian Wilcox, John Stevenson, and Richard Peterson working out of their garage in 1975. The legendary *VTI*(Video Terminal Interface)[a] used with an S-100 machine, employing a software programmable front panel made possible by Robert T. Martin, made modern microcomputing possibe. Here's what Kenyon has to say about the *Poly-88*: "<u>Poly</u> bought BASIC from Wordstar computers, and implemented it to run on the *Poly-88*. This BASIC would run in 8K with room left over for reasonably sized programs. With BASIC, <u>Poly</u> also supported an editor-assembler that allowed assembly from a cassette tape file, or from the keyboard. And, the assembled programs could be saved to the cassette tape. It sure made things easy to have all this stuff. There was even a BASIC program editor that allowed editing BASIC program lines right off the screen. *Poly-88* was ahead of its time in 1976." "<u>Polymorphic Systems</u> closed in 1989 but by then it had implementations for the following languages:

8080 Macro Assembler, LITTLE-ADA, BASIC, Small-C[b], FORTRAN, FORTH, PILOT, UCSD PASCAL[c], PASCAL/MT, and Tiny-BASIC."(Stan Veit, 'The Rise and Fall of Polymorphic Systems," Computer Shopper Dec, 1989: 763.)

[21(a).] An article by Jerry Ogdin in Popular Electronic Sept.1975: 57-61, titled *Hobbyist Interchange Tape System* shows how to make a tape system that can be used to record programs on standard audio cassettes thereby permitting an efficient sharing system.

[21(b).] The first video terminals were referred to as "glass Teletypes".(Al Stevens, "Plumbers, Programmers, and Quincy'96 ", Dr. Dobb's Journal April 1996: 107).

[21©.] An excellent overview of *UCSD PASCAL* is to be found in Byte May 1978: 46.

[22.] Jonathan A. Titus, "Computer! - Build this Minicomputer Yourself," Radio-Electronics July 1974.

[23.] See R. Bompous' article "A User's Reaction to the SOL-10 Computer", Byte Jan. 1978: 86+.

[23(a).] Stan Veit, "The Saga of SOL and Processor Technology," Computer Shopper March 1989: 59.

[24.] *APPLE, COMMODORE* and *TANDY* were called "the 1977 Trinity: the three companies who brought out ready-to-run PCs." [Byte forgot about *Processor Technology's* SOL.] (Byte Sept. 1995: 100)

[25.] See article on Steve Jobs: "The Updated Book of Jobs: A Testament of prophecy, true belief, go-getting and megabucks."(TIME 3 Jan. 1982: 15.)

[26.] Stan Viet, "In Living Color: The Long, Bumpy History of Video Display Terminals," Computer Shopper July 1991: 128,129.

[27.] Jack Tramiel built Commodore...(Computing Now! July 1985: 40). The Commodore *PET* was advertised in the mass-circulation publication Popular Science, August 1977: 118 The price - $495.

[28.] Lee Felsenstein was one of the main designers of the Osborne computer.

[29.] Radio Shack.

[30.] Rogers and Larsen, in Silicon Valley Fever, 3-24, tell the *APPLE* story, in an uncritical fashion. Dvorak, in Computer Shopper July 1982: 754, relates the story of *APPLE*'s III "insanely flawed platform."

[31.] Ron Albright, The Orphan Chronicles.

[32.] One version of the microcomputer price wars is found in S. Veit, Stan Veit's History of the Personal Computer (Asheville, NC.: Worldcomm, 1993) : 180-184.

The home computer price war began in the summer of 1982 essentially between Texas Instruments and Commodore.

By the end of 1982 most of the 8-bit microcomputer manufacturers were involved. By 1983's summers end it was over with the major manufacturers posting very large $(dollar) losses.

[32(a).] Dahmke, "Let Your Fingers Do the Walking," Popular Computing Oct. 1982: 134.

[33.] Adam Osborne founded Osborne Computer Corporation Dec. 1980. He used profits from his book Introduction to Micro-computers, which sold 300,000 copies, and 39 other books, to finance his new company.[He sold his publishing company to McGraw- Hill in 1979.] (Evertt Rogers and Judith K. Larsen, Silicon Valley Fever: Growth of High-Technology Culture 133.)

[34.] IBM's introduction to the microcomputing world is now folklore. Byte was called the best of any magazine at that time.

[35.] Software or hardware emulators were first used in 1967. The name comes from Stewart Tucker of IBM.(Andrew Schulman,"DOS Unbound: Uses of Protected Mode." Byte(IBM Special Edition) Fall 1990: 250.)

One of the first 16-bit microcomputers was the 1976 Alpha Micro Corp., *Alpha Micro*. It used the Western Digital *WD-16 CPU* and the DEC *PDP-11* operating system *AMOS*. Texas Instruments came out with the *T. I. 9900* around the same time.

The first INTEL 16-bit CPU was the *8086*. It was introduced by Seattle Computer Co. It's 16-bit operating system was sold to Microsoft, becoming *PC/MS-DOS*.
(Stan Viet, "What Ever Happened To...The S-100 Bus." Computer Shopper Oct. 1993: 596.)

[35(a).] I have a particular interest in the Coleco *ADAM*. It's storied past is in Appendix 12.

[36.] A debate beginning in the 1940s over what exactly constitutes memory and its role in computing, on a philosophical level, continues today.

[37.] We must add: Minicomputer MAGNETIC CORE memory was 'inexpensive' but very difficult to port to microcomputers.(Popular Electronics Nov. 1974: 107)

Hence it was not used in commercial microcomputers. Hobbyists experimented with this type of memory though. Martin A. Sala gives a good background on how magnetic core memory works and why it didn't catch on in the microcomputer world.("Core Memories - How they work," Radio-Electronics Sept. 1977: 54.)

[38.] Jim Quarishi, "Board with Limited Memory" Yet a New HI - The HI486," Computer Shopper July 1990: 284.

[39.] K is short for kilobyte, in computer parlance 1024 or 2^{12}.

[40.] Memory was expensive. For instance, here's an ad in Jan. 1976, Popular Electronics, page 95, giving the cost of memory modules:

4K - $215 [static memory] 12K - $562 [static memory]
8K - $402   "   "   16K - $696 [dynamic memory]

32K dynamic memory cards were introduced in 1977 and their cost was $995. Popular Electronics July 1977: 13.

A good introduction to microcomputer memory is to be found in Popular Electronics, an article by Hal Chamberlin entitled *Computer Bits: Microcomputer Memory*, March 1978, 96,97.

[41.] Microcomputer Input/Output is briefly discussed by Hal Chamberlin in "Microcomputer Input/Output:, Popular Electronics May 1978: 86,87.

[42.] Robert M. Marsh, "Computer Bits: Computer Users Tape System", Popular Electronics March 1976: 88.

[42(a).] Sight and Sound Marketing, "Wherefore the Computer Market?, reprinted in Creative Computing June 1982: 114.

[43.] Norman Myers, "Computer Readout: The Intercept, Jr.," Elementary Electronics July/Auugust 1977: 67.

[44.] Charles Brannon, "Picking the Right Printer," Compute's Gazette 10 1985: 30.

[45.] Centronics
   It had a short life as dot-matrix printers were faster and cheaper. Many other manufacturers jumped on the bandwagon: *Diablo*, *Ojidata*, *Qume*, *Ricoh*, *Star Micronics* et. Al. Most sold for between $500-$1000.(1982 prices.)

[46.] Barry McConnell, "The HANDICAPPLE: A Low Cost Braille Printer," Creative Computing Oct. 1982: 186, is the opposite of the DEC Writer in cost.

[47.] Stan Veit, "Breaking the One-Grand Printer Barrier Computer," Computer Shopper Sept. 1991: 698.

[48.] Suding

[49.] Stan Veit

[50.] The 8" floppy disk was introduced in 1973 by IBM. Verbatim, created by Reid Anderson in 1969, bought manufacturing rights from IBM and was the major   manufacturer of these drives.

[50(a).] An additional point - 8 inch floppy drives were common place in the early era. Yet only the rich could afford one.[Percom was the major manufacturer.] They were far too expensive for the home computerists. Besides, they generally were larger than the computer itself and were voracious power users. Not exactly a powerful selling point. IBM invented the 8-inch floppy disk in 1971, a read-only device called the 23FD. A read/write version was released in 1973 as the 33FD with an unformatted   capacity of 200K each side. The 8-inch drive was supplanted by the Shugart SA400 mini-floppy drive which used 5.25-inch disks storing around 175K in 1976. (Byte Sept. 1995:102) "The 3.5-inch floppy drive was introduced by SONY in 1981, storing 438K on a disk rotating at 600 rpm. ANSI(American National Standards Institute) committee eventually approved a higher capacity 720K version. One of Sony's arguments for its acceptance was that it could fit into a shirt pocket."

[50(b).] Al Shugart in 1973 founded Shugart Associates that built 8" floppy disk drives. In 1979 Shugart founded Seagate Technology that builds hard disk drives. Incidentally, Shugart Associates developed SCSI(Small Computer Systems Interface) technology in 1979.(Byte Sept. 1995: 102.)

[51.] One of the best articles on floppy disk technology and how to connect one to a microcomputer is David M. Allen's "A Floppy Disk Interface," Byte Jan. 1978: 58. If you want to know how a floppy disk system works see Ira Ramphil's article, *A Floppy Disk Tutorial*, Byte, Dec. 1977: 24+.

[52.] Lemmons, "A Short History of the Keyboard," Lemmons, "A Short History of the Keyboard," Byte Nov. 1982: 386.

[53.] Jim J. Seymour. "The Mouse's Tale," 1993," PC MAGAZINE Oct. 1993: 97.

[54.] Robert Traub, "The Microcomputer Keyboard Story," Computing Now! Jan. 1984: 50-52.

[55.] Hoo-Min D. Toong & Amar Gupta, "Personal Computing", Scientific American Dec. 1982.

[56.] Evans, The Making of the Micro: A History of the Computer (N.Y.: Van Nostrand Reinhold Company, 1981).

CHAPTER FOUR

[1.] Hal Chamberlin, "Computer Bits: Assemblers", Popular Electronics July 1977: 89, gives an excellent introduction to assembly language and assembler programs. He comments: "According to a recent survey, one of the most popular applications of personal computers is software evelopment, or simply writing programs. As anyone who has be bitten by the programming bug undoubtedly knows, each new program is always bigger and fancier than the last. Beyond a certain point in program complexity, however, the use of an assembler program is almost mandatory to eliminate most of the drudgery associated with hand coding in octal and hex. This is particularly true when one wishes to make a 'small improvement' to a hand-assembled program which otherwise requires it to be re-written."

2. Herbert Schildt, C++ From the Ground Up (Toronto: McGraw-Hill, 1994).

3. Mark Garet, "Evolution of the Microprocessor." Byte Sept. 1985.

4. Bill Machrone, in "Discontent with Content", PC Magazine 11 May 1993, says:
    "Historically, programmers controlled all the input and output of a system. Proper procedure for an applications programmer was to say to the user, 'Just tell me what reports you want and how often you need to see them.' He would go off and design the file structure, input formats cards, forms, screens), processing logic, and output formats. What you got was an inflexible, closed-ended system that automated a specific process. With luck, it integrated into other data processing systems, but as often as not, it didn't. Ad hoc reporting helped a lot, but was dependent on proper construction of the underlying data structure. Too often, the answer to your query was, 'You can't get there from here,' or 'I can't even understand the question.'"

5. Bill Machrone, "Discontent with Content", PC Magazine, 11 May 1993: 87.

5(a). Elizabeth Nichols, Data Communications for Microcomputers: With Practical Applications & Experiments (N.Y.: McGraw-Hill, 1982).

6. Ron H. Mitchell, "Me Program? No Way!", AFUG Sept/Oct 1993: 1,2.

7. Somerson

[7(a).] See Bill Machrone's article "Revenge of the Nerds", <u>PC Magazine</u> 21 Dec. 1993: 89, for a new look at nerds and microcomputers. He says: "Brainpower is in; the jocks are in full retreat as Windows programmers write their own tickets in the job market."

[8.] Edward Yourdon, <u>Decline and Fall of the American Programmer</u> (Englewood Cliffs, N.J.: PTR Prentice-Hall, 1992).

[9.] Ivan Flores, <u>The Professional Microcomputer Handbook</u> (N.Y.: Van Nostrand Reinhold Company, 1986).

[10.] Barden, "What Language is best for you", <u>Popular Computing</u> Feb. 1992.

[11.] Al Stevens, <u>Welcome to...Programming: From Mystery to Mastery</u> (New York: MIS Press, Inc., 1994).

[12.] "Admiral Hopper often told the story of how the COBOL project was stalled while the specification languished on the desk of a Department of Defense official. No one could get this bureaucrat to act on the item. Without his approval, COBOL was destined to pass into obscurity, a dead project. In desperation, the team purchased a small tombstone and had it engraved with the name, COBOL. Early one morning they placed the stone on the official's desk. He got the message, moved the paperwork, and the COBOL project resumed. The Smithsonian Institution now has the COBOL tombstone among its collection of computer artifacts."(Al Stevens, <u>Welcome to ... Programming: From Mystery to Mastery</u>. (New York: MIS Press Inc., 1994): 35.)

Shirley Thomas, <u>Computers: Their History, Present Applications, and Future</u>, 115, writing on COBOL: "A major disadvantage of COBOL is that it requires a tremendous amount of computer time to translate the compiler language into machine language. This and other considerations have prompted many leaders in the field to severely question its merits."

[13.] Al Nieburg, "BASIC is Spoken Here," <u>Computer Shopper</u> Oct. 1986.

[14.] Faye Deere has excellent advice for BASIC and all programmers:

    1)Copy programs from magazines or books to get
       you started.
    2) Typos create many headaches. Start slowly.
    3) Debugging skills improve with experience.
    4) Fatigue is the enemy of concentration. Take
       a break.
    5) Boredom takes over when competence level
       isn't challenged. Move to the next level.
      "Classic Computer Column: ADAM News,"
      <u>Computer Monthly</u> Sept. 1990: 96,97.

[15.] GWBASIC - Gee Whiz BASIC.

[16.] <u>Dr. Dobb's Journal of Computer Calisthenics & Orthodontia: Running Light without Overbyte</u> published the first commercial article on TinyBASIC in 1975 several months after the ALTAIR premiered. [a]

[16(a).] According to <u>BYTE</u>, *TinyBASIC* was created by Albrecht and Dennis Allison (implemented by Dick Whipple and John Arnold) running on a microcomputer in 2KB of RAM in (early? [b]) late 1975. At roughly the same time Bill Gates and Paul Allen write a version of BASIC which they sold to MITS. (<u>Byte</u> Sept. 1995: 122)

[16(b)] There is a conflict in the dates. The accepted version appears to be early 1975, but available literature is confusing. I haven't come across a definitive source. The following source puts it in early 1975: <u>Time-Life Books 2:</u>
<u>Understanding Computers – Computer Languages</u> (N.Y.: Time-Life Books, Inc. 1989) 101.

[17.] 8K BASIC, EXTENDED BASIC and finally DISK BASIC (popularly known as DISK BASIC version 5, MBASIC[a] or BASIC-80). For the APPLE , Bill Gates of Microsoft, constructed Applesoft BASIC, short for APPLE BASIC by Microsoft. He did the same for Commodore and Radio Shack. The same was done for Texas Instruments.

Their BASIC wasn't compatible with other Microsoft BASICs. It soon perished.

[18.] Here is the history of BASIC according to Bob Albrecht & Don Inman:

On May, 1964 at 4 AM, John Kemeny and a student simultaneously entered and ran separate BASIC programs at Dartmouth College. Thus was born BASIC, the first computer language designed to be easy to learn and use by just about anyone. It ran on the Dartmouth Time-Sharing System, providing easy access for students and faculty. Original Dartmouth BASIC contained only these statements:

LET, PRINT, END, FOR, NEXT, GOTO,
IF..THEN, READ, DATA, DIM, DEF,
GOSUB, RETURN, and REM.

[19.] D. F. Scott, "The Next Operating System: Some New Ideas," Computer Shopper Oct. 1987.

[20.] Henry Simpson. Serious Programming in BASIC (Blue Ridge Summit, PA.: TAB Books, 1986.)

[21.] Nilsson.

[22.] Hofstadter, Douglas K., Godel, Escher, Bach: An Eternal Golden Braid (New York: Vintage Books, 1979.) "The bug got its name from Grace Hopper, the computing pioneer. While working on an early computer, Ms. Hopper found a dead moth wedged in the electrical circuits that caused a short circuit. As she was removing the moth, someone asked what she was doing.

"Debugging the computer," she replied, and an idiom was born. She stapled the moth to a punched card and posted it on the bulletin board. Henceforth anything in hardware or software that impaired a computer's ability to run and serve its mission was called a *bug*, and the act of finding and removing bugs was called *debugging*.

Historians often try to debunk this story, citing other earlier sources for the debug metaphor. However, I heard Grace Hopper tell her version, which is the one I just related, and I believe it.(Al Stevens, Welcome to...Programming : 302.)[A concise history of the term 'bug' can be found in Byte, Fred R. Shapiro, "The First Bug," April 1994: 308.)

23. Henry Simpson, Serious Programming in BASIC (Blue Ridge Summit, PA.: TAB Books, 1986).

24. Bob Albrecht & Don Inman, 'Your BASIC Backpack," Computer Shopper Oct. 1987: 169.

25. Ibid.

26. Henry Simpson, Serious Programming in BASIC.

27. Bob Albrecht & Don Inman, "Your BASIC Backpack," ibid.

28. Andrew M. Fried, "From 'C' to Shining Sea," Computer Shopper Aug. 1986: 67.

29. Ibid.

30. Hancock, The C Primer (N.Y.: McGraw-Hill)

31. Dave McMillen, "Modula-2: A High Level Language for System Design", Computer Shopper Aug. 1986: 67.

32. Edward Yourdon, Decline and Fall of the American Programmer(Englewood Cliffs, N.J.: PTR Prentice-Hall, 1992).

CHAPTER FIVE

1.   "No one needs a word processor if he has an efficient secretary." (Robertson Davies)

He later added: "I am a technomoron." This goes along with what David Brinton says: The old computer adage of garbage in, garbage out holds true (using Wordstar), but now you can get out garbage that is typographically correct, correctly spelt with excellent footnoting and well documented. You can even edit out all the sexist terms and over-worked clichés. (<u>South African Microcomputer Owner</u>, Nov. 1983: 22).

2.   Here is the history of word processing according to <u>Microcomputer World</u>:

1977	ELECTRIC PENCIL
1977	EASY WRITER -> APPLE II
1977/78	SCRIPSIT -> TRS-80
1979	WORDPRO -> COMMODORE
1979/80	AUTO SCRIBE II -> HEATH/ZENITH H89 MAGIC WAND
1979/82	WORDSTAR

Electronic spelling checker/dictionary

1979/82	HEXSPELL SPELLGUARD MICROPROOF

The term 'word processing' was invented/coined by <u>IBM</u> in 1964. ("Understanding Computer - Computer Languages," Editors <u>Time\Life Books</u> (New York: Time-Life Books, Inc. 1989.)) It introduced the term when it brought a new typewriter to the marketplace in that year. Text editors use specific commands including: Append, Change, Copy, Move, Delete, Insert, Overlay, Print, and Replace - plus pointer- addressing and string searches.

The 6800 Text Editing & Processing System was one of the earliest, circa 1978.

[2(a)] For those using spell correctors the best description of how they work is by Peter Wood, in Microcomputer Printout, April 1982.

[2(b)] *Easy Writer* was written by John Draper (AKA Cap'n Crunch) in 1979 while incarcerated in prison for phone-phreaking. (Byte Sept. 1985: 160) *Easy Writer* is considered to be one of the best 8-bit word processing programs ever written.

[2(c)] *Wordstar* also came with a sophisticated spelling checker. The reason for its speed was a programming technique called *has coding*. Has coding uses a key to determine the address data will be stored at. 'Search routine' using this key can find relevant data very fast. Furthermore, these programs are very small fitting in less than 10KB. (Graham Relf , "Maze Movement: Hash Coding," Practical Computing Sept. 1982: 127.)

Wordstar was created by Seymour Rubenstein, Bill Millard and Bill Lohse, all from *IMSAI*, in 1978. (Stan Viet, "Wordstar 5.5: Review," Computer Shopper Dec. 1989: 770-771.) Early competitors for *Wordstar* were *Easiscript* and *Wordcraft*.

Wordstar employed specific keyboard commands, ie. control, alternate and function key combinations.

[6.] Walters.

[7.] According to Stan Viet, Shrayer orginally wrote a text editor called *ESP-1*, adding formatting and printing features, thereby creating a word processor, naming it *Electric Pencil*.[a] (ii/569)

[7(a)] *Electric Pencil II* was first advertised in <u>Byte</u> May 1978:105. It was successful due to it's CP/M compatibility.

[8] Herb Friedman, "Word Processing," <u>Radio-Electronics</u> 04 1982: 83.

[9] *Magic Wand* word processor was ported to the TRS-100 Model 1 in 1978.

[10] Stan Veit, "Wordstar 5.5: A Review," <u>Computer Shopper</u> 12 1989: 770.

[11] Desktop publishing(DTP) was never an important issue in the early years of microcomputing. It's true microcomputer clubs published newsletters but they didn't use what was later called desktop publishing software to construct and print. Instead they used modified word processors or text editors.

[12] Steven Jong, "Designing a Text Editor? The User Comes First: A System's power is measured in ease of use," <u>Byte</u> April 1982: 284.

[13] Mel Ostler, "From BASICs to BASIC".

[14] Mike Lewis, "What Exactly is a Database," <u>Practical Computing</u> May 1983: 111.

[15] Steven J. Vaughan-Nichols, "Relational Databases: The Real Story - Codd's Commandments," <u>Byte</u> Dec. 1990: 322.

[16] Stan Veit, "Whatever Happened to...The S-100 Bus?" <u>Computer Shopper</u> Oct. 1993: 595.

[17] Marc Schnapp, "Whither xBASE<u>Byte</u> Dec. 1991: 131.
[18] Chris Bidmead, "Dtabases Side by Side," <u>Practical Computing</u> May 1983: 114.

[19] Walters Vol.5.

[20.] *Superfile*, an English competitor to DBASE II, was invented by Dr. Peter Reynolds of Brunel Univ. and named by Mike Healey of Osborne UK., was introduced in 1982. It was never popular on this side of the pond due to its prohibitive cost.

[21.] See "Daniel Bricklin: Software = Hard Cash", Time, Jan. 3, 1982: 18,19.

[22.] Walters Vol. 5.

[23.] *Supercalc* was sold by Sorcim for $295. The least expensive spreadsheet available for 8-bit computers was Radio Shack's *Spectacular*, selling in 1981 for $40.00.(Walters, Vol. 5, 69.)

[24.] *AUTOCAD* began as a CP/M application in the very early 80s.It had limited success due to its demand for memory and processing power. (To my knowledge it never ran on anything less than 64KB.) It was responsible however for wresting control of the design industry from mini-computers. (Byte Sept. 1995: 64.)

[25.] Carl Sagan, in The Dragons of Eden, (N.Y.: Random House, 1977): 216, observes the following:

The two games, *Pong* and *Spacewar*, suggest a gradual elaboration of computer graphics so that we gain an experiential and intuitive understanding of the laws of phsyics. The laws of physics are almost always stated in analytical and algebraic - that is to say, left-hemisphere - terms; for example, Newton's second law is written   F=m a, and the inverse square law of gravitation as F=G M m/r. These analytical representations are extremely useful, and it is certainly interesting that the universe is made in such a way that the motion of objects can be described by such relatively simple laws. But these laws are nothing more than abstractions from experience.

Fundamentally they are mnemonic devices. They permit us to remember in a simple way a great range of cases that would individually be much more difficult to remember at least in the sense of memory as understood by the left hemisphere.

Computer graphics give the prospective physical or biological scientist a wide range of experience with the cases his laws of nature summarize: but its most important function may be to permit those who are not scientists to grasp in an intuitive but nevertheless deep manner what the laws are about.

[25(a)] Leah O'Connor, "Game Corner", <u>INTERFACE AGE</u> June 1082: 28. The 'mysterious' origins of *Spacewar* is 'answered' by Sidney Markowitz in <u>Byte</u> July 1976: 92.

[26] Stewart Brand, "Keep Designing," <u>Whole Earth Review</u> May 1985.

[27] John J. Anderson, "Who Invented the Video Game?" <u>Creative Computing</u> Oct. 1982.

[28] *Pac-Man*, from the Japanese meaning "to eat" became Atari's biggest hit. The female version is called *Ms. Pac-Man. Centipede*, especially attractive to females was   designed by Donna Taylor of <u>Atari</u>. *Pong* was advertised in 1976 for $55.00; *Super Pong* for $79.95.(<u>Popular Electronics</u> Nov. 1976: 126.) The anti-video game movement began around the same time. (Everett Rogers and Judith K. Larsen, <u>Silicon Valley Fever: Growth of High Technology Culture</u> (N.Y.: McGraw-Hill Basic Books, Inc., 1984: 264.)

[28(a)] One of the first games brought from minicomputers and mainframes was *The Game of Life*. (See <u>Scientific American</u> Oct. 1970: 120; Feb. 1971: 112; April 1971: 116)
A paper of the program (is) available for $15 from <u>Cromemco</u> - designed to run on the *Altair 8800*. (<u>Popular Electronics</u> Feb. 1976: 39.)

[29] The story of Jack Tramiel (<u>Computing Now!</u> July 1985).

[30] Katie Hafner, <u>Cyberpunk: Outlaws & Hackers on the Computer Frontier</u>. (N.Y.: Simon & Schuster, 1991.) One of the earliest

organizations of hackers was the *Junior Computer Hackers of America*, of Peoria, Illinois.

[31.] Byte

[32.] There were earlier operating systems: *TOS* - Tape Operating System was a carry-over from the minicomputer world; *COS* - Cassette Operating System was introduced by   APPLE, Radio-Shack(Tandy) and other early microcomputer manufacturers in 1977 to run here assembled machine.[a.]; *BOS* - Basic Operating System. This operating system is based on IBM's *OS*(Operating System). If you didn't have enough memory you could run a scaled-down version of *BOS*. All operating systems use *JCL* - Job Control Language. These commands tell the   operating system what to do, ie., the DIR command tells the OS to list programs of the disk, tape or cassette on the screen.

"Most of these operating systems are based on the work of Frederick Brooks(a major designer of IBM's now-ancient Model 360 operating system.") (Russell Lipton   Multimedia Toolkit: Build Your Own Solutions with DocuSource (N.Y.: Random House Electronic Publishing, 1992: 162.)

[32(a).] For example: The 8080 Cassette Operating System was an adaptation of the CP/M operating system designed to run Micro Designs' digital cassette systems.(Forrest Mims, "Microprocessor Microcourse: Part 3," Popular Electronics May 1978: 88).

[33.] Faye Deere, "American Design Components," NIAD June 1989: 5.

[34.] Kenyon, "The Rise and Fall of Polymorphic Systems," Computer Shopper Dec. 1989: 759.

[35.] Cheryl Peterson, "CP/M Column," Computer Shopper June 1981: 276.

[36.] David Ahl, Getting Started in Classroom Computing.

37. Walters Vol. 5

38. Infosource

39. Bob Linstrom, "Editorial - Why PCs Become Extinct," Computer Shopper Aug. 1989: 227.

40. "Wherefore the Computer Market?" Sight and Sound Marketing. Reprinted in Creative Computing June 1982: 114.

41. Bob Linstrom, ibid.

42. John Weld, "Would you buy a shrink wrapped automobile," Computers and Society Vol. 16, No. 2,3 (Summer/Fall 1986): 29.

43. Ibid.

44. "Businesses wish to maximize profits. To do this you have a monopoly on your product. SO to for software. Getting a copy-right, or even better a patent, will accomplish this goal."(Noel D. Adler & Steven A. Hovani (The Copyright Kit: How to Copyright Your Computer Software (East Setauket, N.Y.: National Attorneys' Publications Inc., 1981.))
     The mass-marketing of microcomputers really began with William Millard and his Computerland franchises.[a] By 1980 there were 160 franchises throughout Canada   and the United States.(Time\Life Vol. 1: 16) Sadly they've been replaced by superstores where service is lacking, price is king.[b]

44(a). The world's first computer store franchise was begun in Dec. 1975 by Paul Terrell. (Byte July 1976: 80).

44(b). See Computer Store Survey Rates Manufacturers.
     This topic is in vogue today considering some 30-40% of microcomputers from major manufacturers are DOA(dead-on-arrival.)

45. Jesse D. Sheinwald, "Is CP/M Dead?" Computer Shopper Aug. 1987: 324.

46. Paul Freiberger, <u>A Consumer's Guide to Personal Computing & Microcomputers, 2nd Edition</u> (Toronto: TAB Books, 1984.)

47. See Stan Veit's article "What Ever Happened To...Software Protection" where he deals with the early years of pirating.

48. Paul Lima, "My Beautiful Friendly Digital Office," <u>Computing Now!</u> May 1994: 22.

CHAPTER SIX

1. The best, early article in a mass-media magazine was "New Home Computers Can Change Your Life-Style: They're cheaper and easier to use - and now they're available
   to everyone" in <u>Popular Science</u> Oct. 1977. It gave the story behind the   most popular
computers: <u>Commodore</u>'s *PET*; <u>Heath</u>'s *H-8*; <u>Radio Shack</u>'s *TRS-80 Model I*; <u>MITS</u>
Altair 8800; <u>IMSAI</u>'s *8048*; <u>Southwest Technical Product</u>'s *6800*; <u>Processor</u>
<u>Technology</u>'s *SOL-20*; <u>Technical Design Labs</u> *Z-80 Xitan*; *Compucolor*; <u>The Digital</u>
<u>Group</u>; <u>Cromeco</u>'s *Z-2*; <u>Polymorphic System</u>'s *Poly 88*; <u>Vector Graphics</u> *Vector +1*; <u>Challenger</u> and <u>EPA</u>'s *6800*.[see Appendix 17]

2. Mickey Williamsom, <u>Artificial Intelligence for Microcomputers: The Guide for Business Decisionmakers</u> (N.Y.: Simon & Schuster, 1986.)
   For an interesting discussion on *Artificial Intelligence* and the contemporary philosophical arguments it's raising see Astro Teller's article in <u>The Globe & Mail</u>.

Here is how <u>International Data Corporation</u> defines the term personal computer: "everything that runs MS-DOS, from low-end hobby units to workstations." (Alvin Toffler, <u>Power Shift</u>: 518.)

[3.] Stan Veit, "The Dragon of Menlo Park," <u>Computer Shopper</u> March 1992: 696.

[4.] Rein Turn, <u>Computers in the 1980s</u> (N.Y.: Columbia Univ. Press, 1974: 157.)

[5.] Don Lancaster, "TV Typewriter", <u>Radio-Electronics</u> Sept. 1973:41.

[6.] John Dvorak & Paul Somerson, "Bean Counters Blast PCs for Zero Productivity Gain," <u>PC/Computing</u> March 1993: 94.

[7.] "The *Scelbi 8H* was the first computer based on a microprocessor advertised for sale.
   The ad appeared in the March 1974 issue of <u>QST, the Amateur Radio Magazine</u>.
      The *Scelbi* was produced by a small company started by Nat Wadsworth and Robert Findley in Milford, Connecticut. Prices for a *Scelbi* kit started as low as $440." (Stan Veit, <u>Stan Veit's History of the Personal Computer: From Altair to IBM, A History of the PC Revolution</u>: 11).

[8.] <u>Byte</u> Sept. 1995.

[9.] "Basic Guide to Computer Buying," <u>Popular Electronics</u> Dec. 1977: 57-59.

[10.] Stan Veit, "TRS-80 Almost Everyone's Computer," <u>Computer Shopper</u> July 1989: 60.
   Dr. David Lein, writer of Radio Shack's User's Manual for Level 1, states the purpose (of the manual) as a tutorial: "...This book is written specifically for people who don't know anything about computers, and who don't want to be dazzled by fancy footwork from someone who does. It is written to teach you how

to use your Radio Shack TRS-80 and start you on a fast track to becoming a competent programmer. To that end, every fair and unfair, conventional and unconventional, flamboyant and ridiculus technique I could think of was used. I want you to have fun with your computer! I don't want to be afraid of it, because there is nothing to fear..." Byte April 1978: 60.)

[10(a).] An article by Dan Flystra, "The Radio Shack TRS-80: An Owner's Report, Byte April 1978: 49, gives an excellent account of the introduction of this 'appliance' microcomputer. Dan writes: "on August 3, 1977, the Radio Shack division of Tandy Corporation announced its entry into the personal computing market with the *TRS-80* microcomputer. The move held special significance for the personal computing   industry, for with parent company sales of nearly a billion dollars and over 6000 retail stores including 500 overseas, Radio Shack is in a unique position to help bring personal computers to the average man or woman."

[11.] The Commodore *VIC*(Video Interface Chip). It was originally called the "Vixen"; then the "VIC-22" and finally the "VIC-20". (Russ Walter, The Secret Guide to Computers Vol. 2 (Boston: Birkhauser Boston, Inc. and Russ Walter, 1984) 22).

[12.] Martin Banks, "The Undiscovered Country," PC Plus Aug. 1993: 183.

[13.] Faye Deere, "ADAM: Modems and Such," Computer Shopper June 1989: 292.

[14.] Russ Walter, The Secret Guide to Computers Vol. 5: Popular Applications (Boston: Birkhauser Boston, Inc. and Russ Walter, 1981):12.

[15.] Ibid.

[16.] Ibid.

17. D. F. Scott, "Mass Macs: APPLE Prepares for the Graphical Melee of '91," Computer Shopper March 1991: 577.

18. Ibid.

19. Faye Deere, "Show Report: ADAMCON 2," Computer Monthly Nov. 1990: 112.

19(a). One of the first computer-specific conventions was the "*First World ALTAIR Computer Convention*, held in Albuquerque, NM, March 26-28, 1976. It attracted over 700 participants. (Electronics July 1976: 40).

20. Silicon Valley wasn't the only place where innovation occurred in the microcomputer industry. One such place was Princeton, NJ. A startup company located there was called Technical Design Labs(TDL). (Stan Veit, "How to Make a Company Disappear: The Story of Technical Design Labs.," Computer Shopper Dec. 1989: 300.)

21. First came newsletters, then magazines. For their history see Appendix 13.

22. Small-computer publishing precedes the microcomputer industry. The first small-computer magazine published was David Ahl's Creative Computing in 1974. In Sept.1975 Byte magazine was
published by Wayne Green. Its success was due to its ability to attract national advertisers. The following 7 to 9 years saw the publication of dozens of microcomputer magazines. In 1978 alone Personal Computing; Kilobaud; Interface; Dr. Dobb's Journal; MicroTeck and ROM appeared.

23. Gregg Williams and Bob Moore, "The Appple Story, Part 1: Early History," History," Byte Dec. 1984.

24. The following article on user groups appears in the July/Aug. 1993, p. 18, issue of

ADVISA:

"Every night of every week, in schools, church halls and libraries, across Canada, computer users gather, to share their common interest. A 'user group' is one of the best ways for computer users to obtain the information needed to make computing, a more 'user-friendly' experience. No matter if you use DOS, or Windows, work with a Macintosh or an Apple, have an Atari or Amiga, or dabble with UNIX there is a user group, out there, with members eager to share their hopes, experiences and failures. (Couldn't say it better than that!)

[25.] One of the first general microcomputer meetings organized and held outside the microcomputer industry centers of Cal., N.Y., Mass., and Texas, was in Des Moines, Iowa, Aug. 21-22, 1977. It was called the *Ham-Computer Meet*. (Elementary Electronics July 1977): 87. The first microcomputer club in Canada, to my knowledge, is the Amateur Microproceesor Club of Kitchener/Waterloo, of Waterloo, Ontario, established in 1975/76.

[26.] See the article by Richard Inmel in Popular Computing. It's light reading.

[27.] Bart Lynch, in "Why an AUG?", states quite succinctly the reasons why it's important to have a user-group and a newsletter: The passive approach...is dead...Today's users must seek out potential users. We need to show understanding of their needs and problems, and show why the virtues unique to ADAM (or any other computer) present the best solution to those problems...It is now up to every ADAM activist to take a positive, deliberate role. This is not going to be easy...And sometimes, I feel that it's now more than just that computer ADAM brought us together, but it's the friendship that endures.

[28.] Stan Veit.

[28(a).] To understand this contention the ADAM community has a yearly convention. See Faye Deere's article in Computer Monthy Nov. 1990.

[29.] Dahmke.

[30.] Lake. Using the Xmodem file transfer protocol, which incidentally Christensen wrote.

[31.] Why do we buy microcomputers asks Don Crabb in <u>PC PCMagazine</u>, p.112: The simple truth is that you don't really buy computers (or you shouldn't), you buy computing solutions. By that we mean you buy software that will do the tasks you want done in an efficient a manner as possible. The computer only becomes important after you have picked the software you like best (because it fits your needs, the way you work, and your budget). The computer, in that scenario is nothing more than the device that can run software.

CHAPTER SEVEN

[1.] R. W. Manning, "One Man's View of Computer Science," <u>ACM Turing Award Lectures</u>, ed. Robert L. Ashenhurst (Don Mills, Ont.: Addison-Wesley Publishing Co., 1987): 207.

[2.] The role computers play in the development of , and in developing world, education is found in <u>Gaps in Technology-Electronic Computers</u>, *Organiztion for Economic Cooperation and Development*, Paris, 1969. [It's somewhat dated but its conclusions still apply while its recommendations haven't been fully implemented to this day.]

[3.] Globe & Mail

[4.] Machrone, "Discontent with Content," <u>PC Magazine</u> 05 11 1993: 87.

[5.] Fereday

[6.] John C. Dvorak & Paul Somerson, "Bean Counters Blast PCs for Zero Productivity Gain," PC/Computing 03 1993: 94,96.

[7.] B. Callahan, "Last Word: Machine Mad," Omni 12 1992: 128.

[8.] Michael Foreman, "How to Cope with a Power Cut," MicroDecision[UK] 11 1992: 53.

[9.] John Bentley Mays, "Citystates: A Detour on the Information Highway," Globe & Mail 30 Jan. 1994: C5.

[10.] Byte, Sept. 1993, 294, early promise of microcomputers. There is a seminal article on the early years of personal computing by Sol Libes entitled "The First Ten Years of Amateur Computing", in Byte, July 1978, pages 64-71.

[11.] Hugh Kenner; A collection of corporate case studies examines the question - Why can't Johnny compute?

[12.] Another thing about keyboard-and-screen: It frees up psyches.
    At the University of Texas-Austin, I one visited a poetry seminar run by John Slatin. Some 30 students sat around a large room, each at a terminal, exchanging comments on the day's assignment and on one another's comments. Any teacher knows how efforts to cause oral 'discussion' will activate -at-most- four articulate people, the rest sitting dumb, but keyboard participation that morning was close to 100%. It was eerie: all of them in the same room, looking not at one another but at monitors, and typing things they wouldn't venture to utter. (Later, everyone received a printout of the hour's interactions.) In that light, think of CEO Pogue getting input from secretaries. "They wouldn't ever call me up. But they feel comfortable sending me a message.'"(334)

[13.] "Computer   games,   reading   programs,   electronic   print programs,and newsletter/story making programs may seem a little pedestrian when discussing the future, but they are the building blocks that will teach children[adults one would think too] to be comfortable with the tools[a.] that will drive the computer age."(Bennett\12).

[13(a).] Martin Heidegger, the German philosopher, "recognized, right at the dawn of the   computer age, that man's relationships to his tools was undergoing a revolutionary transformation."(Lipton\110)

[13(b).] "Has anybody ever questioned whether more, faster, bigger brighter are necessarily better? We all seem to have accepted that the advance of technology is somehow synonymous with reason, logic, and ultimately nature." (Gregoire\A16)

[14.] Peter Suber, "Teaching in a Blizzard of Information," Issues in Science and Technology (Summer 1989): 29.

[15.] Selby Bateman, "Putting Computers to good use: The Innovative School," Compute's Gazette 10 1985: 22.

[16.] Jack Nimershein, "DOSier: The Experiences of a Typical PC user," Vulcan Computer Monthly Oct. 1990: 72.

[17.] M. J. Perenson, "Electronic Field Trips for the '90s, " PC Magazine 8 Feb. 1994: 30.

[18.] Robert Bullis.

[19.] Stewart Brand, The Media Lab: Inventing the Future at M.I.T. (Markham, Ont.: Penquin Books, 1987.)

[20.] Neil Postman[a/b] writes of an infoglut[c] overwhelming our knowledge processes in UTNE Reader. He says that "we have transformed information into a form of garbage."(35)

However, Edna St.Vincent Mallay states the problem far more eloquently:

Upon this gifted age, in its dark hour,
Rains from the sky a meteoric shower
Of facts...They lie unquestioned, uncombined.
Wisdom enough to leech us of out ill
Is daily spun, but there exists no loom
    To weave it into fabric ...

[20(a)] Neil Postman's theory is rebutted by Kerchove who argues that "our brains will be capable of so much more processing once we abandon our alphabetic mindset." (Radge\C21).

[20(b)] Noam Chomsky agrees with Postman by declaring 'that consent is manufactured through narrowing the range of media debate" (Radge\C21) while control of computerized information knowledge by transnational corporations and world-wide government-database networks limits our freedom.

[20(b)] According to Lipton *trail making* can solve information glut - "that is, a knowledge-poor culture drowning in apparent information wealth because information is not receiving adeqaute interpretation."(11)

[21] "The goal of information software is to teach concepts and skills in the most expedient way."(Swenson\139) (see Appendix 18)

[22] Globe & Mail.

[23] Will LOGO change this situation? As the editors of <u>Micro-Computer Printout</u> (July 1983:3) report: "Strictly speaking the Turtle is a miniature robot which draws graphical images on the floor - but in reality it is a 'device for thinking with.' It forms part of the LOGO system intended to create an environment in which children can learn how to learn." "Teaching machines were initially conceived by Professor Sidney Pressey at Ohio State University in the 1920s. Interest was revived in the 1950s, however, largely through the work of Professor B. F. Skinner at Harvard University. He suggested that simple teaching machines

could be developed, which would not only test whether a student had learned information correctly, but which would actually present new information to the student." (Lawrence A. Cremin: Focus on Education," The 1967 World Book Year Book: 41.)

24. "Tutor by Computer" by Carl Zimmer in Discover is an excellent article on computers in education.[a.] See the *new & timely* section in Radio-Electronics, Aug. 1974, p. 6, for an article on calculators and their role in education.

24(a). Myles White makes an excellent case for computers in education in his article in The Toronto Star, Oct. 5, 1995, H4.

25. Alan Kay established the rules for portable computing with his discovery of the *Dynabook* while at Xerox PARC in the 1970s.(Lipton/213-215) See Amanda Illes's article in MacWeek to get a good view of why this research centre played such a crucial role in early microcomputing history.

25(a). The story of The story of Dynabook can be found in Byte Feb. 1991: 203. [See appendix 18]

26. Stan Veit, Stan Veit's History of the Personal Computer (Asheville, NC.: WorldCOmm, 1993) 238,239).

27. Economist

28. Globe & Mail.

29. H. Dominic Covvey, Computer Choices: Beware of Conspicious Computing (Reading, MA.: Addison-Wesley Publishing Co., 1982).

30. "The investigation of the chess-playing problem is intended to develop techniques that can be used for more practical applications. The chess machine is an ideal one to start with for several reasons. The problem is sharply defined, both in the allowed operations(the moves of chess) and in the ultimate goal(checkmate). It is neither so simple as to be not too difficult for satisfactory solution. And such a machine could be pitted

against a human opponent, giving a clear measure of the machine's ability in this type of reasoning." (Hsu, 44,45.)

Chess, since the earliest days, has been at the heart of game-playing microcomputer science. The science of game playing as noted above was pioneered by C. Shannon. In 1950 he proposed a way for computers to play chess. One of the first chess playing programs was written by Richard Greenblatt and friends at MIT. The first minicomputer program was Chess 4.9 (Walter/I/257).

[31.] Evans; Seth Feldman - Techno-boosters
    a)   What is the microcomputers meaningful impact on class structure? Who gets what?
    b)   Technology is power. It can liberate society and make people work smarter and faster.
    c)   Who'll pay for it? Will the rich & corporations have the most access and use it advantageously?
    d)   For the press. Is freedom only for those who own it or control it?

Likewise, is freedom limited to those who make the hardware and software? In other words who *controls* knowledge? Yet are we to blame? If we insulate ourselves from the outside world becoming ultimate couch potatoes in which we entertain, work and shop at home as an escape from the violent outside world. Yet isolating us from it. Severely limiting social interaction perpetuating our fears.

[32.] Crane.

[33.] The computer industry is a greed machine. My 1989 XT is obsolete. Software is upgraded as soon as users come close to mastering it. Thousands of users will never learn to use computers because of the fear that they can't catch up. Thank goodness for DOS and the 640K barrier, or computer whizzes would be completely out of control. The buck stops with my 486. I'm not upgrading again until my two-year-old daughter needs the latest technology for college or I've sucked the last byte out of this over-qualified machine.(Mike Wayne, "The Buck Stops Here," PC/Computing Sept. 1993: 37).

[33(a).] Seymour Papert writes in Mindstorms: Many children are held back in their learning because they have a model of learning in which you have either 'got it' or 'got it wrong'. But when you program a computer you almost never get it right the first time. Learning to be a master programmer is learning to become highly skilled at isolating and correcting 'bugs', the parts that keep the program from working. The question to ask about the program is not whether it is right or wrong, but if it is fixable. If this way of looking at intellectual products were generalized to how the larger culture thinks about knowledge and its acquisition, we all might be less intimidated by our fears about 'being wrong'. (quoted in Brand\126).

[34.] In the Feb. 1990 Byte Robert Newcomb described a project based on Etch-a-Sketch.
    It's low technology yet it hasn't been duplicated in the PC world. Today's plotters are very expensive and very high tech. Such projects are rare because of the low return to developers. It seems innovation and practising one's hobby for its own sake is passé in the PC world.

[34(a).] Geoffrey Rowan, "Expect Home Computers to become more Personal", Globe & Mail 5 Jan. 1990: B1.

[35.] Tim Albano, "Read Only", PC Magazine 17 May 1994: 73.

[36.] Morgan.

[37.] Jane Gaughan, "Futuristics as a Subversive Activity", Trend (Spring 1971): 11.

[37(a).] What have we learned from a decade of research (1983-1992) on "The Pyschological Impact of Technology". This excellently titled article can be found in Larry D. Rosen and Michelle M. Weil, Computers & Society March 1994 (Vol. 24, No. 1): 3-5.

[38.] W. B. Riley, "Wanted for the '70s: Easier-to-program Computers", <u>Electronics</u> 13 Sept. 1971.

[39.] Wienberg, <u>The Psychology of Computers</u> tells explicitly why programmers must write with regard to 'people issues' not just to technical issues. Programmers must keep in mind that few of their inventions are on the scale of Einstein's work. Thomas Kuhn, <u>The Structure of Scientific Revolutions </u>(Chicago: University of Chicago Press, 1970) writes of paradigm shifts and how it drives computer programming: Programmers begin as young *radicals*; mature as *conservatives* due to financial and social constraints defending his/her paradigm at all costs; finally accepting the inevitable - the arrival of a new and 'better' paradigm. (paraphrasing Wienberg; italics mine.)

CONCLUSION

[1.] <u>Compute Now!</u>

[2.] Nick Sullivan, "Buyer's Guide to Personal Computers: Shopping Do's and Don'ts", <u>Family Computing</u> 06 1986: 29. Used computers have been around since the earliest days of small-computing. See <u>Byte</u>, Dec. 1977, *Where to Get Bargains in Used Computer Equipment*, 154,155.

[3.] Steven Jong, "Designing a Text Editor? The User comes first: A System's power is measured in ease of use", <u>Byte</u> 04 1982: 284.

[4.] Faye Deere, "Troubleshooting ADAM", <u>Computer Monthly</u> 11 1990: 112.

[5.] Christos J. Georgiou, "Machine Intelligence: A Function of Human Ingenuity", <u>Creative Computing</u> 06 1982: 124.

[5(a).] Marin Banks, "The Undiscovered Country", <u>PC Plus</u> 08 1993: 183.

[5(b).] One such addition to word processing is *Grammatik*. An excellent early review is found in <u>Creative Computing</u> by Steven Kimmel, "I Sing the Editor Electric", <u>Creative Computing</u> 05 1982: 75.

[6.] Martin Banks, Ibid.

[7.] There is a special application that has been around for years, a true software innovation that deserves special   attention - it's called *hypertext*. (Stan Veit/Kilarski, "Hypertext for PCs", <u>Computer Shopper</u> 09 1988: 27. A program built around hypertext theory – a term coined by Ted Nelson[a.] In 1973 in <u>Computer Lib/Dream Machines</u> (Chicago:

Hugo's Book Service, 1974), uses linked lists, - what is essentially relational database technology - is available to ADAM users. The objective of the program is to link note cards(nodes) in an associative fashion: *"By linking related bits of information, users can follow a chain of data and view parts that fit your specific needs, and not have to browse through large quantities of irrelevant fluff."* (Stan Viet, History of the Personal Computer (Asheville, NC.: WorldComm, 1993) 174. The process is similar to word processing, except that Hypertext organizes ideas logically rather than by words. However, processing and storage demands severely curtail the number of nodes and associated links one has on an ADAM. [The original concept of 'hypertext' theory was developed by Douglas Engelbart at SRI in the early 70s. (Ron Albright, "PC Insights", Computer Monthly 04 1991: 7.]

7(a). An excellent article on the *Zanadu* project is in Wired, July 1995. It's visionary, Ted Nelson, is the reason both for its external success and internal failure,b. according to the author.

7(b). This may be construed as a perverse view of not-discovered-here syndrome.

8. Aldous Huxley. The Human Situation: Lectures at Santa Barbara, 1959 (Toronto: Clarke, Irwin & Co. Ltd., 1977).

9. The ultimate in anti-technology statements is arguably that of the Una-bomber's Manifesto. One that is considerably less threatening is Chellis Glendinning's Utne article "Notes toward a Neo-Luddite Manifesto".

10. Editors, "Fear of technology is the phobia of the '90s", The Computer Paper Sept. 993: 54.

11. Unequal Distribution: The Information Haves and Have-Bots by R. Furger.

[12.] Florman; *"What happens to people who get sideswiped from low-tech jobs in the displacement that is coming?"* [12a.] This was predicted decades ago in contemporary form, but actually going back to the Luddites,[b.] by such visionaries as Turing, Asimov, et al. (Toronto Star, 29 Jan. 1994: B1,B5). [See Appendix 20]

[13.] Buerger; The argument, begun in the mid 70s with the arrival of microcomputers, is electronic technology will end the printing era. Information
moving electronically or optically is stored then viewed at one's leisure. Furthermore, its environmentally friendly, so the argument was and is. (Jogn C. Dvorak, "Sure, Paper Publishing is Evil Waste, But Media Junkies Prefer It", (PC/Computing Oct. 1993: 166).

[14.] See Appendix 21.

[15.] Christopher C. Evams, "Can a Machine Think". *Futurism*[a.] Gone mad! Or not! Here are four books that elucidate an enigmatic future:
>   1) Arthur Kroker, Data Trash: The Theory of the
>   Virtual Class.
>   2) Douglas Coupland, Microserfs.
>   3) Richard Dawkins, Out of Eden.
>   4) Derrick de Kerchove, The Skin of Culture.

[15(a).] "Benjamin Franklin was wrong in one respect. Although it is true that we can never escape death and taxes, we can also be certain of the heightened acceleration of change. We hurtle forward into a future that is forever unknown while history watches, daily transforming the future into the past. Like our ancestors, we live on the razor's edge of time, poised between the known and the possible, hoping to discover in ourselves and in our past some small clue as to what awaits us". This quote is from Microsoft Encarta '95 *TIMELINE: The Future*.

[16.] Scott Nesbitt, "Gutenberg Alert", The Globe & Mail 25 Nov. 1993: A11, "The wearing of an old-fashioned watch, with hands, may become the mark of a neo-Luddite, like refusal to learn metric, let alone FORTRAN and COBOL".(Ed. Hailwood, "Science",

[17.] Farewell to the 70's, Ed. Anna Porter and Marjorie Harris (Toronto: Thomas Nelson & Sons, 1979: 249).

[18.] Ibid., :A22. This situation reminds me of E. M. Forster's flat people - those who led one dimensional lives. Today there are rounded or portfolio people who when asked what they do reply, "It will take a while to tell you it all, which bit would you like.'

[19.] Christopher Harris, "Review of the Creation of the e-nation", The Globe & Mail 20 Nov. 1995: C1. William Thorsell, ed. The Globe & Mail, conversing on a two day visit to MIT's *Media Lab* in Boston excites humility in the face of technological change, envy over the opportunity of these young people to explore it and greed at the   commercial potential of their inventions. The future is arriving much more quickly than it did...The rate of change in the human environment has never been faster. We are not going nearly slow enough to describe and comprehend it."

[20.] Jacques Leslie, "Ambiguity Machine", Byte Oct. 1995: 250. In this regards Tetsuya Mizuguchi writes:

> *Unlike the arts, where it is often a matter of*
> *taste whether something is good or not,*
> *creating good interactive entertainment is*
> *easily more definable.*
>   (Edge, Sept. 1996: 17).

[21.] Ross Laver, "Mobile Madness", Maclean's 08 Jan. 1996: 29.
   An interesting argument is put forth by Sean W. Fleming in an E-mail message (sfleming@oce.orst.edu) quoted in Wired June 1996; 122: "One key benefit of the increasing power and pervasiveness of computers is seldom mentioned in polite

conversation: the virtually unlimited opportunity they provide for scapegoating. Disenfranchised classes make decent scapegoats, but as sentient beings they can fight back. So such annoyances befall the person who blames failure on an inanimate object. A manager knows she needs to hire another worker, but that the powers that be will reject this proposal. The solution? Upgrade from run-of-the-mill 486s to Pentiums" It was all the computer's fault. Undoubtedly, the few seconds saved each day, which would otherwise be wasted waiting for WordPerfect to open, will turn the company around."

[22.] Charles Macli, "Futurist's cheerleading fitfully entertaining", Globe & Mail 23 Jan. 1996: D3.

BIBLIOGRAPHY

PRIMARY SOURCES

Ahl, David H. Getting Started in Classroom Computing.
    Maynard, MA.: Digital Equipment Corp., 1974.

American National Standards Institute(ANSI). Minimal BASIC.
    Publication Number X3.60. NY.: ANSI, 1977.

Jobs, Steven. "The Personal Computer: A New Medium."
    Personal Computer Forum, Lake Geneva, Wis., 1981.

Corliss, William R. Computers. U. S. Printers, U. S. Atomic
    Energy Agency, 1973.

Digital Equipment Corporation. PDP 10 Multiprogramming Batch
    Programmer's Reference Manual(DEC-10 TBA-D).
    Maynard, MA.: Digital Equipment Corporation, 170.

Drushel, Richard F., Ph.D. A Tour Inside the Coleco ADAM, Or,
    What Do All Those Chips Do?. Paper presented at
    ADAMCON 06, Oct. 8, 1994.

Felsenstein, Lee. "Build 'Pennywhistle' The Hobbyist's Modem."
    Popular Electronics March 1976: 43+.

Gasseé, Jean-Louis. The Third APPLE. NY.: Brace Harcourt &
    Jovanovich, 1987.

Dictionary IEEE Standard of Electrical and Electronics Terms
    (3rd ed.). NY.: Whiley, 1984.

Intel Corporation. Intel 8080 Microcomputer System User's
    Manual. Santa Clara, CA.: Intel Corp., 1975(July).

Intel Corporation. Intel: Architect of the Microcomputer
    Revolution. Sanata Clara, CA.: Intel Corp.

Jensen, Kathleen and Niklaus Wirth. <u>PASCAL User Manual and Report</u>. NY.: Spring Verlag, 1974.

Kay, Alan and The Learning Research Group. "Personal Dynamic Media". <u>IEEE Computer</u> March 1977: 31-41.

_____. "Microelectronics and The Personal Computer". <u>Scientific American</u>. Sept. 1977: 231+.

Kernighan & Dennis Ritchie. <u>The C Programming Language</u>. Englewood Cliffs, NJ.: Prentice-Hall Software.

Kurtz, Thomas. "On the Way to Standard BASIC." <u>Byte</u> June 1982: 182+.

Lancaster, Don. <u>TV Typewriter Cookbook: Complete Guide to Low-cost Television Display of Alphanumeric and Graphic Data for Microprocessor Systems, Computer Hobbyists, Ham RTTY, TV Titling, Word Processing, and Video Games</u>. Indianapolis, IN.: Howard W. Sams, 1977.

_____. "Build an ASCII Keyboard Encoder." <u>Radio-Electronics</u> April 1973: 55+.

_____. "Build the TVT-6: A Low-Cost Direct Video Display, Part 1", <u>Popular Electronics</u> July 1977: 47+.

_____. "Build the TVT-6: A Low-Cost Direct Video Display, Part 2", <u>Popular Electronics</u> Aug. 1977: 47+.

Larter, Sylvia(Principal Investigator). <u>The Impact of Microcomputers in Elementary Education</u>. Toronto: Ministry of Education, (Queens' Printer)1983.

Mawby, Ronald, et. al. <u>Structured Interviews on Children's Conceptions of Computers</u>. Wash., DC.: U. S. Dept. of Education, Office of Educational Research and Improvement(OERI), 1984.

MOS Technology, Inc. <u>KIM-1 Microcomputer Module User Manual.</u> Morristown, NJ.: MOS Technology.

<u>National Computer Security Association (NCSA)</u>. Carlisle, PA.

Osborne, Adam. "Commentary on Microcomputing Industry". <u>Practical Computing</u> Jan. 1978: 5.

_____. <u>16-Bit Microprocessor Handbook</u>. Berkeley, CA.: Osborne/McGraw-Hill, 1981.

Ostler, Mel. <u>From BASICs to BASIC</u>. Las Cruces, NM.: Mel Ostler(Roadrunner Publications), 1988.

Ragsdale, R. G. <u>Computers in the Schools: A Guide for Planning</u>. Toronto: OISE(Ontario Institute for Studies in Education), 1982.

Raymond, Eric S. <u>The New Hacker's Dictionary, Second Edition</u>. Cambridge: MIT Press, 1993.

Science Council of Canada.<u>Sur les technologies de projection de la vis priv au Canada</u>. Ottawa: Science Council of Canada, 1985.

Sculley, John. <u>Odyessy</u>. NY.: Harper & Row, 1987.

Solomon, Leslie and Stan Veit. <u>Getting Involved With Your Own Computer: A Guide for Beginners</u>. Short Hills: R. Enslow Publishers, 1977.

Special Altair. "MITS-MAS Christmas Catalogue". <u>Popular Electronics</u> Dec. 1975: 33+.

SYBEX. "Programming Courses on Cassette: S1 Introduction to Microprocessors". Berkeley, CA: Sybex, 1977.

Viet, Stan. "The Night Fifth Avenue Stood Still". <u>Computer Shopper</u>. Aug. 1991: 128+.

Walker, Terry, Roger Melen, Harry Garland, Ed Hall. "Build the TV DAZZLER: Unique computer accessory provides alpha-numerics and graphics in full color". <u>Popular Electronics</u> Feb. 1976: 31+.

<u>Webster's New World Computer Dictionary</u>. Toronto: Prentice-Hall, 1992.

SECONDARY SOURCES

Adler, Noel D. and Steven Hovani. The Copyright Kit: How to Copyright Your Computer Software. Sautuket, N.Y.: National Attorney's Publications Inc., 1981.

Ahl, David, ed. The Best of Creative Computing, Vols. 1&2. Morristown, NJ.: Creative Computing, 1977.

_____. Basic Computer Games: Microcomputer Edition. (Revision of 101 BASIC Computer Games) Morristown, NJ.: Creative Computing, 1978.

_____ and Carl T. Helmers, eds. The Best of Byte, Vol. 1. NY: McGraw-Hill Publications, 1977.

Albrecht, Bob. Teaching BASIC to Kids. Sebastopol, CA.: BASIC for Kifs, Inc., 1991.

Albright, Ron. The Orphan Chronicles. (Very Difficult book to get???)

Allaby, Michael. Inventing Tomorrow : How to Live in a Changing World. Abacus Books, 1977.

Arnold, D., ed. The Sociology of Subculture. Berkeley, CA.: Glendessary Press, 1970.

Barbier, Ken. CP/M Assembly Language Programming. Hall Books.

Barden, William. How to Buy and Use Minicomputers and Microcomputers. Peterborough, NH.: BITS, Inc., 1977.

Baron, Naomi S. Computer Languages: A Guide for the Perplexed. NY.: Doubleday, 1986.

Basalla, George. The Evolution of Technology. NY.: Columbia University Press, 1990.

Beasley, Jack. Microcomputers on the Farm. Indianapolis, IN.: H. W. Sams, 1983.

Bernstein, Jeremy. The Analytical Engine: Computer – Past Present & Future. Morrow, 1981.

Binder, Robert M. A Practical Guide to Small Computers For Business & Professional Use. NY.: Monarch Press, 1981.

Bishop, Peter. Fifth Generation Computers.

Boyce, Jefferson C. Digital Computer Fundamentals. Peterborough, NH: BITS, Inc., 1977.

_____. Microprocessor and Microcomputer Basics. Englewood Cliffs, NJ.: Prentice-Hall, 1979.

Brand, Stewart. The Media Lab: Inventing the Future at M.I.T. Markham, Ont.: Penguin Books, 1987.

Brod, Craig. Technostress: The Human Cost of the Computer Revolution. Reading, MA.: Addison-Wesley, 1984.

Brooner, E. G. Microcomputer Data-base Management. Indianapolis, IN.: H. W. Sams, 1982.

Brown, Gerald R. Instant Freeze-Dried Computer Programming in BASIC. Menlo Park, CA.: Dymax, 1978.

Brown, Peter J. Writing Interactive Compilers and Interpreters. NY.: Wiley, 1979.

Burks, Alice R. and Arthur Burks. The First Electronic Computer: The Atanasoff Story. Ann Arbor, MI.: Univ. of Michigan Press, 1988.

Chandor, Anthony. The Facts of File Dictionary of
        Microcomputers. NY.: Facts on File, Inc., 1981.

Chartrand, Marilyn and Constance D. Williams. Educational
        Software Directory: A Subject Guide to Microcomputer
        Software. Littleton, CO.: Libraries Unlimited, 1982.

Clarke, Arthur C. 2001 - A Apace Odyssey. NY.: New American
        Library, 1968.

Conniffe, Patricia. Dictionary of Computer Terms Made Simple.
        Toronto: Scholastic Inc., 1984.

Constantine, Larry. Constantine on Peopleware. Englewood,
        Cliffs, NJ.: Yourdon Press (Prentice-Hall), 1995.

Consumer Guide, eds. Home Computers. N. Y.: Bechman House,
        1978

The Hacker's Handbook. Alexandria, MN.: Arthur Brown, 1986.
        [First published in Great Britain – London: Century
        Communications Limited, 1985. This early edition was
        banned but it's now available through the NET???]

Coupland. Douglas. Microserfs, NY.: Regan Books(Harper-
        Collins), 1995.

Covvey, Dominic and Neil Harding McAlister. Computer
        Choices: Beware of Conspicuous Computing. Reading,
        MA.: Addison-Wesley Publishing Co.,
        1982.

_____. Computer Consciouness: Surviving the Automated
        80s. Reading, MA.: Addison-Wesley Publishing Co.,
        1980.

Cremin, Lawrence A. "Focus on Education", The 1967 World Book Year Book. Toronto: World Book Encyclopedia, 1967.

Crevier, Daniel. A.I.: The Tumultuous History of the Search for A.I.. NY.: Basic Books, 1993.

Curran, Susan & R. Curnow. Overcoming Computer Illiteracy. NY.: Penguin Books, 1983.

DaCosta, Frank. How To Build Your Own Working Robot. Blue Ridge Summitt, PA.: TAB Books, 1979.

Dahmke, Mark. Microcomputer Operating Systems. Peterborough, NH.: Byte Books, 1982.

Deken, Joseph. The Electronic Cottage: Everyday Living With Your Personal Computer in the 1980s. Morrow, 1981.

Derfler, Frank J. Microcomputer Data Communication Systems. Englewood Cliffs, NJ.: Prentice-Hall, 1982.

Dewdney, A. K. The Armchair Universe: An Exploration of Computer Worlds.

Dewar, Robert B. K. and Matthew Swosna. Microprocessors: A Programmer's View. NY.: McGraw-Hill, 1991.

Dirksen, A. J. Microcomputers: What They Are and How to Put Them to Productive Use. Blue Ridge Summitt, PA.: TAB Books, 1978.

Dowling, Colette. The Techno/Peasant Survival Manual. N.Y.: Bantam Books, 1980.

Dwyer & Critchfield. CP/M and the Personal Computer. Reading, MA.: Addison-Wesley Publishing Co., 1983.

Editors. The Pre-Computer Book. Toronto: TAB Books, 1984.

Evans, Christopher. The Mighty Micro: The Impact of the Micro-Chip Revolution. Kent, England: Coronet Books, 1979. [Released in the U.S. by Victor Collancz Ltd., 1979.)

_____. The Making of the Micro: A History of the Computer. NY.: Van Nostrand Reinhold Company, 1981.

Fishman, Katherine Davis. The Computer Establishment, NY.: Harper & Row, 1981.

Flores, Ivan. The Professional Microcomputer Handbook. NY.: Van Nostrand Reinhold Company, 1986.

Rational Search for Scapegoats. NY.: St.Martin's Press, 1981.

Forester, Tom. High-Tech Society: The Story of the Information Technology Revolution. Cambridge, MA.: MIT Press, 1987.

Forester, Tom and Perry Morrison. Forester, Computer Ethics: Cautionary Tales and Ethical Dilemmas in Computing. Cambridge, MA.: The MIT Press, 1990.

_____. Ed. The Microelectronics Revolution: The Complete Guide to the New Technology & Its Impact on Society. Cambridge, MA.: 1981.

Frieberger, Paul & Chew. A Consumer's Guide to Personal Computing & Microcomputer, 1st Ed.. Toronto: TAB Books, 1978.

_____. A Consumer's Guide to Personal Computing & Microocmputers, 2nd Ed. Toronto: TAB Books, 1984.

Frieberger, Paul & Michael Swan. <u>Fire in the Valley</u>.

Gallo, Michael and Robert K. Henno. <u>Computers & Society with BASIC and Pascal</u>. Boston: Prindle, Weber & Schmidt, 1985.

Gerrold, David. <u>When Harlie was One</u>. NY.: Doubleday, 1972.

GFN Industries Inc., eds. <u>Design of Digital Systems: Books 1-6, New Teach Yourself Courses</u>. Hicksville, NY.: GFN Industries, Inc., 1977.

Giarratano, Joseph C. <u>Foundations of Computer Technology</u>. Indianapolis, IN.: H. W. Sams, 1982.

Goldstein, Larry J. <u>Computers and Their Applications</u>. Prentice, 1986.

Goldstine, H. H. <u>The Computer from Pascal to Von Neuman</u>. Princeton: Princeton Univ. Press, 1972.

Goodwin, James C. <u>The S-100 & Other microcomputer abuses</u>. Indianaplois, IN.: H. W. Sams, 1981.

Greenberger, Martin, ed. <u>Computers and the World of the Future.</u> Cambridge, MA.: The MIT Press, 1962.

Greenblatt, Stanley. <u>Understanding Computers Through Common Sense</u>. NY.: Cornerstone Library, 1983.

Grosswirth, Marvin. <u>Beginner's Guide to Home Computers</u>. Garden City, NJ.: Dolphin Books, 1978.

<u>Outlaws and Hackers on the Computer Frontier</u>. NY.: Simon & Schuster, 1991.

Hahn, Harley. <u>Open Computing: UNIX Unbound</u>. Toronto: Osborne, McGraw-Hill, 1994.

Hancock & Krieger. The C Primer. NY.: McGraw-Hill.

Handel, S. The Electronic Revolution. London: Penguin Books, 1967.

Hanson, Dirk. The New Alchemists: Silicon Valley and the Microelectronics Revolution. Boston: Little, Brown & CO., 1982.

Heinlein, Robert A. The Moon is a Harsh Mistress. NY.: Putman, 1966.

Helms, Harry. The McGraw-Hill Computer Handbook. NY.: McGraw-Hill, Inc., 1983.

Hiserman, David L. Build Your Own Working Robot.

Hoffman, Lance A. Rogue Programs: Viruses, Worms and Trojan Horses. NY.: Van Nostrand Reinhold, 1990.

Hofstadter, Douglas K. Godel, Esher, Bach: An Eternal Golden Braid. NY.: Vintage Books, 1979.

Hogan. Osborne CP/M User Guide. Toronto: McGraw-Hill.

Hardeski, Michael. Illustrated Dictionary of Microcomputer Terminology. Blue Ridge Summit, PA.: TAB Books, 1978.

Horgan, John. The End of Science; Facing the Limits of Knowledge in the Twilight of the Scientific Age. Reading, MA.: Addison-Wesley Publishing CO., 1996.

Huxley, Aldous. The Human Situation: Lecturers at Santa Barbara, 1959. Toronto: Clarke, Irwin & Co., Ltd., 1977.

Ichbiah, Daniel and Suan L. Knepper. The Making of Microsoft: How Bill Gates and his team created the world's most successful software company. Prima Publishing.

Ide, T. R. The Computerized Society: Implications for Canada. Toronto: Canadian Studies Foundation, 1979.

IEEE. IEEE Symposium on Small Computers in the Arts. Philadelphia, PA.: IEEE Computer Society, Nov. 20-22, 1981.

Image Resource. Computer Store Survey Rates Manufacturers. Westlake Village, CA.: Image Resource, 1977.

James, Peter and Niel Thorpe. Ancient Inventions. NY.: Ballantine Books, 1994.

Jones, D. F. Colossus:(aka: The Forbin Project). NY.: Putman, 1967.

Karin, Sidney and Norris Barker Smith. The Supercomputer Era. NY.: Harcourt, 1987.

Katzan, Harry, Jr. Microcomputer Graphics & Programming Techniques. NY.: Van Nostrand Reinhold Co., 1982.

Kelly & Aspray. Computer: A History of the Information Machine. NY.: Basic Books, 1996.

Kernighan & Plauger. Software Tools.

Kespret, Istok. PKZIP, LHARC & Co.: Using Data Compression Utilities. Grand Rapids, MI.: Abacus Books, 1995.

Kidder, Tracy. The Soul of a New Machine. NY.: Little, Brown, 1981.

Kleinberg, Harry. How You Can Learn to Live With Computers.

Kuhn, Thomas. The Structure of Scientific Revolutions. Chicago: Univ. of Chicago Press, 1970.

Knight, K. E. A Study of Technological Innovation: The Evolution of Digital Computers. PhD.. Diss. Carnegie Institute of Technology, 1963.

Knuth, D. E. The Art of Computer Programming, Vol. 3: Sorting and Searching. Reading, MA.: Addison-Wesley, 1973.

Koffman, Elliot B. Pascal: A Problem Solving Approach (APPLE II). Reading, MA.: Addison-Wesley, 1982.

Kraft, George D. Microprogrammed Control and Reliable Design Of Small Computers. Englewood Cliffs, NJ.: Prentice-Hall,1981.

Lammers, Susan. Interviews with 19 Programmers who shaped the computer industry. Tempus Press/Microsoft Books.

Lancaster, Don. Enhancing Your APPLE II. NY.: Howard W. Sams & Company, 1983.

_____. The TTL Cookbook. Peterborough, NH.: Byte Books, 1976.

_____. The Case Against Patents. Thatcher, AZ.: Synergetics, 1996.

Landauer, Thomas K. The Trouble with Computers. Boston: MIT Press, 1995.

Laurel, Brenda. Computers as Theater. Reading, MA.: Addison-Wesley Publishing Co., 1995.

Laurie, Edward J. Computers, Automation, and Society. Homewood, IL.: R. D. Irwin, 1979.

Layton, Edwin T., Jr., ed. <u>Technology and Social Change in America</u>. NY.: Harper & Row, 1973.

Lechner, H. D. <u>The Computer Chronicles</u>. Belmont, CA.: Wadsworth Publishing Co., 1984.

Levering, Robert, Michael Katz and Mark Moskowitz. <u>The Computer Entrepreneurs</u>.

Levy, David. <u>Chess and Computers</u>.

Levy, Steven. <u>Hackers: Heroes of the Computer Revolution</u>. NY.: Dell Press, 1984.

Lien, David A. <u>Learning BASIC for the Tandy Computer</u>. San Diego: Compusoft Publishing, 1988.

Lipton, Russell. <u>Multimedia Toolkit: Build Your Own Solutions with DocuSource</u>. NY.: Random House Electronic Publishing, 1992.

Littman, Jonathan. <u>Once Upon a Time in Computerland</u>. Los Angeles: Price Stern Sloan, Inc., 1987.

Logan, Robert K. <u>The Alphabet Effect: The Impact of Tie Phonetic Aphabet on the Development of Western Civilization</u>.

Logsdon, Thomas S. <u>Computers & Social Controversy</u>. Computer Science, 1980.

Loofbourrow, Tod. <u>How to Build a Computer-controlled Robot</u>.

Loop, Liza, Julia Anton and Ramon Zamora. <u>ComputerTown, Bringing Computer Literacy to Your Community</u>. Reston, VA.: Reston Publishing Co., 1993.

Manes, Stephen and Paul Andrews. Gates - How Microsoft's mogul reinvented an industry. Simon & Shuster Pub.

Markus, John. McGraw-Hill Electronics Dictionary. Blacklick, OH.: McGraw-Hill Companies, 1996.

Martin, Campbell-Kelly and William Aspray. Computer: A History of the Information Machine. NY: Basic Books, 1996.

Martin, James and Adrian R. D. Norman.The Computerized Society. NY.: Prentice-Hall, 1970.

Margolin, Joseph B. and Marion R. Misch, eds. Computers in the Classroom. NY.: Spartan Books, 1970.

Margolis, Art. Troubleshooting & Repairing Personal Computers. Blue Ridge Summit, PA.: Tab Books, 1983.

Matt, Stephen K. Electricity and Basic Electronics(rev). NY.: Goodheart, 1982.

Maynard, Jeff. Computer Programming Made Simple. London: Allen, 1972.

McCarthy, John. "Information." Rochlin, Gen I., Ed. Scientific Technology and Social Change. San Francisco, CA.: W. H. Freeman and Company, 1974.

McCumm, Donald H. Computer Programming for the Complete Idiot. San Francisco, CA,: Design Enterprises of San Francisco, 1979.

Mercer, Donald G. Introduction to Microcomputer Programming in BASIC. Cobourg, Ont.: Northumberland & Clarington Board of Education, 1985.

McDermott, Vern and Diana Fisher. <u>Learning BASIC Step by Step</u>. Rockville, MD.: Computer Science Press, 1982.

Menzies, Heather. <u>Computers on the Job: Surviving Canada's Microcomputer Revolution</u>. Toronto: Lorimer, 1982.

Metropolis, H., J. Howlett & Gian-Carlo Rota. <u>A History of Computing in the Twentieth Century: A Collection of Essays</u>. NY.: Academic Press, 1980.

Mims, Forest. <u>Siliconnections</u>.

Minsky, Marvin. <u>The Society of Mind</u>. NY.: Simon & Schuster, 1986.

_____ and Seymour Papert. <u>Perceptons: An Introduction to Computational Geometry</u>. Cambridge, MA.: MIT Press, 1969.

Moody, Fred. <u>I Sing the Body Electronic: A Year with Microsoft on the Multimedia Frontier</u>. Toronto: Penguin Books, 1995.

Moscoe, Vincent. <u>Pay-per Society, Computers and Communication in the Information Age: Essays in Critical Thinking and Public Policy</u>. Norwood, NJ.: Ablex Pub., 1989.

Mumford, Lewis. <u>The City in History: Its Origins, Its Transformations, and Its Prospects</u>. NY.: Harcourt Brace & Company, 1989.

Myers, Roy E. <u>Microcomputer Graphics</u>. Reading, MA.: Addison-Wesley, 1982.

Nash, Andrew & Derek Hall. <u>An Introduction to Microcomputers</u> in Teaching. London Hutchinson,1982.

Nelson, Theodor H. Computer Lib. Chicago: Hugo's Book
     Service, 1974.

Newman, William M. and Robert F. Sproull. Principles of
     Interactive Computer Graphics.

Nevison, John M. The Little Book of BASIC Style. Reading,
     MA.: Addison-Wesley, 1983.

Nichols, Elizabeth Agnew. Data Communications for
     Microcomputers: With Practical Applications and
     Experiments. NY.: McGraw-Hill, 1982.

Niman, John. A Teacher's Companion to Microcomputers.
     Lexington, MA.: Lexington Books, 1985.

Oakman, Robert L. The Computer Triangle. NY.: John Wiley &
     Sons, 1995.

Osborne, Adam. An Introduction to Microcomputers, Vol. 0: The
     Beginner's Book. Berkeley, CA: Osborne & Associates,
     1976.

_____. An Introduction to Microcomputers, Vol. I:
     Basic Concepts. Berkeley, CA: Osborne & Associates,
     1976.

_____. An Introduction to Microcomputers, Vol. II: Some Real
     Products. Berkeley, CA: Osborne & Associates, 1977.

_____. Running Wild: The Next Industrial Revolution.
     Berkeley: Osborne/McGraw-Hill, 1979.

_____, and David Bunnell. An Introduction to
     Microcomputers, Vol. 0, The Beginner's Book. Berkeley,
     CA.: McGraw-Hill, 1982.

Pagnoni, Mario. Computers & Small Fries. Avery, 1987.

Palferman, Jon and Doron Swade. The Dream Machine: Exploring The Computer Age. London: BBD Books, 1991.

Pask, Gordon and Susan Curran. Microman: Living and Growing with Computers. London: Century Publishing, 1983.

Penrose, Roger. Emperor's New Mind: Concerning Computers, Minds, & the Laws of Physics. Oxford: Oxford Univ. Press, 1989.

Perry, Greg. Absolute Beginner's Guide to C. Indianapolis, IN.: Prentice-Hall Computer Publishing, 1994.

Petersen, Dale. Big Things from Little Computers: A Layperson's Guide to Personal Computing. Englewood Cliffs, NJ.: Prentice-Hall, 1982.

_____. Intelligent Schoolhouse: Readings onComputers & Learning. Reston, VA.: Reston Pub. Co., 1984.

Poe, Elmer and James C. Baldwin, II. The S-100 and Other Micro Buses. Indianapolis, IN.: W. H. Sams, 1981.

Ramierez, Edward V. and Melyvn Weiss. Microprocessing Fundamentals, Hardware & Software. McGraw-Hill, 1980.

Raskin, Robin and Kaire Christian. Your Child's Education: Teaching Your Kid How to Use Computers.... NY.: Ziff-Davis, 1995.

Rheingold, Howard. Tools for Thought: The People and Ideas Behind the Next Computer Revolution. NY.: Simon & Schuster 1985. [Available on the net.]

Richardson, R. L. Computers: Understanding & Using Them: A Hands-On Approach. Gorsuch Scarisbrick, 1985.

Rinder, Robert N. <u>A Practical Guide to Small Computers for Business and Professional Use</u>. Rochester & Gantz.

The Naked Computer. NY.: Morrow.

Rochlin, Gene. <u>Trapped in the Net: The Unanticipated Consequences of Computerization</u>. Princeton, NJ: Princeton, Univ. Press, 1997.

Robillard, Mark J. <u>Microprocessor Based Robotics</u>. NY.: Howard W. Sams, 1983.

Rogers, Everett and Judith K. Larsen. <u>Silicon Valley Fever: Growth of High-Technology Culture</u>. NY.: McGraw-Hill Basic Books, Inc., 1984.

Roszak, Theodore. <u>Bugs</u>. NY.: Doubleday & Co., 1981.

Rutland, David. <u>Why Computers are Computers: The SWAC and the PC</u>. Philomath, OR.: Wren Publishers, 1995.

Sagan, Carl. <u>The Dragons of Eden</u>. NY.: Random House, 1977.

Sammett, Jean. <u>Programming Languages</u>.

Sargent, Murray, III and Richard L. Shoemaker. <u>Interfacing Microcomputers to the Real World</u>. Reading, MA.: Addison-Wesley Pub. Co., 1981.

Saxon, James A. <u>COBOL A Self-Instructional Manual 2ndEd.</u> Englewood Cliffs, NJ.: Prentice-Hall Inc., 1971.

Schildt, Herbert. <u>C++ From the Ground Up</u>. Toronto: McGraw-Hill, 1994.

<u>Scientific American Reader</u>. NY.: Scientific American Inc. 1963.

Scott, E. F. Beginner's Guide to Microprocessors andComputing. Toronto: TAB Books, 1984.

Shallis, Michael. The Silicon Idol: The Micro Revolution & Its Social Implications. Toronto: Oxford Univ. Press, 1984.

Shurkin, Joel. Engines of the Mind: A History of The Computer. NY.: W. W. Norton, 1984.

Siegel, Lenny and John Markoff. The High Costs of High Tech. NY.: Harper & Row, 1985.

Silver, G. and J. Silver. Computer Algorithms and Flowcharting. NY.: McGraw-Hill Book Co., 1975.

Simon & Schuster. The Way Things Work Book of the Computer. NY.: Simon & Schuster, 1975.

Simpson, Henry. Serious Programming in BASIC. Blue Ridge Summit, PA.: TAB Books, 1986.

Sims, Forrest. Siliconnections.

Sippl, Charles J. and Charles P. Sippl. Computer Dictionary & Handbook. NY.: Smas, 1985.

Smith, Douglas K. and Robert C. Alexander. Fumbling the Future: How Xerox Invented, then Ignored, the First Personal Computer. NY.: William Morrow & Company, 1988.

Spencer, Donald D. An Introduction to Computers: Developing Computer Literacy. Columbus, OH.: C. E. Merrril Pub., Co., 1983.

Spencer, Donald D. Webster's New World Dictionary of Computer Terms, 4th Ed. New York: Prentice-Hall, 1992.

Squire, Enid. Computer: An Everyday Machine. Don Mills, Ont.: Addison-Wesley Canada, 1977.

Steele. The Hacker's Dictionary. NY.: Harper & Row.

Stern, Robert A. Concepts of Information Processing with BASIC. NY.: Wiley, 1983.

Stevens, AL. Al Steven's Teaches C: An Interactive Tutorial. NY.: MIS Press Inc., 1994.

_____ . Welcome to ... Programming: From Mystery to Mastery. NY.: MIS Press Inc., 1994.

Steyer, Wesley W. and James A. Saxon. Basic Principles of Data Processing, 2nd. Englewood Cliffs, NJ.: Prentice-Hall, 1970.

Stockley. Computer Jargon.

Swan, Tom. Type & Learn C. Boston: IDG Books, 1994.

Taylor, Charles F. The Master Handbook of Microcomputer Languages. Blue Ridge Summitt, PA.: TAB Books, 1984.

Taylor, Robert. The Computer in the School: Tutor, Tool,Tutee. NY.: Columbia Univ. Press, 1980.

Thomas, Shirley. Computers: Their History, Present, Applications, and Future. NY.: Holt, Rinehart and Winston, Inc., 1965.

Time-Life Books. "Understanding Computers – The Personal Computer". NY.: Time-Life Books, Inc., 1989.

_____. "Understanding Computers – Computer Languages". NY.: Time-Life Books, Inc., 1989.

Toffler, Alvin, ed. Learning for Tomorrow: The Role of the Future in Education. NY.: Random House, 1974.

_____. Power Shift: Knowledge, Wealth, and Violence at the Edge of the 21st Century. Toronto: Bantam Books, 1990.

Turkle, Sherry. The Second Self: Computers and the Human Spirit. NY.: Simon & Schuster, 1984.

Turn, Rein. Computers in the 1980s. NY.: Columbia Univ. Press, 1974.

Van Tessel, Dennis L. Compleat Computer. Palo Alto, CA.: Science Research Associates, 1976.

Veit, Stan. Stan Veit's History of the Personal Computer: From Altair to IBM, A History of the PC Revolution. Asheville, NC.: WorldComm, 1993.

Wadsworth, Nat. Understanding Microcomputers and Small Computer Systems. NY.: DaCapo Press, 1980.

Waite, Mitchell and Robert Lafore. Soul of CP/M - How to Use the Hidden Power of Your CP/M System. Sams & Co., Books.

Waite, Mitchell and Michael Pardee. Microcomputer Primer. Indianapolis, IN.: Howard W. Sams & Co.,1977.

Wallace, James and Jim Erickson. Hard Drive: Bill Gates and the Making of the Microsoft Empire. John Wiley & Sons Books.

Walter, Russ. <u>Beginning with BASIC: An Introduction to Computer Programming</u>. NY.: NAL/Plume, 1984.

_____. <u>Hassles in BASIC</u>. Boston: Birkhauser Boston, Inc., and Russ Walter, 1984.

_____. <u>The Secret Guide to Computers Vol. 1</u>. Boston: Birkhauser Boston, Inc. and Russ Walter, 1984.

_____. <u>The Secret Guide to Computers Vol. 2</u>. Boston: Birkhauser Boston, Inc. and Russ Walter, 1984.

_____. <u>The Secret Guide to Computers Vol. 5</u>. Boston: <u>Applications</u>. Boston: Birkhauser Boston, Inc. and Russ Walter, 1981.

_____. <u>The Secret Guide to Computers 17th Ed</u>. Boston: Birkhauser Bsoton, Inc. and Russ Walter, 1989.

Weinberg, G. M. <u>The Psychology of Computer Programming</u>. NY.: Van Nostrand Reinhold Company, 1971.

Wienberg, Sanford H. & Mark Lawrence Fuerst. <u>Computer Phobia: How to Slay the Dragon of Computer Fear</u>. Wayne, PA.: Banbury Books, Inc., 1984.

Weisskopf, Gene. <u>Murpy's Laws of PCs: Getting the Best of Your Computer Before It Gets the Best of You</u>. Alameda, CA.: Sybex Inc., 1993.

Weizenbaum, Joseph. <u>Computer Power and Human Reason: From Judgment to Calculation</u>.

White, James. <u>Your Home Computer</u>.
_____. <u>Your Personal Computer</u>.

Williams, Brian K, Stacey C. Sawyer, Sarah E. Hutchinson. Using Information Technology: A Practical Introduction to Computers & Communications, 2nd Edition. Toronto: Richard D. Irwin, 1997.

Williams, Gene B. How to Repair & Manintain Your Apple Computer: All II Series Including the IIc. Radnor, PA.: Chilton Book Co., 1985.

Williams, Michael R. The PC Is Not A Typewriter.Berkeley, CA.: Peachpit Press, 1992.

Williamson, Mickey. Artificial Intelligence for Microcomputers: The Guide for Business Decisionmakers. NY.: Simon & Schuster, 1986.

Willis, Jerry and Merl Miller. Computers for Everybody. Beaverton, OR.: Dilithium Press, 1983.

Winograd, Terry and Fernando Flores. Understanding Computers and Cognition: A New Foundation for Design. NY.: Ablex, 1986.

Wright, Edward C. and Richard C. Forcier. The Computer: A Tool for the Teacher. Belmont, CA.: Wadsworth Publishing Company, 1983.

Wu, M. S. Introduction to Computer Data Processing With BASIC. NY.: Harcourt, Brace, Jovanovich, 1980.
Youdon, Edward. Decline and Fall of the American Programmer. Englewood Cliffs, NJ.: PTR Prentice Hall, 1992.

_____. The Rise and Resurrection of the American Programmer. Englewood Cliffs, NJ.: Prentice-Hall, 1996.
Zaks, Rodnay. From Chips to Systems: An Introduction to Microprocessors. Sybex Books.

Zuboff, Shoshana. <u>In the Age of the Smart Machine</u>. NY.: Harper-Collins, 1988.

SERIALS, JOURNALS & OTHER PERIODICALS

Abtan, P. "Education: Bringing the PC Home." <u>Computing Canada</u> 9 Nov. 1992: 13.

Adams, Scott. "In the '90s, Computer Skills Mean Sex Appeal." <u>Windows Magazine</u> May 1995.

Ahl, David. 'The First West Coast Computer Faire." <u>Creative Computing</u> Sept/Oct 1977.

_____. "The First Decade of Personal Computing." <u>Creative Computing</u> Nov. 1984.

Albano, Tim. "Computers in Canadian Education." <u>Computing Now</u> May 1985: 64-66.

Albreacht, Bob & Don Inman. "Your BASIC Backpack." <u>Computer Shopper</u> Oct. 1987: 165-166,314-315.

_____. "Your BASIC Packpack." <u>Computer Shopper</u> Dec. 1987: 171-174.

_____. "Your BASIC Packpack." <u>Computer Shopper</u> Jan. 1988: 170-173.

Albright, Ron. "PC Insights." <u>Computer Monthly</u>. April 1991: 72-76.

Allason, Julian. "Newsletter: Is the press biased?" <u>Microcomputer Printout</u> July 1983: 12.

_____. "Newsletter: Microsoft." <u>Microcomputer Printout</u> July 1983: 13,14.

_____. "Newsletter: Profitable Prophet." <u>Business Micro</u> Oct. 1983: 6.

Allen, David M. "A Floppy Disk Interface." <u>Byte</u> Jan. 1978: 58+.

Alpert, D. and D. L. Bitzer. "Advances in Computer Based Education." <u>Science</u> (Vol. 167) 20 March 1970: 1582-1590.

Amdahl, Gene and Jon Schiell. "The Mainframe Perspective." <u>MIPS</u> March 1989: 54-55.

Anderson, John J. "Who Invented the Video Game." <u>Creative Computing</u> Oct. 1982: 190-196.

Anderson, T. M. "The Future." <u>ECOAUG</u> Vol. 1, Nos 2,3, 1995: 6-8.

Archer, Sr., Rowland. "COBOL for the TRS-80 Models I and III." <u>Byte</u> March 1982: 384-412.

Asimov, Isaac. "Interview." Ed. Bill Moyers. <u>A World of Ideas</u>. Toronto: Doubleday, 1989.

_____. "The Last Question", <u>Science Fiction Quarterly</u> Nov. 1956: 6.

Aubrey, David. "Brain Waves: Neural network design brings Artificial intelligence to life." <u>Computer Shopper</u> March 1996: 566-568.

_____. "Now Hear This: Speech Recognition reaches a new level of sophistication – and a mainstream audience." Computer Shopper Jan. 1996: 622-623.

Austill, L. C. "BASIC Programming Course." The ADAM- User-Friendly Group Jul/Aug 1993: 8.

Banks, Martin."The Undiscovered Country." PC Plus Aug. 1993: 183.

Baran, Nick. "The Loneliness of the Low Budget User: Are computer companies forgetting the people who put them where they are today?" Byte Aug. 1989: 344.

Barden. "What Language is Best for You." Popular Computing Feb. 1982: 68+.

Barker, Dennis. "Working in the Code Mines." Byte Oct. 1995: 49.

Barron, Janet. "Birthing the Visible Calculator." Byte Dec. 1989: 326-328.

Barry, Tim. "Komputer Korner: Stacks - what they are and how they're used." Radio-Electronics March 1977: 22+.

Bateman, Selby. "Putting Computers to Good Use: The Innovative School." Compute's Gazette. Oct. 1985: 22.

Bennett, Graeme. "Buying a Computer for Your Kids." The Computer Paper Sept. 1993: 12+.

Bidmead, Chris, "Clearway: A low-cost local networking system." Practical Computing Sept. 1982: 61-64.

_____. "Databases Side by Side." Practical Computing May 1983: 114-118.

_____. "Superfile." <u>Practical Computing</u> Sept. 1982: 69-71.

_____. "The Big Memory Machine." <u>Electronics &
Computing</u> April 1982: 26-29.

Bigelow, Stephen J. "Microprocessors: Two Decades of
Microprocessor History." <u>Electronics Now</u> June 1995:
35-44.

_____. "PC Cards: The PC Card standard is changing the
shape of mobile computing." <u>Electronics Now</u> June
1995: 31-36.

Bissell, Don. "The Father of Computer Graphics: Today's
graphics systems owe their existence to an innovative
graduate school project called *Sketchpad*." <u>Byte</u>
June 1990: 380-381.

Bitzer, D. L. and R. L. Johnson. "*PLATO*: A Computer Based
System Used in the Engineering of Education". <u>IEEE
Proceedings</u> (Vol. 59, No. 6) June 1971: 960-968.

Blechman, Fred. "BASIC Anatomy I - A Menu Program."
<u>Vulcan's Computer Monthly</u> July 1990: 135-136.

Bobo, Ervin. "Classic Computer Column: The AMIGA
Connection." <u>Computer Monthly</u> Aug. 1990: 82+.

Boraiko, Allen A. "The Chip: Electronic Mini-Marvel That is
Changing Your Life." <u>National Geographic</u> Oct. 1982:
420+.

Bourque, Joseph. "An Apple for the Teacher: Classroom
Computers." <u>Popular Computing</u>. March 1982: 50.

Bowden, Lord. "Language of Computers." <u>American Scientist</u>
Jan.-Feb. 1970: 43+.

Bowles, Kenneth L. "UCSD PASCAL: A (Nearly) Machine Independent Software System (for Microcomputers and Minicomputers)." Byte May 1978: 46+.

Brand, Stewart. "Keep Designing." Whole Earth Review May 1995.

Brannon, Charles. "Picking the Right Printer." Compute's Gazette Oct. 1985: 85+.

Brinton, David. "Computer Literacy Project gets a boost." South African Microcomputer Owner Nov. 1983: 75.

Brody, Herb. "Video Games That Teach." Technology Review November/ December 1993: 50-57.

Buerger, David. "Power Pundit." Wired March 1995: 123.

Bullis, Robert. "A Look At Computermania: Personal computers were supposed to change our homes. Why are so many underused today?" Candian Consumer Jan. 1986: 11-12.

Bullough, Vern L. "The Computer & The Historian - Some Tentative Beginnings." Computers & The Humanities Vol. 1, 1996.

Burnett, Gerald and Richard Nolan. "At last, major roles for minicomputers." Harvard Business Review My/June 1975.

Bush, Vannevar. "As We May Think." Atlantic Monthly July 1945.

BYTE. Special Issue(20 Years). Sept. 1995.

Callahan, P. "Last Word: Machine Mad." Omni Dec. 1992: 128.
Campbell, Tom. "How to get started with programming." Compute Oct. 1990: PC-15+.

Canter, S. "Not SO BASIC Anymore." PC Magazine 28 Sept.
      1993: 233+.

Card, Stuart, William English, and Betty Burr. "Evaluation of
      Mouse, Rate-Controlled Isometric Joystick, Step Keys for
      Text Selection on a CRT." Ergonomics Vol. 21, No. 7,
      1978: 601+.

Carroll, Jon. "A Nation of Evil Geniuses: The soul of the new
      machine is inevitably malign, and when it escapes it
      causes all sorts of havoc." ComputerLife Jan. 1996: 248.

_____. "The Cozy Glow of the Cyberfire." ComputerLife Dec.
      1995: 306.

Castleman, Kenneth R. "The Intelligent Memory Block." Dec.
      1995: 306.

Castleman, Kenneth R. "The Intelligent Memory Block." Byte
      March 1978: 186-192.

Chamberlin, Hal. "Computer Bits: Assemblers." Popular
      Electronics July 1977: 89-90.

_____. "Computer Bits: Mass-Storage Systems." Popular
      Electronics Nov. 1976: 106-109.

_____. "Computer Bits: Microcomputer Memory". Popular
      Electronics March 1978: 97-97.

Christian, Charles. "Programming it's not for everyone!."
      MicroComputer Printout. March 1983: 40.

Coles , Roy. "The 44 million chip question." Practical Computing
      May 1983: 39.

Compute! "Getting Down to BASICs." Compute! July 1986: 18+.

Computer Shopper. "Changing Times: The Rise and Fall of Venture Capital." Computer Shopper March 1991: 245.

Crichton, Michael. "Installer Hell." Byte Sept. 1993: 294.

Dahmke, Mark. "let Your Fingers Do The Walking." Popular Computing Oct. 1982: 134-136.

_____. "Osborne 1 - Hardware Review." Byte June 1982: 48+.

Dash, Glen. "Build this Video Modulator: Permits direct connection of composite video from video games and microcomputers to the antenna terminals of your TV set," Radio-Electronics Aug. 1977: 33+.

Davis, Harry M. "Mathematical Machines." Scientific American Reader 509-525.

Dickinson, J. "The New PC Lingo: Counterintuitive, Anti-revolutionary, and Most Uncool." PC/Computing June 1993:106.

D'Ignazio, Fred. "The World Inside the Computer: The Talking Head." Compute! Sept. 1982.: 78-80.
_____. "D'Inversion: Tiny Talented Machines: Desktop Fusion." Compute Oct. 1990: G-18.

Deep ROM."Heard On-Line." Computer Shopper Sept. 1988: 157+.

Deere, Faye. "ADAM: Modems and Such." Computer Shopper June 1989: 292+.

_____. "Classic Computer Column: ADAM News." Computer Monthly Sept. 1990: 96,99.

_____. Computer Monthly Oct. 1990: 136-138.

_____. Computer Monthly Nov. 1990: 97-98.

_____. "Exploring CP/M 2.2." Computer Shopper Nov. 1989: 689-690.

_____. "Show Report: ADAMCON 2." Computer Monthly Nov. 1990: 112+.

_____. "Troubleshooting ADAM." Computer Monthly Dec. 1989: 718+.

_____. "American Design Components." NIAD June 1989: 5.

De Palma, Paul. Review of *The Evolution of Technology*, by George Basalla. Computers & Society (March 1994) Vol. 24, No. 1: 33.

Ditlea, Steve. "Word Processing." Byte Oct. 1986.

Dvorak, John C. "What Ever Happened To...(Series)" Computer Shopper

_____. "The First Personal Computer?" June 1992: 720.

_____. "IBM's Stretch Supercomputer?" March 1992: 58,659.

_____. "MSX Computers?" Feb. 1992: 685.

_____. "The APPLE III: APPLE's Insanely Flawed Wonder Platform?" July 1992: 754-756.

Dvorak, John C. "Technologies of the Past? PC Magazine Nov. 1995: 89.

_____. "Forget Politically Correct Packaging Give Us Functional Software." PC/Computing May 1993: 100.

_____. "Inside Track." <u>PC/Magazine</u> 26 Dec. 1989: 75.

_____. "Can the Glitz - Only Boring Computer TV Shows Will Win." <u>PC/Computing</u> Nov. 1993: 156.

_____. "The Servant Becomes the Master: The Computer is Killing Us." <u>PC/Computing</u> Aug. 1993: 90.

_____. "Sure, Paper Publishing is Evil Waste, But Media JunkiesPrefer It." <u>PC/Computing</u> Nov. 1993: 166+.

_____. "Future Shock." <u>PC/Computing</u> Oct. 1995: 73.

_____ & Jim Seymour. ""Dvorak dismisses standards, Seymour upholds them. Two sides of the story." <u>PC/Computing</u> March 1989: 29,30.

_____ & Paul Somerson. "Bean Counters Blast PCs for Zero Productivity Gain." <u>PC/Computing</u> March 1993: 94+.

Edge. "Cyberlife: Artificial life". <u>Edge[UK edition]</u>. Oct. 1996: 58+.

Editors. "New Hobby Computers You Can Build From A Kit." <u>Radio-Electronics</u> Aug. 1977: 42-44.
_____. "Lifetime Achievement: Jack St. Clair Kilby and Robert N. Noyce." <u>PC Magazine</u> 21 Dec. 1993: 151.

_____. "Special Report: Computer Languages.: <u>Popular Computing</u> Sept. 1993.

_____. "Special Report: Computer Languages." <u>Popular Computing</u> Sept. 1995: 113.

_____. "Computing Now!" in <u>A Beginner's Guide to Computers and Microprocessors with Projects</u>. Toronto: TAB Books, 1984.

Editors. "Building a PC - On Your Own." Personal Computing
     Aug. 1990: 22.

_____. "Basic Guide to Computer Buying." Popular
     Electronics Dec. 1977: 57-59.

_____. "DYNAMICRO: Build an 8080 Microcomputer Parts
     I-III." Radio-Electronics May/June/July 1976.

_____. "Electronic pocket calculators take over a classroom."
     Radio-Electronics Aug. 1974: 6.

_____. "Fear of Technology is the phobia of the 90s." The
     Computer Paper Sept. 1993: 54.

_____. "Multiprocessing Systems." Radio-Electronics Sept.
     1976: 98+.

_____. "Product Evaluation: North Star Micro-Disk – Why a
     Floppy Disk System." Personal Computer News Sept.
     1977: 1.

_____. "Pricing Patterns: Commodore versus Radio-Shack."
     Personal Computer News Sept. 1977: 1.

Enea, Horace & John Reykjalin. "Introducing SPEECHLAB: The
     First Hobbyist Vocal Interface for a Computer." Popular
     Electronics May 1977: 43+.

Englebart, Douglas. "Dreaming of the Future." Byte Sept. 1995:
     330.

English, David. "Compute's Getting Started With Desktop
     Publishing." Compute July 1991.

Evans, Christopher R. "Can a Machine Think?" Philosophy and
     Contemporary Issues. Burr and Goldinger.

Exon, Senator Jim. "Dialog Box." Windows Magazine Oct. 1995: 81+.

"Fear of Technology is the phobia of the 90's: Dell Computer Survey." The Computer Paper Sept. 1993: 54.

Ferrel, Keith. "New Wave Appliances: Home Computers Make a Comeback." Compute Oct. 1990: 15+.

Ferguson, III, Withworth. "Deming's Legacy: TMQ is Alive and Well. Creativity in Action (No.241) May 1994: 3.

Fitzgerald, Pat. "BASIC to Assembly Language Linkage". Byte July 1978: 112-114.

Flamm, Kenneth. "Semiconductors & pseudoscience." Issues in Science and Technology (National Academy of Sciences) Spring 1990: 79-82.

Ford, Gary A. "Comments on PASCAL, Learning How to Program Small Systems." Byte May 1978: 136+.

Frenzel, Lou. "How to Choose a Microprocessor". Byte July 1978: 124+.
_____. "The Personal Computer - Last Chance for CAI?" Byte July 1980: 86-96.

Fried, Andrew M. "From 'C' to Shining Sea." Computer Shopper Aug. 1986: 67+.

Friedman, Herb. "Data Base Management." Radio-Electronics April 1982: 91+.

_____. Word Processing." Radio-Electronics April 1982: 83+.

_____ and Lawrence Friedman. "Computers Phone The Future." Elementary Electronics Sept/Oct. 1977: 41.

_____ and Stan Veit. "Before DOS – Recollections."
Computer Shopper Jan. 1987: 162+.

Foreman, Michael. "How to Cope with a Power Cut."
MicroDecision [UK] Nov. 1982: 53+.

Freed, Les. "A Brief History of BBSs." PC Magazine Aug. 1995:
NE6.

Gannon, Robert. "Big Brother 7074 is Watching." Popular
Science March 1963.

Gardner, W. David. "Will the Inventor of the First Digital
Computer Please Stand Up." Datamation Feb. 1974: 84+.

Garetz, Mark. "Evolution of the Microprocessor." Byte Sept.
1985.

Gaughan, Jane. "Futuristics As a Subversive Activity." Trend
(Spring 1971): 11-28.

Georgiou, Christos J. "Machine Intelligence: A Function of
Human Ingenuity." Creative Computing June 1982: 124+.

Gray, Stephen B. "Building a Computer of Your Own." The Best
of Creative Computing:107-108.

_____. 'Computer Bits: Computer Stores." Popular Electronics
Feb. 1977: 90,90.

Grossblatt, Robert. "Drawing Board – Understanding Memory
ICs." Radio-Electronics Sept. 1985: 92+.

Hailwood, Ed. "Science." Farewell to the 70s. Eds. Anna Porter &
Marjorie Harris. Toronto: Thomas Nelson & Sons,1979.

Hamming, R. W. "One Man's View of Computer Science." <u>ACM Turing Award Lecturers</u>. Ed. Robert L. Ashenhurst. Don Mlls, Ont.: Addison-Wesley   Publishing Company, 1987.

Handy, Jim. "Introduction to NSC TinyBASIC: The Language of he INS8073." <u>Byte</u> April 1982: 472+.

Hart, Glenn A. "A Hard Disk's Night: An In-Depth Look At Mass torage Options." <u>Creative Computing</u> June 1982: 35+.

_____. "The Little Computer That Could." <u>Creative Computing</u> une 1982: 11+.

Harvey, David. "A Faster, Tougher Drive: Plus Hardcard II XL." <u>omputer Shopper</u> March 1991: 444+.

Hauck, Lane T. "Who's Afraid of Dynamic Memory". <u>Byte</u> July 978: 42+.

Heilmeier, George. "The Future of Artificial Intelligence." <u>Radio-Electronics</u> May 1987: 85+.

Helmers, Carl. "Is PASCAL the Next BASIC?" <u>Byte</u> Dec. 1977: 6+.

_____. "Personal Computing: New Prospects for Art and Science." <u>Byte</u> April 1978: 6+.

_____. "What Is This Phenomenon Personal Computing." <u>Byte</u> Jan. 1978: 6+.

_____. "Some Thoughts About Modems". <u>Byte</u> July 1978: 6+.

Hercz, Robert. "Growing Up Digital: How computers are changing your kids." <u>Canadian Business Technology</u> Fall 1995: 22+.

Hey, Wilf. "How a Turing Machine Works." PC Plus Aug. 1993: 321.

Hillis, Burton. "High-Tech Notes." Better Homes & Gardens May 1991: 204.

Hiserman, David L. "Minicomputers - What They Are and What They Can Do." Popular Electronics June 1972: 32+.

Hoban, Phoebe. "Artificial Intelligence: Literate Computers." Omni Sept. 1983: 24.

Holtzman, Jeff. "Computer Connections: Ten Years of progress – for better or worse." Radio-Electronics Feb. 1995: 89+.

Honan, Patrick. "The Personal Computing 500 – PC Industry Trivia". Personal Computing Magazine Oct. 1986.

Hsu, Feng-hsing, Thomas Anantharaman, Murray Campbell and Andreas Nowatzyk. "A Grandmaster Chess Machine." Scientific American Oct. 1990: 44+.

Hughes, Elizabeth M. "The IRS and the Computer Entrepreneurs." Byte Jan. 1978: 27+.

Hunt, Morton. "What The Human Mind Can Do That The Computer Can't." Philosophy and Contemporary Issues, Burr and Goldinger.

Ickes, Bob. "Die, Computer, Die: First We Kill All The Computers." New York 24 July 1995: 22+.

Illes, Amanda. "The Fountain of Ingenuity at PARC." MacWEEK 5 April 1985.

Immel, A. Richard. "Silicon Valley: The Wild West of Computer Technology." Popular Computing March 1982: 108.

_____. "Electric Pencil's Rise & Fall." Popular Computing
    Aug. 1984.

Johnson, Arthur. "Why the future isn't what it used to be."
    Canadian Business Technology Summer 1995: 9.

Johnson, Bill. "Bits, Bytes and Baud - Parts 1-6". Electronics
    Today. Sept. 1977 - Feb. 1978.

Johnston, Moira. "High Tech, High Risk, and High Life In Silicon
    Valley." National Geographic Oct. 1982: 459+.

Jones, James R. "Coincident Current Ferrite Core Memories."
    Byte July 1976: 6+.

Jong, Steven. "Designing a Text Editor? The User Comes First: A
    System's power is measured in ease of use." Byte April
    1982: 284+.

Kahaner, Larry. "Teletypewriter Fundamentals For Hams,
    SWL'ers & Computer Hobbyists". Popular Electronics.
    Oct. 1977: 43-48.

Karakotsios, Ken. 'Artificial life in cell automata." Algorithm 3.3
    July 1992: 16+.

Kaufman, Pat. "Cyberpunk - Readings on High Tech Antisocial
    Notoriety." Computer Monthly Dec. 1991: 151.

Kelly-Bootle, Stan. "Devil's Advocate - The Mouse That
    Yawned." UNIX Review (Vol. 8, No. 4) May 1990: 72.

Kenyon, Ralph. "The Rise and Fall of Polymorphic Systems."
    Computer Shopper Dec. 1989: 759+.

Kenner, Hugh. 'Electronic Books: Quick, someone please tell all those CR-Rom publishers that most books are better left on paper." Byte Nov. 1993: 404.

_____. "Somewhere Out There." Byte Aug. 1989: 340+.

_____. "Bicycles for the Mind." Byte 334.

Kilarski, Douglas E. "Editorial - Who Invented the Single-Chip Computer?" Computer Monthly Nov. 1990: 2.

Kimmel, Stephen. "I Sing the Editor Electric." Creative Computing May 1982: 75+.

Kinnucan, P. "A New Use for Core Memory", Mini-MicroSystems (Vol. 10, No. 3) March 1977: 23-26.

Kitteredge, F. H. "Old PCs Never Die." PC/Computing June 1993: 43.

Knight, Tim. "Probots and People - 'Big Robot'." Computer Shopper April 1986: 54+.

Lake, Matthew and Timothy E. Downs. "Modem Communication: ow Modems and Ma Bell Link PCs   with Serial Transfer." PC/Computing Sept. 1992: 330,331.

Lancaster, Don. "What's a RAM?" Radio-Electronics Sept. 1974: 50+.

_____. "Hardware Hacker." Radio-Electronics May 1988.

Larsen, David, Peter Rony, and Jonathan Titus. "Computer Corner: Moving Data Inside the Machine." Radio-Electronics Sept. 1977: 74+.

_____. "Komputer Korner: The 8080 Microprocessor." Radio-Electronics July 1976: 22+.

Lautsch, John C. "The Software Are Coming: A Horror Story for Educators." Future Life Nov. 1981: 25-26.

Ledder, Wayne H. "A Novice's Eye On Computer Arithmetic." Byte Jan. 1978: 150+.

Ledgard, Henry and Andrew Singer. "Elementary BASIC - Adventures with Sherlock Holmes and the Analytical Engine." Popular Computing Oct. 1982: 120+.

Leibson, Steve. "Input/Output Primer, Part 5: Character Codes." Byte June 1982: 242+.

Lemmons, Phil. "A Short History of the Keyboard." Byte Nov. 1982: 386-387.

_____. "Chuck Peddle: Chief Designer of the Victor 9000 Byte Nov. 1982: 256+.

Lenk, Frank. "Streaming Tape (How to Safeguard Data)." Computing Now! May 1985: 48+.

_____. "Solutions in APL." Computing Now! Feb. 1986: 36+.

_____. "Did Canada Invent the Microcomputer." Computers in Education April 1986: 41.

Leslie, Jacques. "Ambiguity Machines." Byte Oct. 1995: 250.

Leuhrmann, Arthur. "Computer Illiteracy - A National Crisis and a Solution for It." Byte July 1980: 98-102.

Leventhal, Lance A. "Microprocessors in Computer Education." Computers and People Oct. 1976: 11+.

Levine, Ronald D. "Supercomputers." Scientific American Jan. 1982: 118+.

Lewis, Mike. "What exactly is a Database?" <u>Practical Computing</u> May 1983: 111-112.

Libes, Sol. "Notes on Bringing up a Microcomputer." <u>Byte</u> Jan. 1978: 162-164.

_____. "The First Ten Years of Amateur Computing", <u>Byte</u> July 1978: 64+.

Licklider, Tracy Robnett. "Ten Years of Rows and Columns. <u>Byte</u> Dec. 1989: 324+.

Lima, Paul. "My Beautiful Friendly Digital Office." <u>Computing Now!</u> May 1994: 22-24.

Linstrom, Rob. "Editorial - Why PCs Become Extinct." <u>Computer Shopper</u> Aug. 1989: 171+.

Lloyd, Seth. "Quantum Mechanical Computers." <u>Scientific American</u> Oct. 1995: 140+.

Loewer, Bob. "The Z-80 in Parallel". <u>Byte</u> July 1978: 60+.

Lowe, William C. "The PC in Retrospect." <u>Personal Computing</u> Oct. 1986.

Machrone, Bill. "Discontent with Content." <u>PC Magazine</u> 11 May 1993: 87,88.

_____. "Revenge of the Nerds." <u>PC Magazine</u> 21 Dec. 1993: 89,90.

_____. "Giving hackers back their good name." <u>Infoworld</u> 5(48): 43+.

Majumber, Diganta. "Dialog Box." <u>Windows Magazine</u> June 1995: 55+.

Marsh, Robert M. "Computer Bits: Computer Users Tape System." Popular Electronics March 1976: 88+.

Martin, R. R. "Electronic Disks in the 1980s." Computer (Vol. 8, No. 2) Feb. 1975: 24.

Masters, Gary. "Computer Literacy." Microsoft *ENCARTA* '95. CD-ROM. Redmond, WA.: Microsoft Inc./Funk & Wagnalls, 1994.

McCarthy, J. P. "Automatic File Compression", Proceedings of the International Computing Symposium 1973. Davos, Switzerland - North Holland, Amsterdam, Netherlands: 1974: 511-516.

McConnell, Barry. "The Handicapple: A Low Cost Braille Printer." Creative Computing Oct. 1982: 186+.

McCormack, John. "Software Patents." Computer Shopper Dec. 1988: 295+.

McGath, Gary. "A Look at LISP". Byte Dec. 1977: 156-161.

McMillen, Dave. "Modula-2: A High Level Language for Systems Design." Computer Shopper Aug. 1986: 67+.

McMullen, Barbara E. & John F. McMullen. "New York's School Banishes Computer Illiteracy." Computer Shopper 20+.

McNutt, Dinah. "Doing it Over." Byte Nov. 1995: 94,95.

Melymuka, Kathleen. "Honey, I Shrunk the Mainframe." CIO Magazine Sept. 1989.

Meyer, Salome. "Striving toward the Elusive HAL." South African MicroComputer Owner Nov. 1983: 4,5.

_____. "The computer as scientific pioneer." <u>South African MicroComputer Owner</u> Nov. 1983: 6-8.

Mims, Forrest M., III. "Microprocessor Micrcourse: Parts 1-4." <u>Popular Electronics</u> March-June, 1978.

_____. "Experimenter's Corner: Flip-Flops and Decade Counters - Part 1." <u>Popular Electronics</u> Feb. 1977: 75,76.

_____. "The Altair Story." <u>Creative Computing</u> Nov. 1984.

_____. "The Tenth Anniversary of the Altair 8800, Setting the Story Straight." <u>Computers & Electronics</u> Jan. 1985.

_____ and Edward Roberts. "Basic Digital Logic Course." <u>Popular Electronics</u> Nov. 1974: 57,58.

Mitchell, Eugene H. "In's and Out's of Computers for Beginners." <u>Popular Electronics</u> June 1976: 47+."

Mitchell, Ron H. "Editor's Wanderings." <u>AUFG</u> Sept/Oct. 1993: 1,2.

_____. "Me Program? No Way! "Paper presented at <u>ADAMCON 5</u>, Salt Lake City, Utah, July 22-25, 1993.

_____. "AUFG Product Review - School Daze." <u>AUFG</u> Sept/Oct. 1989: 9,10.

Moran, Brian. [Junior Computer Hackers of America].

Morgan, Chris. 'PC 77." <u>Byte</u> Dec. 1977: 74,75.

Mother Jones. "First reports how Silicon Valley companies pollute air with CFCs." July/Aug. 1989.

Muller, Jim. "The Friendly Computer Language." <u>Creative Computing</u> Oct. 1982: 55+.

Myers, Norman. "Computer Readout: The Intercept, Jr." Elementary Electronics July/Aug. 1977: 67+.

Neeley, Alan. "Product Review: School Daze." ADAMLink of Utah July/Sept. 1989: 22,23.

Negroponte, Nicholas. "The Next Billion Users." Wired June 1996: 320.

Nelson, Robin. "Word Processing." Personal Computing Aug. 1990: 49,50.

Nicita, Mike and Ron Petrusha. Review, *The Human Factor*.

Nicolaisen, Nancy. "FORTRAN Rebirth: FORTRAN gets a facelift for the 90s." Computer Shopper June 1995: 573-575.

Nieburg, Hal. "BASIC is Spoken Here." Computer Shopper Oct. 1986: 117+.

Nimershein, Jack. "DOSSier: The Experiences of a Typical PC User." Vulcan Computer Monthly Oct. 1990: 72+.

_____. "DOSSier - Experiences of a Typical PC User: Turning On and Off Computer Hardware." Computer Monthly Nov. 1990: 85+.

_____. "Modem Madness - The Terminology of Telecommunications." Vulcan's Computer Monthly July 1990: 122,123.

Noll, Edward M. "Learning Electronic Theory with Hand Calculators". Popular Electronics. Sept. 1976: 70-73.

Nordier, Robert. "Taking the Mystique out of Assembly Language." South African MicroComputer Owner Nov. 1983: 85,86.

Nottingham, Ralph with Al Frazer. "Who Says CP/M is Dead?"
Computer Shopper Oct. 1986: 98.

O'Connor, Leah and Patrick. "Game Corner." Interface Age June
1982: 28,29.

O'Malley, Chris. "Analyzing the People Factor: Explore the
relationship between people and their PCs in the ever-
changing world of computer technology."
Computer Shopper Aug. 1995: 443,444.

Ogdin, Jerry. "Computer Bits: Hobbyist Interchange Tape
System." Radio-Electronics Sept. 1975: 57-61.

Ostler, Mel. "The Microprocessor." ADAM-Link of Utah
Sept/Oct. 1988: 10,11.

Pack, S. Hughes. "Teacher Training is Key." Byte Nov. 1994:
366.

Papert, Seymour. "New Cultures from the New
Technologies." Byte Sept. 1988: 230+.

Patton, Phil. "How to Bring History to Life: Youngsters learn
timeless truths about survival as they head west-bound,
circa 1840." Computerlife Nov. 1995: 69.

Paul, Marianne. "MicroComputers for Micro Users." Computing
Now! Oct. 1983: 24+.

_____. "Educational Software." Computing Now! Nov. 1984:
20+.

Pawson, Richard. "Frontline: Animal Farm."
MicroComputer Printout March 1983: 5.

_____. "Frontline: Learning vs Teaching."
MicroComputer Printout July 1983: 5.

Peace, Love and the Rise of IBM. Computers & Society (Vol. 23, No. 1-2) July 1993.

Persenson, M. J. "Electronic Field Trips for the 90s." PC Magazine 8 Feb. 1994: 30.

Pescovitz, David. "The Future of Schools." Wired June 1996: 82.

Peterson, Cheryl. "CP/M Column." Computer Shopper June 1989: 273+. [Uses for CP/M machines, p. 276.]

Petzold, C. "Move Over, ASCII! UNICODE is Here." PC Magazine 26 Oct. 1993: 374-376.

Philips, Curt. "Celebrating Ten Years of BBSing." Computer Shopper June 1988: 86+.

Phillips, Dwayne. "Networks That Think: Neural Networks Learn to Remember." Computer Shopper July 1992: 757,758.

Platt, Charles. "Music on Demand: Bell Lab's Ken Thompson, the father of Unix, has invented a new technology that could mean never having to buy a CD again." Wired Aug. 1995: 82+.

Postman, Neil. "Currents Comment." UTNE READER July/Aug. 1995: 35.

Pountain, Dick. "The Joy of J." Byte Sept. 1995: 267,268.

_____. "Functional Programming Comes of Age." Byte Aug. 1994: 183,184.

_____. "Standard Fare." Popular Computing Sept. 1985: 48+.

Preston, Chris. "How it Works: Floppy Disk Drives." Micro-computer Printout Oct. 1982: 36+.

Popular Science. "ENIAC." August 1992: 79.

_____. "Home Computers." Aug. 1992: 85.

_____. "Supercomputers." Aug. 1992: 87.

_____. "Word Processing." Aug. 1992: 91.

_____. "Electronics: Buzzwords - Paging the
        Digerati." Aug. 1992: 43.

Pournelle, Jerry. "A Slew of Languages, a Slap at Documentation,
        and a Curse at Keyboards: Unaccustomed as he is to
        voicing his opinions, Jerry drops a few hints." Byte 1982:
        222-224.

_____. "BASIC Instinct." Byte Aug. 1993: 209+.

Quraishi, Jim. "Board with Limited Memory? Yet a New HI - The
        AMS HI486." Computer Shopper July 1990: 284+.

Rampil, Ira. "A Floppy Disk Tutorial." Byte Dec. 1977: 24+.

Reed, Sandra R. "The Person in Personal Computing." Personal
        Computing Aug. 1990: 5.

Reid-Green, Keith S. "A Short History of Computing". Byte July
        1978: 84+.

Relf, Graham. "Maze Movement: Has Coding." Practical
        Computing Sept. 1982: 127+.

Reynolds, Louis R. and Stephen J. Derose. "Electronic Books."
        Byte June 1992: 263+.

Richardson, Ronny. "Learning DOS." Computer Shopper Oct.
        1987: 312.

Riley, W. B. "Wanted for the 70s: Easier-to-Program Computers." <u>Electronics</u> 13 Sept. 1971.

Rimmer, Steve. "Down to the Ships on C." <u>Computing Now!</u> Nov. 1984: 65+.

Ross, Jacob. "BEAMing up the Robots." <u>Algorithm 3.3</u> July 1992: 5.

Rossman, Michael. "Demanding More of Manuals." <u>Popular Computing</u> Aug. 1983: 136-138.

Rowney, Don. "The Historian and the Microcomputer." <u>Byte</u> July 1982: 166+.

Ruber, Peter. "Anatomy of a Microchip." <u>Computer Monthly</u> March 1992: 52+.

Ryan, B. "Dynabook Revisited with Alan Kay." <u>Byte</u> Feb. 1991: 203+.

_____. "Digital Research: A New Era." <u>Computer Shopper</u> July 1988: 181+.

Sala, Martin A. "Core Memories - How they work." <u>Radio-Electronics</u> Sept. 1977: 54,55.

Sale, Kirkpatrick. "Dialog Box: Did my political opposition to technology precede my personal revulsion." <u>Windows Magazine</u> Dec. 1995: 93+.

Salsberg, Art. "The Future of Home Computers". <u>Popular Electronics</u>. Oct. 1977: 4.

Sandler, Corey. "Innovators: The Next Generation." <u>Computer Shopper</u> April 1990: 121.

Savon, Carl. "State of Solid State: Microprocessors – assembling a system, software and system modules." <u>Radio-Electronics</u> Sept. 1976: 36+.

Schnapp, Marc. "Wither xbase?" <u>Byte</u> Dec, 1991: 131+.

Schulman, Andrew. "DOS Unbound: Uses of Protected mode." <u>Byte</u> (*IBM Special Edition*) Fall 1990.

Scott, D. F. "The Next Operating System: Some New Ideas." <u>Computer Shopper</u> Oct. 1987: 191+.

_____. "STOS: Old Bottles for New Wine." <u>Computer Shopper</u> April 1989: 251+.

_____. "Mass Macs: APPLE Prepares for the Graphical Melee of '91." <u>Computer Shopper</u> March 1991: 575+.

"Semiconductors." <u>Wired</u> March 1996: 70.

Seymour, J. "The Mouse's Tale, 1993." <u>PC Magazine</u> Aug. 1993: 97,98.

Shannon, Claude E. "A Chess Playing Machine." <u>Scientific American Reader</u>: 538-544.

Shapiro, Fred R. "The First Bug." <u>Byte</u> April 1994: 308.

Sheinwald, Jesse D. "Is CP/M Dead?" <u>Computer Shopper</u> Aug. 987: 324-326.

Shell, Ellen Ruppel. "The Brain Behind BASIC." <u>Technology Illustrated</u> Dec./Jan. 1983.

Shipley, Chris. "Whatever Happened to AI?" <u>PC/Computing</u> March 1989: 64+.

Smallbridge, Justin. "The Video Tycoons. "Canadian Business: 18-24.

Solomon, Leslie. "Anatomy of a Robot - HERO 2000." Computer Shopper Aug. 1986: 69+.

_____. "Computer Bits: Music Generators and Other Items." Popular Electronics Feb. 1978: 92+.

_____. "Computer Terminals are Coming." Popular Electronics Feb. 1974: 78.

_____. "Test Equipment Scene: The Microprocessor Revolution." Popular Electronics Dec. 1975: 99,100.

_____. "Computer Bits: Remote Control." Popular Electronics Aug. 1977: 88,89.

Somerson, Paul. "Everything You Always Wanted To Know About Batch Files." PC/Computing Nov. 1991: 171+.

Spindle, Les. "History of Computers in Education." Radio-Electronics April 1982: 112,113.

Stafford, David. "What's the Code?: Curing Those Unsightly Bugs." Computer Shopper Dec. 1992: 890+.

Stern, Marc. "Touchscreen Technology." Radio-Electronics (Computer Digest) Sept. 1985: 8-10.

Stern, Richard. "Case of the Purloined Object Code: Can It Be Solved(Part 1)." Byte Oct. 1982: 420.

_____. Case of the Purloined Object Code: Can It Be Solved (Part 2)." Byte Oct. 1982: 210+.

Stevens, Al. "Plumbers, Programmers, and Quincy 96." Dr. Dobb's Journal April 1996: 105-111.

Steven, Daniel. "What's an Orphan to Do?" Computer Shopper Dec. 1987: 336+.

Suber, Peter. "Teaching in a Blizzard of Information." Issues in Science and Technology Summer 1989: 29-31.

Suding, Dr. Robert. "Why Wait? Build a *FAST* Cassette Interface." Byte July 1976: 46-53.

Sullivan, Nick. "Buyer's Guide to Personal Computers: Shopping Do's and Dont's." Family Computing June 1986: 29.

Suzuki, David. "Science." Farewell to the 70s. Ed. Anna Porter & Marjorie Harris. Toronto: Thomas Nelson & Sons, 1979.

Swartzlander, Earl. "Calculators." IEEE Annals of the History of Computing (Vol. 17, No. 3) Fall 1995: 75-77.

Tenny, Ralph. "How to Interface Microprocessors." Popular Electronics Dec. 1977: 66+.

Thompson, H. Bradford. "Text Editing with Compuviews's VEDIT." Byte March 1982: 262+.

Thompson, Tom. "The World's Fastest Computers." Byte Jan, 1996: 45+.

Thornburg, David D. "Compilers, Interpreters, and Flow: Conclusion." Compute! Sept. 1985: 104.

_____. "Of Babbages and Things." Compute! Oct. 1985: 107.

TIME. "*The Computer Society*. TIME. Feb. 20, 1978: 28+.

Titus, Jonathan A. "Computer! - Build This Minicomputer Yourself." Radio-Electronics Jan. 1975: 2-15.

_____, Peter Rony, and David Larsen. "Komputer Korner: Substituting microcomputer software for hardware." Radio- Electronics Sept. 1876: 22+.

Toong, Hoo-Min D. & Amar Gupta. "Personal Computing." Scientific American Dec. 1982.

Traub, Robert. "Operating Systems." Computing Now! Oct. 1983: 56,57.

_____. "The Microcomputer Keyboard Story." Computing Now! Jan. 1984: 50-52.

Turing, Alan. "Computing Machinery and Intelligence". Reprinted in Computers and Thought. Eds. E. Feigenbaum and J. Feldman. NY.: McGraw-Hill, 1963.

"TX-0: Its Past and Present." Computer Museum Report Spring 1984.

Tymon, Frank. "That Dangerous Thing - A Little Learning." Computer Shopper April 1986: 43+.

Uttal, Bro. "The Coming Struggle in Personal Computers." Fortune 29 Jan. 1981.

Vaughan-Nichols, Steven J. "Realational Databases: The Real Story - Codd's Commandments." Byte Dec. 1990:322.

Veit, Stan. "If I Had Four APPLES." Computer Shopper.

_____. "Trends in Computer Languages." Computer Shopper Aug. 1986: 7+.

_____. "A Funny Thing Happened in San Diego: The Story of PASCAL." Computer Shopper Aug. 1986: 7+.

_____. "The State of the Eight: 8-Bits Alive and Running."
Computer Shopper June 1988: 44+.

_____. "Editorial." Computer Shopper Sept. 1988: 149.

_____. "The First Decade." Computer Shopper Nov. 1989: 28+.

_____. "How to Make a Company Disappear: The Story of
Technical Design Labs." Computer Shopper Dec. 1989:
300-303.

_____. "WORDSTAR 5.5: Review." Computer Shopper Dec.
1989: 770,771.

_____ and Douglas E. Kilarski. "Hypertext for PCs." Computer
Shopper Sept. 1988: 27+.

Stan Veit. History of the Microcomputer.
Computer Shopper.

Feb. 1987, Computer Camelot II: 291,292.

Nov. 1988, 10 Years Since The First Comdex: 12+.

Jan. 1989, Rashomon or the First PC: 29+.

Feb. 1989, IMSAI: The Foundation: 84-86.

March 1989, The Saga of SOL and Processor Technology: 59+.

July 1989, TRS-80 Almost Everyone's Computer: 60+.

March 1991, UCSD Pascal: 248+.

April 1991, IBM's PCjr: 240.

May 1991, The Day of the Clone is Gone: 253.

July 1991, <u>In Living Color: The Long, Bumpy History of Video Display Terminals</u>: 128,129.

Sept. 1991, <u>Breaking the One-Grand Printer Barrier</u>: 698.

Feb. 1992, <u>Are We Having Fun Yet? Rolling Your Own</u>: 680.

March 1992, <u>The Dragon of Menlo Park</u>: 696.

April 1992, <u>Uncle SOL's Toys</u>: 671.

May 1992, <u>The Most Popular Computer Ever</u>: 662-664.

June 1992, <u>PCs That Never Made It</u>: 686+.

July 1992, <u>What IBM Borrowed from APPLE</u>: 734.

Stan Veit, *What Ever Happened To...(*Series), <u>Computer Shopper</u>.

Sept. 1992, <u>Time-Sharing, MultiUser Personal Computers?</u>: 743-745.

Nov. 1992, "<u>Personal Robots?</u>: 794,795.

Dec. 1992, <u>UCSD Pascal and the P-System?</u>: 860,861.

March 1993, <u>IBM?</u>: 772,773.

May 1993, <u>Zilog?</u>: 648,649.

Oct. 1993, <u>The S-100 Bus?</u>: 595,596.

Nov. 1993, <u>Early Computer Magazines?</u>: 610+.

Dec. 1993, <u>R2D2-Style Robots?</u>:638,639.

Jan. 1994, <u>Cassette Data Storage?</u>: 643+.

April 1994, <u>Kit Computers?</u>: 595+.

May 1995, <u>Word Processing?</u>: 568+.

June 1995, <u>Carmen and the Gray PC Market?</u>: 580,581.

Aug. 1995, <u>The Big PC Designs?</u>.

Sept. 1995, <u>Time-Sharing?</u>: 598,599.

Oct. 1995, <u>Memory?</u>: 588,589.

Jan. 1996, <u>the PC Stock Market?</u>: 630,631.

March 1996, <u>Garage-based Computer Factories?</u>: 569+.

Waddington, D. E. O'N. "Microprocessors: An introductory discussion of the principles of design, programming and application." <u>Wireless World</u> Dec. 1975: 550+.

Wakefied, Rowan A. "Home Computers and Families: the empowerment revolution." <u>The Futurist</u> 20(5), (Sept/Oct.1986): 18+.

Walter, W. Grey. "Imitation of Life." <u>Scientific American Reader</u>: 545+.

Walton, Marcus. "The Birth of an Industry." <u>Impact</u> Dec. 1984.

Watt, Roy. Quoted in <u>Wired</u> March 1995: 84.

Wantz, Sherman. "Computer Stores: A New Retailing Phenomenon." <u>Popular Electronics</u> Dec. 1977: 70-72.

Watt, Dan. "LOGO: What Makes It Exciting." <u>Popular Computing</u> Aug. 1983: 106+.

_____. "Teaching in the Computer Age." <u>Popular Computing</u> Aug. 1983: 65-67.

_____. "The Two Cultures: Science and the humanities split over computers in the school." <u>Popular Computing</u> April 1983: 58+.

Watt, Molly. "What is LOGO?" <u>Creative Computing</u> Oct. 1982: 112+.

Webster, Bruce F. "The Real Software Crisis." <u>Byte</u> Jan. 1996: 218.

Weld, John. "Would you buy a shrink wrapped automobile?" <u>Computers and Society</u> (Vol. 16, Nos. 2,3) Summer/Fall 1986: 29+.

Weisbecker, Joseph A. "Build the PIXIE Graphic Display." <u>Popular Electronics</u> April -July 1977.

_____. 'ELF Microcomputer Project." <u>Popular Electronics</u> Aug. 1976.

"Wherefore the Computer Market?" <u>Sight and Sound Marketing</u>. Reprinted in <u>Creative Computing</u> June 1982: 114.

Williams, Gregg and Bob Moore. "The Apple Story, Part 1: Early History." <u>Byte</u> Dec. 1984.

Williams, James M. "Antique Mechanical Computers: Part 1: Early Automata". <u>Byte</u> July 1978: 48+.

Williams, Linda. "Guide to Computer Repair." <u>Family Computing</u> March 1987: 47-49.

Winograd, Terry. 'Thinking Machines: Can There Be? Are we?" In <u>Understanding Computers and Cognition: A New Foundation for Design</u>. Terry Winograd and C. Fernando Flores. Norwood, NJ.: Ablex, 1986.

Woehr, Jack. "An Interview with Donald Knuth." <u>Dr. Dobb's Journal</u> April 1996: 16+.

Wolfe, Tom. "The Tinkerings of Robert Noyce." <u>Esquire</u> ec.1983.

Woteki, Thomas H. and Paul A. Sand. "Four Implementations of Pascal: Programming Language Terms." <u>Byte</u> March 1982: 316+.

Yakal, Kathy. "C and the 68000." <u>Compute!</u> July 1986: 28-33.

Yob, Greg. "Personal Electronic Transactions." <u>Creative Computing</u> Oct. 1982: 298+.

Young, John E. "Using Computers for the Environment." <u>State of he World: 1994</u> Eds. Lester K. Brown, et al. NY.: W. W. Norton & Company, 1994.

Yule, Dave, and Ed. Hoornaert. "Birth of a Hero." <u>Computing Now!</u> Sept. 1984: 84-86.

Zimbardo, Philip g. "The Hacker Papers." <u>Psychology Today</u> 14 Oct. 1980: 62-69.

Zimmer, Carl. "Tutor by Computer." <u>Discover</u>: 36.

CD-ROMs

<u>Hacker Chronicles: A Tour of the Computer Underground</u>. P-80 Systems, 1993.

Microsoft Encarta '95 (ENC\95). Yearly release 1995. Redmond, WA.: Microsoft Corp., 1994.

<u>Smash hilites for Programmers Vol. 1.1(Catalog #58)</u>, The Software Developers Company, Inc., 1994.

Superpac - ComputerLife. *ComputerLife Magazine* NY.: Ziff-Davis, 1995.

NEWSPAPERS

Auerbach, Jon. "PC makers' screens show limits to sales growth: the scenario of saturation at high income levels and poor penetration at all others seems to be playing out." The Globe & Mail 27 Feb. 1996: C7.

Blackwell, Gerry. "Class Act: Taking Technology to the Classroom." The Toronto Star 26 Oct. 1995: H1,H4.

Gregoire, Lisa. "There's just no time to think." Globe & Mail 20 Nov. 1995: A16.

Emerson, George. "Wiring up the school: Is the goal of connecting every classroom to the Internet a democratizing initiative, or an invasion of public space by corporate interests?" Toronto Star April 21, 1996: F6.

Harris, Christopher. "Review of Creation of the e-nation." Globe & Mail 20 Nov. 1995: C1.

Ingram, Mathew. "A short history of hackers, phreaks and worms." The Globe & Mail 27 Feb. 1996: C1,C2.

Johnston, Mike. "Farley Mowat: On computers, big cities and life in Port Hope." Northumberland News 6 Feb. 1994: 1,4.

Lester, Lee. "Aged are getting wired." The Globe & Mail 27 Feb. 1996: C10.

Levin, Martin. "Climate of Ideas: Cruising with the Inter-nuts." The Globe & Mail 25 May 1995: A22.

Letters to the Editors. "Learning to buy or learning to think?" The Toronto Star 9 Sept. 1995: D7.

Little, Bruce. "Poor left behind in computer revolution." The Toronto Star 15 Jan. 1996: B11.

Markoff, John. "Computing in America: A Masculine Mystique." The New York Times 13 Feb. 1989.

Mays, John Bentley. "Citystates: A Detour on the Information Highway." The Globe & Mail 30 Jan. 1994: C5.

Nessbitt, Scott. "Gutenberg Alert." The Globe & Mail 25 Nov. 1993: A30.

Postman, Neil. "Information has become a 'form of garbage." The Globe & Mail 25 Nov. 1993: A29.

Radge, Prabhakar. "No new wrinkles of thought in *Skin of Culture* a review." The Globe & Mail 8 July 1995: C21.

Ritter, Jonathan. "The World View of a Computer Hacker." The Globe & Mail 29 March 1994: A22.

Rowan, Geoffrey. "Expect Home Computers to Become More Personal." The Globe & Mail 5 Jan. 1990: B1+.

_____. The Globe & Mail 14 March 1995: B10.

Strauss, Stephen. "Mind & Matter." The Globe & Mail 7 Jan. 1995: D8.

Tannenbaum, Jeffrey A. "Small Businesses Learn That A Computer Without Software IS 'Dumb Hunk of Iron'." Wall Street Journal April 2, 1980.

"Technophobia." The Globe & Mail 25 Oct. 1993: A18.

Taylor, Fabrice. "Portrait of a Hacker." <u>The Globe & Mail</u> 27 Feb. 1996: C1,C2.

Thompson, Allan. "Information Highway Endangers French Language, Chirac says." <u>The Toronto Star</u> 3 Dec. 1995: A1,A24.

Thorsell, William. "Days of wonder: Imagining the future as it zooms towards us." The <u>Toronto Star</u> 8 June 1996: D6.

White, Myles. "Computer Wares: A big byte out of school budgets; MORE = BETTER Debate over computers in class brings up thorny issues of access, cost, obsolescence." <u>The Toronto Star</u> 9 Sept. 1995: E1,E5.

_____. "Computer Wares: Computer a great tool for learning." <u>The Toronto Star</u> Oct. 5, 1995: H4.

FILMS

<u>Digital Computer Techniques: Computer Introduction</u>. *U. S. Dept. of the Navy*. Wash., DC.: 1962.

<u>Digital Computer Techniques: Computer Units</u>. *U. S. Dept. of the Navy*. Wash., DC.: 1962.

<u>Digital Computer Techniques: Computer Logic</u>. *U. S. Dept. of the Navy*. Wash., DC.: 1962.

INTERNET

Frontline(PBS). "High Stakes In Cyberspace." 1995.
    http://www.pbs.org

MAGAZINES

Brand, Stewart. "Fanatic Life and Symbolic Death Among the
    Computer Bums." Rolling Stone 1972: 15.

Boorstin, Daniel J. "Tomorrow: The Republic of Technology."
    Time 17 Jan. 1977.

Friedrich, Otto. "Glork! A Glossary for Gweeps: Even users
    should grok this cuspy sampler of computerese." Time 3
    Jan. 1983: 24.

Laver, Ross. "Mobile Madness." Maclean's 8 Jan. 1996: 29.

Ratan, Suneel. "A New Divide Between Haves and Have-nots?"
    Time (Spring 1995 -Special Issue): 25,26.

Rosenblatt, Roger, et al. "A New World Dawns: Machine of the
    Year." Time 3 Jan. 1983: 5,24.

Taylor, A. "Small-Computer Shootout." Time 2 March 1981.

Uttal, Bro. "The Coming Struggle in Personal Computers."
    Fortune 29 Jan. 1981.

Wallace, Claudia. "The Learning Revolution." Time (Spring 1995
    - Special Issue): 49-51.

"Clive Sinclair's Little Computer That Could." <u>Fortune</u> 8 March
     1982.

"Other Maestros of the Micro." <u>Time</u> 3 Jan. 1983.

RADIO/TELEVISION

Delaney, Frank. "History of the Microcomputer: Part 13- A

Walk in the PARC." <u>Computer News this Week</u> MTA, (Micro
     Technology Associates) Spokane, WA.: May 3, 1995.

_____. "Raw Bytes." <u>KPBX, National Public Radio</u>. MTA,
     Spokane, WA: 1997.

Rooney, Andy. "A few minutes with Andy Rooney(Transcript).
     <u>Sixty Minutes(CBS)</u> (Vol. XVI, No. 4) 9 Oct. 1983.

<u>Bits & Bytes</u> [No. 2, 4, 6] *TVO(TVOntario)* Sept. 1993.

<u>CANADA Online</u>. *CBC News (Canadian Broadcasting
     Corporation)* 19 Sept. 1995.

"Facts and myths about hardware and software; computer
     philosophy." <u>Discovery Television Entertainment(DIS)</u>.
     19 Sept. 1995.

<u>VISTA</u>. "From books to Bytes: The Impact of Technology on
     Education." *TVO (Ontario Film Library)* Peterborough,
     Ont.

<u>VISTA</u>. "The Strange Life and Death of Dr. Turing." *TVO*. 24
     Jan. 1994.

<u>VISTA</u>. "Tour of 'Cyberpunk' World." *TVO*. 28 June 1993.

INDEX

www.ingramcontent.com/pod-product-compliance
Lightning Source LLC
Chambersburg PA
CBHW051225050326

40689CB00007B/808